Practical Marketing and Public Relations for the Small Business

For Paul, Spike and Ellie

THE SUNDAY TIMES

BUSINESS ENTERPRISE GUIDE

Practical Marketing and Public Relations for the Small Business

2ND EDITION

MOI ALI

RECOMMENDED BY
INSTITUTE OF DIRECTORS

KOGAN
PAGE

First published in 1998
Second edition 2002

Kogan Page Limited
120 Pentonville Road
London N1 9JN

The views expressed in this book are those of the author, and are not necessarily the same as those of Times Newspapers Ltd.

British Library Cataloguing in Publication Data

A CIP record for this book is available from the British Library.

ISBN 0 7494 3823 1

Typeset by Saxon Graphics Ltd, Derby
Printed and bound in Great Britain by Clays Ltd, St Ives plc

Contents

About the author

Moi Ali is a PR and marketing consultant who runs her own business – The Pink Anglia Public Relations Company – which specialises in communications, marketing services and PR training for small companies and charities. For nearly two decades she has practised public relations and marketing. She has worked for companies, PR consultancies, charities and the public sector. Moi is a member of the Institute of Public Relations, the professional body which represents PR practitioners.

Moi has written books on PR, marketing and copywriting.

Introduction

Scan the shelves of any decent business bookseller and you will see plenty of PR and marketing books. But if you run a small business, you won't be spoilt for choice; most of what is available has been written for those with an academic interest in the subject. As a result, they can be over-theoretical and not very 'hands-on'.

This book is different. It is jargon-free, accessible, readable and, above all, practical, showing how to do it – and how not to! Packed with true stories and fictitious examples, this book bursts at the seams with hundreds of helpful tips, hints and ideas.

Written specially for small businesses by someone who runs her own business – and is therefore acutely aware of the financial constraints you face when it comes to PR and marketing – this book is highly relevant to the entrepreneur. Though tailor-made for businesses who are new to public relations and marketing (or very inexperienced), and who have limited budgets for PR/ marketing activity, it also contains plenty of good advice for bigger and more affluent companies. It will help you to get the most from your PR/marketing spend, and will show you how to develop your own PR and marketing programmes in order to be more effective and, ultimately, more profitable.

Read this book from cover to cover if you wish, or just look up chapters as you need to – it has been designed so that you can dip in whenever necessary.

Marketing is an immense discipline; each of the subjects covered here could easily be a book in its own right. Certainly it would be impossible to do justice to everything there is to know about PR and marketing in just one volume. That said, you will find between these covers most of what you need to consider, in the amount of detail you require. So whether you are a sole practitioner, or you run a fair-sized enterprise, get reading and start reaping the benefits of effective PR and marketing.

How to use this book

This book has been divided into three parts and the appendices.

Part 1: The principles

This part covers marketing theory – the spicy way! Theory can be rather dry and boring: here it has been presented in a lively and readable style. Nevertheless, it's still theory and is therefore inevitably less practical than the other sections. It has been written in plain English to make it as accessible as possible to 'theory-phobes' – those who hate and fear anything too theoretical. It provides a useful information base, but it is not essential that you read it straight away. If you are raring to get into a particular aspect of PR or marketing, go to the relevant chapter and miss out the theory for now. But do make the time to read it later; it will be useful.

Part 2: The practice

Now for the really hands-on bit! This section deals with the nuts and bolts and will be the most useful part of the book to you. Find out how to do everything from customer care to market research. Step by step you will be guided through the various subject areas, and given practical tips and hints along the way. Amusing anecdotes will bring each subject to life.

Part 3: The professionals

This book aims to make you as self-sufficient as possible when it comes to marketing. Inevitably, though, there will be occasions when you need to bring in the experts. This section will show you how to choose and use various external consultants and how to get the best out of them.

Appendices

In the appendices you will find a really useful glossary of marketing terms and a listing of useful addresses.

Part 1

The principles

Introduction

This section will introduce you to the key concepts of marketing. It is not essential reading, at least initially. You can undertake effective marketing without a thorough understanding of the theory that lies behind it. So if you are eager to get on with a promotional brochure, a piece of marketing research, or some other activity, just go straight to Part 2 and refer to the relevant chapter. But if you plan to take marketing seriously, you will need to prepare a marketing strategy. This section will lead you through the main areas of marketing, culminating in advice on how to produce your own strategy. Part 2 will help you put your strategy into action. Part 3 will advise you on how to buy in external help, and the information in the Appendices will point you in the right direction if you want to know more.

Happy marketing.

1

Back to basics:
a look at definitions

This introductory chapter explains what is meant by the terms 'marketing' and 'public relations'. It also sets out some of the benefits small firms can derive from a marketing-led approach to running a business.

Few small businesses use PR and marketing effectively – if they use them at all. The fact that you have bought this book is a good sign for your business. You already believe that PR and marketing can enhance your company's profile, its image and, of course, its profits. Great. You're off to a good start. You are committed to the principle and want to know the techniques. But before I give you a blow-by-blow guide on how you can use PR and marketing effectively, it makes sense to be certain that you and I mean the same thing when we use the terms 'marketing' and 'PR'.

What is marketing?

We need to begin with a look at definitions. First, the meaning of 'marketing'. Contrary to what you may think, marketing is not just another word for sales promotion – even though we all tend to use the word in everyday speech as a synonym for selling and for promotion. How often have you said that you were really impressed with how a new product was *marketed*, when really you meant that you were impressed with how it was *advertised* or *promoted*? Confuse marketing and promotion and you're in trouble. Promotion is a part of marketing, just as a wheel is part of a car. But you would never talk about a wheel when really you meant the car. Just as a car has components other than wheels, marketing comprises more than just promotion.

Promotion is product-led; you already have a product or service which you are trying to sell. If you only begin to think about marketing when you reach the stage where sales promotion is required, you have started too late. Marketing techniques should be used before the product is even conceived. Indeed, a marketing approach will help you to come up with the kinds of products that will satisfy your customers' needs and wants. By finding out what customers want before you develop a product or service, you avoid any potential mismatch between your service and their needs. As you can see, marketing should be customer-led, not product-led.

Another way of looking at it is to see marketing as making what you can sell, not selling what you can make. If every business concentrated only on trying to sell what it could make, rather than on responding to changing consumer demands in a fast-changing world, their products would be fixed in a time warp. We would have no labour-saving devices in our homes, no computers in our offices and no cars on our streets. Progress would stop. A marketing-led company is not stuck in a rut, churning out the same old products regardless. It stays ahead by altering its products to meet changing consumer need.

It is clear, then, that marketing is about so much more than just promotional activity. It embraces all aspects of the way you run your business.

What is public relations?

Next to public relations – PR for short. In some ways it is easier to say what PR is *not*. PR is not the art of putting a gloss or a spin on something unattractive. It has nothing to do with using hype and false claims. It does not involve white-washing or concealing a business's mistakes and shortcomings – although a few businesses do use PR in this way, thereby helping to add to its bad name. (It is ironic that PR – the discipline of managing reputations – should have such a poor reputation itself.) Companies misusing PR in this way deserve to have their actions branded mere 'PR stunts'.

A lot of businesses wrongly believe that PR involves little more than attracting positive media coverage. In my work as a PR consultant I am often asked to do what I can to notch up a few column inches for a client. Companies do not always realise that PR is much more wide-ranging than that. The Institute of Public Relations defines PR as: 'the planned and sustained effort to establish and maintain goodwill and mutual understanding between an organisation and its publics'.

If it is to be planned and sustained, PR cannot be a knee-jerk reaction nor a 'one-off'. It must be an integral part of how you do business. Once you under-stand what your 'publics' (customers, staff and others) need, want and can legiti-mately expect from you, and so long as you can consistently meet those needs and expectations, you will have (and deserve) a good reputation. It is upon good reputations that successful businesses are built.

Are PR and marketing the same?

Public relations practitioners like to think of PR as a separate discipline. Marketers too often regard public relations as a mere branch of marketing. Marketing focuses on products (or services) and their price, promotion and place (distribution). These are known as the 'four Ps' or the 'marketing mix'. The late Norman Hart, Britain's first professor of PR, suggested that added to the classic four Ps of marketing should be P for 'perception'. That's where PR comes in. It is about relationships and reputation, both of which help shape people's perceptions of a company. If customers have a poor perception of a business, they will be loath to buy its products, however good or affordable they are. So without effective PR to build a good reputation, effective marketing cannot take place.

Why bother with PR and marketing?

Enterprises large and small need PR and marketing techniques in order to build their business and make a good profit. There are tell-tale signs which show that a company takes PR and marketing seriously. Here are some of them:

- A look at its product range will demonstrate the company's commitment to products and services that are customer-focused and superior to others on the market.
- They deal with enquiries in a prompt, courteous and efficient manner.
- Their promotional material is attractive and persuasive.
- They know their customers and their customers know them.
- The whole business is well-organised, forward-thinking, focused, flexible and responsive.

The benefits for marketing-led companies include:

- They are less likely to go out of business.
- They make a healthy profit.
- They are envied by competitors.
- They attract and keep customers.
- They attract the best staff – and keep them.
- They are ahead of the game in every way and they stay that way.

Would you like your business to have these attributes? Then take your marketing seriously. Don't see it as a quick fix. Regard PR and marketing as a way of thinking, a part of your company's approach and philosophy. Work through this book, put the techniques you read about into action, and you too will have a growing and successful business.

2 Getting to know you: finding out about your customers

Customers should be centre-stage in your business. This chapter will help you get to know your customers better. It will explain how to classify them, how to find out why your customers buy, and how to give them what they want.

Without customers you don't have a business. Companies that fail to recognise their customers' needs and wants will go to the wall – sooner rather than later. Some initially successful companies make the mistake of failing to keep up with the changing needs of their customers. They carry on in the same old way, year after year, without realising that their customers have moved on. One day, when the bills pile up and the creditors close in, they discover too late that their customers have deserted them. Don't let that happen to your business.

Let's take a look at a fictitious company to illustrate why it is so important to keep up with your customers. Imagine yourself back in the 1950s. You are in your late 20s, married with two young children. Your holiday aspirations do not exceed a week in a Skegness bed and breakfast establishment. A major travel company, Travelogue, arranges bed and breakfast packages to all the favourite British family resorts. Naturally you book your holiday through them.

OK. Now whiz forward to 21st century Britain. You are the same age, but this time you are cohabiting and you have no children. Your partner also works and you take two foreign holidays a year – usually long-haul adventures. You want a fortnight's beach holiday in Goa, or maybe a safari in Kenya. You remember from your childhood happy holidays booked through Travelogue. You call them to see what's on offer. You are disappointed: the prospect of a week in Margate has lost its appeal!

It's obvious that a successful 1950s holiday company will not be successful in the 21st century if all it can offer is 1950s favourites. These days few people turn their nose up at foreign food. We crave the exotic – and we can have it. Advances in jet technology have made international travel faster and cheaper. In line with these changes, holiday companies have altered their wares for their new cosmopolitan, travel-hungry clientele. They have taken serious notice of what their customers want, and can offer it to them in an attractive, appealing and affordable way. The company specialising in bed and breakfast holidays in Blackpool is catering for an ever-dwindling market.

Even household names like Butlins have had to go with the flow. Butlins has said 'bye-de-bye' to its 'hi-de-hi' image. It has met the needs of holiday-makers for excitement and good weather by transforming its outmoded holiday camps into indoor climate-controlled themed spaces. Any business failing to keep up with, or even ahead of, what its customers want is doomed.

That's all pretty obvious stuff, yet you would be amazed at how many companies are stuck in a time warp. They no longer stop to think about who their customers are or what they might want. They carry on working on a kind of 'autopilot'. Does any of that apply to you? Can you say who your customers are? How much do you know about them? When did you last try to find out what they might want? When did you last modify your service or product range to meet the changing needs of your customers?

Who are your customers?

For some businesses, it is fairly easy to know who the customer is. A grocer's shop in the middle of an inner-city housing estate will probably draw its custom from those living on the estate. They are likely to be of a similar socio-economic group and the grocer may even know most of them by name. For other enter-prises, it may not be so straightforward. (Later in this chapter you can pick up some ideas to help you build up a profile of your customers.)

To complicate the picture, you need to know not only your customer – the person who *buys* your product – but also the person who uses it: they are not always the same. Take the case of children's snack foods, for example. Although children eat the food, adults pay for it. Even so, the product packaging and branding are devised to appeal to children. Parents buy what they hope their children will eat. Products bearing pictures of the latest cartoon hero, pop star or footballer are more likely to appeal to children, who in turn are more likely to eat them. End result: happy parents and happy children. By understanding what motivates both the customer and the user, you can create the right kind of products.

Here's another example. Suppose you make men's socks. You need to know whether men themselves buy your hosiery, or whether they leave it to their wives or mothers. If the latter, you will need to aim your promotional activity at women. You would be missing the target by advertising in men's magazines.

Market segmentation

Perhaps you find that your socks are bought by three distinct customer groups:

- men who buy their own socks;
- wives who buy their husbands' socks;
- mothers who buy their sons' socks.

Within these three broad groups there will probably be differences. It is likely that what a young woman is looking for in a pair of socks will be very different to the features an older woman seeks. Perhaps stylish design and colour range are paramount to the younger woman, while quality and durability appeal mostly to the older woman. The type of woman who buys socks for her grown-up son is very different to the kind of man who buys his own socks. You can now begin to see why it is so important that you know your customer.

It is likely that, like the sock manufacturer, you will have different customer groups. Each may require a separate marketing strategy. This is known as 'market segmentation' – the recognition that you have a range of different customers with very different characteristics, preferences and tastes. By splitting your market into different segments you can begin to meet those varying needs and wants.

Putting customers in pigeon-holes

Various ways of categorising customers have been developed over the years. Categories have been based on social class, occupation, income and education. The categorisation designed by the Institute of Practitioners in Advertising, the advertising agencies' professional body, has been adopted as the standard by advertisers, marketers, market researchers and a host of others involved in marketing:

AB   managerial and professional
C1   supervisory and clerical
C2   skilled manual
DE   unskilled manual and unemployed

No classification is perfect. Take the example of classification based on household income. It is probable that two families on the same income will have very different interests and lifestyles, depending on their social class. Look at these two fictitious families:

Mr and Mrs Jones

Mr Jones, an accountant, earns £30,000 a year (plus a company car). His wife gave up her job when baby Benjamin was born. They live in a detached house in the suburbs, read the *The Times*, holiday in Tuscany, and eat sushi. They like watching current affairs programmes and documentaries on TV and they love listening to Radio 4.

Mr and Mrs Smith

Mr Smith, a mechanic, and Mrs Smith, a school dinner lady, have three children. Their combined income, including overtime, is £30,000. The Smiths have bought their council house, they read the *Sun*, holiday in Marbella, and like oven-ready frozen pizzas. Favourite TV programmes include soaps and gameshows, and they love their local commercial radio station.

The Smiths and the Joneses are stereotypes, but they help illustrate how wary you should be of simplistic classifications. Having said that, it is helpful to categorise customers; it has been proved that groups of customers share characteristics. By understanding the characteristics of particular groups, you can begin to target those groups which are more likely to be disposed towards buying from you.

If you discover that your typical customer is female, middle-aged and reads the local evening newspaper, you can target your advertising to reach her. Your adverts should use the kind of language and imagery that will appeal to this type of woman.

In order to segment your market and build up an accurate picture of your many customer types, you will need to undertake research. This can be very basic, simply involving the analysis of information you already have (desk research) or it can be more in-depth, involving your company in commissioning primary research among your customers. You can read about how to do this in Chapter 18.

Business to business

When you are selling to another company, working out exactly who your customer is requires an understanding of the buying/decision-making process. Let's imagine you run a courier business. You get regular work from around 100 local firms including:

- small design studios that need important artwork biked quickly;
- medium-sized law practices that need to move confidential legal documents around the town;
- a few large companies that use you to deliver from town to town.

Already you have some clear market segments. But perhaps you need to take an even closer look at these businesses in order to pinpoint the customer more accurately. Companies are not entities in their own right; they comprise people, some of whom have power and autonomy and others who don't. The customer, then, is not the law firm or the design studio, but certain key individuals within it. In the case of the large company it is probably a secretary who decides which courier firm to use. There's no point in wooing the MD if he or she does not care which courier firm is used, so long as they are reliable and affordable. You'd be far better targeting the secretary. Finding out who your customer is involves asking:

- Who decides to buy?
- Who are the key decision-makers in the buying/commissioning process?
- Who inside the company influences the decision?
- Who makes the final decision?

In order to answer many of the above questions you need to carry out some marketing research (see Chapter 18). Once you understand the purchasing process, and its influencing factors, you are in a better position to know how, and to whom, you should promote your product. You will also need to find out:

- What does the company buy?
- How often? At the year end? Every three years? Once a week?
- How long is the pre-purchase decision period? (Do they start considering the options six months before a final decision is reached? Do they buy after they have run out of the product?)
- What are the key dates in the process? (eg, is there a cut-off date after which they will not accept tenders or proposals?)
- At what stage, if any, can you influence the decision?
- How does the company decide who to buy from? (Do they consult a list of approved suppliers? Do they shop around for the best deal? Do they ask for tenders? Do they use personal contacts?)
- How does the company arrive at a purchase decision? By appraising the options in a formal way? By holding a meeting?

True story

A courier company wanted to win new customers. Its research showed that senior staff decided when to courier something, but secretaries were charged with sending it. The decision about which courier company to use lay with them. The company therefore direct-mailed secretaries at all the target companies to offer them vouchers for Next, the high street fashion chain, as a reward for switching their courier business. It worked.

Four ways to get to know your business customers

Research is essential if you want to get to know your customers better. But without spending too much time or money there are some simple ways of getting to know them:

- *People*   List the five most important companies (and people within them) whom you need to interview in order to find out what they want from your business. Go and talk to them.
- *Questions*   List the principal enquiries you want to make of them. Ask about these when you go to see them.
- *Magazines*   List any important magazines or journals that will tell you more about your customers, the issues that concern them etc. Go out and buy them.
- *Events*   List any exhibitions and events you need to attend which will give you a chance to get to know your customers better. Book tickets and attend them, or exhibit at them.

The psychology of buying

No one buys anything just for the sake of it. Even shopaholics buy for a reason, even if the reason is just to satisfy their addiction to shopping! To make money for your business you need to be able to sell, but effective selling requires a good insight into why your customers buy. What motivates them? Much work has been done in this area, for obvious reasons. If we could unlock the reasons why people buy, what a head start we would have in selling! But life is not that easy. There is no neat set of reasons why people buy, but there are some broad motivators:

- *Need*   Food, heating, lighting, etc, come into this category.
- *Want*   Sweets, cosmetics, luxury items. Often we buy not from need but from desire. We might not need yet another new pair of shoes; we just want them.
- *To make a statement*   Sometimes we buy something as a way of making a statement about ourselves. For example, a flamboyant tie, a Labour Party mug or recycled envelopes. These items are bought in order to make a statement about us, our moral/religious beliefs, political affiliations or just our personality. Ties, mugs and envelopes are practical objects, but we buy them not only for their practical value, but also because they say something about us.
- *To resell*   Wholesalers buy in order to resell to retailers, who buy to resell to customers.
- *For entertainment*   Theatre or cinema tickets, entrance to horse races, lottery tickets, videos and DVDs.
- *Impulse*   Often we buy on impulse, particularly when it comes to things we don't really need. They catch our eye, they might come in handy later, or they are a bargain.

People tend to buy for a complex variety of motivations. Someone might buy a snazzy black and white 'op art' tie because he wants to show his extrovert personality, because it goes with his red shirt, because he wants to irritate his boss, because he loves op art, because he thinks the tie looks stylish, because he likes its silky fabric, because he knows that the woman he fancies is into op art, for nostalgic reasons (he had something similar during his student days in the 1960s) – or, more likely, for a combination of these factors.

Finding out who buys from you and why enables you to promote your product more effectively. If most of your customers are female and buy your silk blouses because they are attractive, affordable, fashionable and versatile, your promotional material might read:

> Beautiful blouses in the finest silk, the brightest colours, the highest quality but the lowest prices. Look smart in the office, or dress up your blouse with gold jewellery for a stunning evening look. The wear-anywhere shirt that always looks great and feels terrific…

But suppose your research shows that your customers are mainly men buying for women as a romantic present. You would need to take a different angle:

> Show the woman in your life how special she is with one of these sumptuous silk blouses, beautifully gift-wrapped and delivered straight to her door. She will love the delicate fabric, the vibrant colours, the tailored cut. But above all, she'll adore the sheer sensual luxury of silk next to her skin. No other fabric is quite like it. No woman can resist it. So next time you want to say how much you love her, forget flowers: do it in style. Pure silk. She's worth it.

If you sell your blouses through wholesalers for resale, their motivation is profit. They want to buy cheap and sell dear. To them you might say:

> Quality silk blouses in ten fashionable colours, sizes 10–14. Only £120 per dozen. Will easily retail at £20 plus each.

Hopefully you can begin to see the benefits of knowing as much as you can about your customers. The more you know about who they are and why they buy, the easier it is to target them and to brand your products to appeal to them. By so doing, you should be able to maximise sales and thus profits.

3

Products: taking a fresh look

This chapter will help you take a fresh look at your products. Find out how you can use your existing products to enter new markets, and how incentives, endorsements and testimonials can help boost profits.

I began the last chapter by pointing out the obvious: without customers you have no business. It is perhaps equally obvious that without products (or services) you have no business. But what exactly are your products? If your business is manufacturing, you should be able to reel off, without hesitation, a list of them. It is not always so easy for the service sector. Suppose you run a large hotel. Is the hotel the product? Or your conference facilities? Or the weekend break packages you offer? Or the fixed-price afternoon tea menu? Or the hotel health club? The bar? It's all of them, and you need to think of each – and manage each – as a separate product, while at the same time ensuring that each is promoted as part of an integrated marketing strategy. It is marketing madness to waste money advertising your weekend packages if you always get vastly overbooked and can easily fill rooms without the expense of press adverts. Perhaps you should tackle your weekday occupancy problems instead. Unless you regard each of your services as a product in its own right, it can be difficult to concentrate marketing effort where it will be most profitable.

The success of one product often depends on the success of another. If the hotel is full of conference delegates, you probably do not need to worry too much about the bar's profits. If your hotel is quiet over winter, it might make sense to entice local residents into the otherwise empty bar by providing a welcoming log fire and laying on entertainment (ie creating a new seasonal product).

By seeing your business as a series of products you can measure the effectiveness and performance of each, and develop separate promotional programmes. If one product shows itself to be in difficulty, you can act to ensure that it does not pull other products (or indeed the whole company) down with it. Even if you are involved in just one line of business, such as hotels or catering, you will still have a range of different products as in the example above. List all of your products. Do you currently treat each as separate? Is each one promoted, costed and evaluated separately? Do you run one at a profit in order to subsidise a less profitable (or even loss-making) but nevertheless important service (eg, your hotel bar might not be profitable on its own, but without it you would be unable to attract the highly lucrative conference market)?

Some companies employ 'product managers' to oversee the development and promotion of individual products. For example, a bank might have a VISA product manager, one for current accounts, one for business borrowing, one for mortgages and one for savings accounts. Although banks are in the business of borrowing and lending, each of their products has an individual role to play within that.

The idea behind the product

Is there an idea behind your product? Let me explain. A cosmetics manufacturer makes, well, cosmetics – lipstick, mascara, blusher and so on. But what does it sell? It sells beauty. A washing powder manufacturer sells cleanliness, not soap powder. A well-known brand of athlete's foot powder has 'Healthy Feet' as its strapline, despite the fact that you buy the product precisely because you have unhealthy feet! Look behind your products and see what you are really selling. You can then build a promotional strategy around the idea behind your product.

Going for growth

Usually, the bigger a company grows, the more profitable it becomes. You can look for growth through:

- *Market penetration* This is where you take your existing products to your existing markets in order to capture a bigger share of this market, or to reach previously unreached potential customers.
- *Market development* Here you take your existing products, but you promote them to new target markets.
- *Product development* This is where you develop new products for your existing markets.
- *Diversification* This involves developing new products and offering them to new markets, a risky strategy unless you really know what you are doing.

The low risk option is to grow through market penetration. But even this may not be straightforward. Suppose your market is well-off elderly people who need domestic lifting devices to enable them to get into the bath, and in and out of bed with ease. To penetrate the market you must reach wealthy elderly people who currently have no lifting devices. How do you know who they are? How do you reach them? There is no easy answer, though you can read more about targeting customers later on in the book.

Market development involves taking your existing products to new markets. It might be that you run a successful architectural practice in Manchester, specialising in small domestic alterations. You could develop your market by opening up in Bolton, Bury and Rochdale.

A strategy of product development has to be based on research. You should not offer your customers new products until you have unearthed any unmet needs. If research reveals that customers using your hairdressing chain would also like facials, leg waxing, manicures and other beauty treatments, you can then consider developing these new services.

For obvious reasons, diversification as a means to growth is risky. Developing new products and taking them to new and unfamiliar markets is not something you would want to undertake on a whim.

Give an incentive

Incentives can help encourage sales of your product. An incentive is an inducement which you can use to:

- *Persuade people to buy from you rather than a competitor*   For example, offering a free carrying case with every laptop computer might tip the balance in your favour, and persuade customers to buy from you rather than a competing computer supplier.
- *Get people to respond*   If you offer customers a free gift, but only if they buy/respond before a certain deadline, this could prod people into action.
- *Get people to buy more of your product*   If you offer an incentive for sales over a certain number, this can encourage people to buy more than they might otherwise do. For example, offering mail order customers free postage on orders over £30 might be enough to persuade some to increase the total of their purchases.

If you are considering offering an incentive, ask yourself:

- What incentive?
- Would this incentive be likely to boost sales?
- Would it boost them by enough to cover its cost?
- What is the evidence?

The dos and don'ts

- ✓ *Do* offer something appropriate that ties in both with with your business or product and with your customers' interests.
- ✗ *Don't* go over the top – customers will know that ultimately they are paying for it.
- ✓ *Do* offer something that will be valued, however small.
- ✗ *Don't* offer shoddy or tacky incentives that will reflect the wrong image.
- ✓ *Do* work out your figures very carefully to ensure you see a good return in the form of new business. The only reliable way to know what effect an incentive will have is to offer it to one group but not to another similar group. Measure take-up and see if the incentivized group was significantly more responsive than the control group. The easiest way to do this is to split your mailing list (see Chapter 16 on direct mail to find out more about 'test mailings'). You can also use questionnaires to find out whether an incentive is likely to affect whether someone buys from you (and to assess the popularity of different incentive options).

True story

A bank, promoting motor loans in July, decided to offer an incentive linked with motoring: snow shovels. Unfortunately, snow shovels were far from motorists' minds, as Britain basked in one of the hottest summers for years. The incentive campaign was a flop!

Get an endorsement

Endorsements can be used to enhance products and boost sales. You don't need to use a real person to offer the endorsement: you could describe an ingredient as the one professional cooks prefer. (We all know which pet food manufacturer says that it makes the dog food that top breeders recommend!) This gives buyers confidence in the quality of the product.

Testing out testimonials

A testimonial quotes someone's words. Big companies can afford to use famous faces to provide testimonials. Perhaps their budget will stretch to a Premier League footballer saying how great their sports shoes are, or a top chef singing the joys of their pasta. But you do not have to use a celebrity. The words of ordinary customers can be every bit as powerful, if not more so. Take the following fictitious example:

> I'm a bit sceptical when I see advertising making great claims. So when I read that Dazzo washing powder gave the cleanest wash ever, I took it with a pinch of salt. But now that I've tried it out on my husband's mud-encrusted rugby kit, my children's chocolate-drenched T-shirts, our gravy-stained tablecloth, and my own make-up-marked white silk shirt, I have to say that I'm more than impressed. It really does work. But don't take my word for it. Try it for yourself.

Customers are far more likely to believe an independent third party talking about your products than they are to believe you. Even big companies use the voice of the people to give testimony to the quality of their product. Kwik Fit leave folders in the reception areas at each of their tyre depots containing compliments and 'thank yous' from ordinary customers. So test out some testimonials and get them working for you.

True story

The manufacturer of a horse shampoo and disinfectant used the following endorsement, by a well-known jockey, in an advert: 'When it comes to my horses' health I can't take any chances. I need a product that gives me 100 per cent protection from any infection. My choice is...' It landed them in trouble with the Advertising Standards Authority, who asked them to remove the testimonial, as the implied efficacy could not be substantiated. Make sure you are able to support any claims made in testimonials.

If you are using a photo as part of your testimonial, don't just caption it: 'Mrs Smith'. Instead say: 'Mrs Smith runs Britain's biggest laundry. She will only use Dazzo washing powder.' Captions attract twice the readership of the main text and you should use them to get your key selling messages across.

Bright idea

Testimonials which look hand-written (even in printed publicity) add authenticity. If the author consents, use their name and a photograph too. It all helps make your testimonial really believable.

4

How to fight the competition – and win!

This chapter shows you how to keep an eye on what your competitors are up to, how to get one over on them, how to keep one step ahead of them, and how to develop a competitive edge.

In business the threat from competition is ever present. It is what keeps us on our toes. Legal means such as patents and trade marks can keep competitors at bay, but there's nothing you can do to prevent legitimate competition from taking place. Competitors will always be around to steal your ideas, your customers, even your staff. The best way to beat your rivals is to keep one step ahead of them. You don't work in a vacuum, so you cannot blithely go about your business unconcerned about what they are up to. Monitor competitors' actions, though forget the Mata Hari stuff because there's no need to bug their boardroom to discover their plans.

Eight ways to keep your eye on the competition

1. *Talk to them* – your competitors will not reveal their trade secrets to you, but you can sometimes discover their plans by getting friends and relatives to pose as potential customers. Of course you don't always have to be underhand to get information. Chatting to competitors at events – Chamber of Commerce meetings and other events which bring you together – does at least give you a chance to eye them up and to get a feel for how they are doing. Keep in mind that while you are monitoring them, they are likely to be monitoring you!

2. *Talk to their customers* – although it is not always easy to do, you can find out a lot about your competitors from their customers. Perhaps interviewing people as they come out of a competing store, or sending a questionnaire to

known customers of a rival, can throw some light on what they are doing that is so good.

3. *Visit trade exhibitions* – this is a useful and enjoyable way of keeping up to speed with developments in your field. Use exhibitions as an opportunity both to suss the competition, and to forge partnerships with non-competing businesses. Perhaps your chain of upholstery stores could team up with the nationwide interior design service you saw at a trade exhibition. At exhibitions, look out for new friends, not just enemies.

4. *Monitor local and specialist press* – successful companies promote their work to the media. By creating a file of press cuttings you can build up a dossier of what a particular business, or a particular sector, has been doing.

5. *Look out for their advertising* – if you attract a major slice of your custom from advertising, it is essential that you monitor your competitors' advertising activities. What special offers, discounts or incentives are they offering? Where are they advertising? (It might be in publications you would not have expected, and that in itself could be useful marketing intelligence.) How are they promoting and positioning their product? (eg as the cheapest/the best/the most exclusive.)

6. *Collect their literature* (annual reports, promotional leaflets, sales brochures, price lists) – to find out what they are doing that you are not.

7. *Visit their Web site* – take a trip into cyberspace to see what they are up to.

8. *Sample their product* – as the saying goes, 'The proof of the pudding is in the eating.' Try out rival products and see for yourself. Spend a night in a rival's hotel, eat your competitor's meat pies, have a look round their showroom, ask them for a quote for double glazing. If it can be sampled, sample it now.

Don't be paranoid

It makes sense to watch your rivals but don't become paranoid, seeing competition where none exists. Some people are so preoccupied with so-called competitors that they have little time left to build their business. That's no route to success. I am a Scotland-based PR consultant but I do not regard all Scottish PR agencies as competitors. Most of the big consultancies are pitching to a very different market. It would be crazy of me to monitor their activities; I prefer to focus on what my real competitors are up to – those who also specialise in my branch of PR.

I was once asked to do some promotional work for a company producing a unique product. They said they didn't want too much publicity because they were worried someone else would come along and steal their idea. I asked them how they expected potential customers to know about the product if they were too fearful of promoting it. And I pointed out that, like it or not, it was inevitable that their idea would eventually be copied. Their objective should be to become the

---

True story

I saw an advert for a firm of designers specialising in housing association annual reports. My own company writes reports for housing associations, but as I do not have an in-house designer I need to buy in design work. I called the designers to get some information. I needed a designer and was eager to try someone new. The person I spoke to was clearly suspicious of me and let it show. He regarded me not as a customer, but as a competitor. I wanted to buy his services, not steal his clients. Rather than answer my genuine questions, he interrogated me about my motivation in calling him. Eventually I issued an ultimatum; send me some information and I will consider giving you some business, or ignore my request and miss out on some well-paid commissions. I never heard from the company again. They have lost out on a great deal of work, and all because they feared competition where none existed.

---

leading name for the product so they would have an edge over any 'Johnny come latelies'. Make sure you do not silence yourself for fear that your competition will find out; if they are any good, they will make it their job to find out anyway. Ensure you know at least as much about your competitors' activities as they know about yours.

Monitoring the competition is just one weapon in the fight. A great way to get ahead of competitors is to develop a competitive edge.

How to develop a competitive edge

The problem with many products is that they are pretty standard. One roll of roof insulation is very much like another. Even if your products are similar (or even identical) to those of your main competitor, you can help differentiate yours by developing a 'competitive edge', that is offering something that is recognized and valued by the customer, that helps make your company appear different to and better than the rest.

Five winning ways to give you the edge

1. *Quality of service* Every customer wants quality service and some are willing to pay handsomely for it. You don't have to be in Harrods' league to use quality as a selling point, so long as your quality claims are matched by reality. Don't raise customers' expectations by claims of fantastic quality, only to dash them by offering an inferior service. Small businesses should be able to offer a higher quality of service than their larger competitors because

True story

Following glowing reports on the founder of sandwich chain Prêt à Manger in the press, in which he claimed to speak to every customer who phoned him (Prêt à Manger bags at that time carried the founder's name and number and an invitation to call him with comments), a *Financial Times* journalist decided to call. Needless to say, she was unable to speak to the 'great man' and was quizzed about who she was. She then wrote in her newspaper: 'My main complaint now about Prêt à Manger is not that I don't like their sandwiches... but that I don't like the way they are better at making grand mission statements than at living up to them.'

people working for a small company, or running their own business, are often acutely aware that the business's success is down to them. Use quality of service as a selling point to give you an edge over the bigger names who might otherwise have a head start on you.

2. *Flexibility*   Do you often find yourself up against much bigger businesses? Use your size as a strength, not a weakness. Smaller businesses ought to be able to be more flexible, less bureaucratic, more responsive, and more able to provide a non-standard service or a more tailored product than larger companies.

3. *Personal service*   The managing director of a small engineering firm is far more likely to know what is happening there than the MD of a major national or international business specialising in engineering. Use this to your advantage. Make sure you meet your customers, talk to them, show an interest in them and make them feel important. Give them a genuinely caring and personal service.

4. *Value for money*   Some small companies have relatively low overheads, offer few perks (private health insurance, company cars) to their staff, and do not run up large expenses bills. As a result, they are able to offer a better value service than competitors, while maintaining the same high standards. Make the most of this by explaining to clients and customers how you are able to offer the same service (or perhaps even a better one) for less.

5. *Image*   Image is a powerful source of competitive advantage; that's why big companies spend so much on PR, design and advertising. Develop a good image that will help you stand out from the crowd. (You can read more about image in the next chapter.) Don't forget that a genuine competitive edge involves not just promoting a positive image, but ensuring that everything you do lives up to that image.

Spotting your edge

What's your competitive edge? To find out, ask yourself:

True story

A famous baked beans company promoted itself as having a family image, which helped its brand develop a competitive edge. However, when parents wrote to the company for information to help their children with school projects, many never received replies. This was uncovered when a major piece of independent research was commissioned to expose the gap between organisations' image and reality. The company received bad press as a result. The family-friendly image that was promoted differed from the reality. Proper marketing involves getting both the image and the reality right.

- Do we do anything different to/better than our competitors? (Eg perhaps you bake everything on the premises, or only use precision instruments.)
- What's in it for the customer who buys our products/services? (Do they get a friendlier welcome, a lower price, better quality, less hassle?)
- What's the gain for them? (Do we have a bigger product range? Are we more efficient?)
- Are we more responsive than the 'big boys'?
- Are we more customer-centred?
- Is our service or product better? How?
- Do we represent better value for money? How?

Find and use your USP

A USP (unique selling point) can give you an edge over the competition. You might run the only Russian vegetarian restaurant in the whole of Britain. Or the largest paper recycling depot in the West Midlands. Or the oldest established bespoke tailors in the world. Or Britain's first telephone evaluation service. Do you have any USPs that you can use to give you a head start? To find out if you have a USP, answer the following questions:

- Are you the only company providing that particular service or product?
- Are you the only one providing it locally?
- Are you the oldest in your field (locally, nationally, internationally)?
- Are you the newest?
- Are you the largest?
- Are you the best on price?
- Is there something about your product or company that is pioneering or unique?
- Do you have a piece of performance-enhancing machinery or equipment that your competitors do not have?

- Were you the first to introduce something that is now commonplace?
- Do your customers get something from you that they do not get with similar companies? (Eg a regular customer newsletter containing special offers, a free extended warranty, invitations to sale previews, corporate hospitality.)

Remember that a USP must be meaningful to your customers. Having a performance-enhancing piece of machinery is not a USP in its own right, it is merely a means to it. The USP arising from that might be that you can turn an order round in 24 hours, unlike the 48 hours offered by your rivals.

True story

Sainsbury's offers shoppers a free breakdown or tow service if they get into car trouble at any of their stores. They also offer free nappies for customers changing their baby at a store, a guide for visually impaired customers, and a replacement if you drop an item before you get it home. Their range of unique selling points gives them an impressive competitive edge. And they promote these services by printing leaflets and handing them out to customers.

Beware price as your competitive edge

In retailing, price can be *the* determinant factor. When shoppers want bargains, the shop offering the best price may have the competitive edge. In business-to-business deals, too, price is a factor. In competitive tendering the bottom line may be cost. Consequently, for many businesses, there can be pressure to undercut in order to gain the edge over competitors and win the contract. But price-cutting can be a dangerous route to take. There are many price-war casualties. Often it will cost you the same to provide a service or make a product as it will cost another company. The only way to do it for less may be to cut corners and provide an inferior product. Do you really want to be known for your shoddy service or products? There may, of course, be times when you can provide the same service for less, perhaps because you operate in a more efficient way or you have lower overheads. In such cases it is quite legitimate to promote price as your competitive edge.

While you don't want to offer cheap, inferior products or services, you also have to be careful not to charge too much, pricing yourself out of the market and ending up with no customers. Sometimes quality must be compromised. Marketing decisions often involve a trade-off between minimising costs and maximising service and customer satisfaction. (You can read more about pricing in Chapter 6.)

Don't be a feature freak

Knowing the difference between a 'feature' and a 'benefit' can help you gain a big advantage over your competitors. A mistake many companies make when selling a product is to focus on its features. You'll sell more if you talk about the *benefit* to customers of the features. Here's a real-life example which shows very clearly the difference between features and benefits. Clarks, the shoemaker, include a leaflet with their 'City' range of men's shoes. It sets out the features, advantages and benefits of its shoes (see Table 4.1):

Table 4.1 Clarks' (the shoemaker) leaflet on their 'City' range of men's shoes

Feature	Advantage	Benefit
Flexon sole	Wears extremely well	Longer-lasting value
Padded uppers	Surrounds the foot with softness	Extra comfort
Extra padding underheel	Cushions heel strike	Less shock
Latex sole	Cushions the heel of the foot	Less fatigue

If you have an edge over your competitors, make sure your customers know about it! Clarks and Sainsbury's give leaflets to customers drawing attention to the benefits their products offer. Take their lead. Get promoting those benefits that set you apart.

Other threats

We have looked at competitors and the threat they pose to your business. Of course rival companies are not the only threat you face. Other threats in the marketplace include the following.

Technological changes

Technological breakthroughs have transformed the way we live and work. (Imagine life without computers, washing machines, microwave ovens, etc!). New inventions can put companies out of business. CDs have replaced vinyl records and DVDs are fast replacing videotape. Such innovations can have major implications for businesses large and small. Will satellite, cable and Internet online shopping affect the way we shop for business and pleasure? If we stop using the high street to shop, how will that affect bus and train operators? The knock-on effects of technology must also be considered.

Legislative changes

Although there is little you can do to prevent changes in the law (other than taking part in trade campaigns to try to avert threatening legislation) you need to be aware of any legislative changes that will affect you. When legislation was introduced to allow a national lottery, did pools operators, betting shops and bingo halls anticipate the effect a lottery and scratch cards would have on their businesses? Most did not. Do not wait for the impact of new legislation to be felt before you act: it may be too late. Legislative change can also herald new opportunities. Keep an ear to the ground so you get the head start necessary to exploit these opportunities before your competitors. Take the example of legislation introduced in 1995 requiring landlords to service gas appliances annually. Wised up gas fitters contacted residential letting agents, housing departments, housing associations and other landlords in a bid to win all that new business.

Changes in fashion

Even really successful companies can be fashion victims. If their products go out of fashion, they could go out of business. What is the next trend? Can you jump in before the others follow? Perhaps there is scope for being a trend-setter. Turn style guru and tap into profitable tastes and trends.

Social trends

Emerging social trends can pose threats. Rising unemployment, for example, leaves families with less disposable income to spend on your products. Of course social trends can offer opportunities too. More mothers work now than in the past, creating opportunities for those in the professional childcare business. We are living longer and the State is unable to look after us in old age. This has created a boom in private nursing homes. What social trends can you use to your advantage?

5 *Building an image*

A poor image is bad for business; if you don't care about your image, you might find that your customers don't care about you. This chapter will show you how to build an all-round positive company image, with a strong brand identity that will help you sell your products and services.

A company with a good image will generally do better than one with a poor image. So take a close look at your image and how you can transform it to help make you a really successful company. (*Image* is the way you are regarded. *Identity* is the visual image you shape for yourself, something I will explore later in this chapter. Ideally there should be a fit between the two.) Image is not a cosmetic afterthought, it is central to how your business is regarded. Let's say you have an old-fashioned image, as British Homes Stores used to. Your products might be really fashionable and appealing, but people will have difficulty getting beyond their own prejudices about you. BHS tackled this by dropping its outdated name (and using just the BHS abbreviation), introducing a livelier logo, running trendier advertising and aiming for a younger market. With products on sale that matched its more fashionable image, its fortunes have turned. What does your image say about you? Is your image the right one for your target customers?

You cannot change your image overnight, suddenly becoming funky, slick and sophisticated, loved and trusted or the tops for customer care. You will have to do some groundwork first.

Examine the image you have just now. Try writing it down. Get others in the company to contribute their thoughts (though bear in mind that what you come up with will be your own perception of how you are seen. The only way to find out for real is to ask those outside your company – customers, the general public, etc. This can be costly if you bring in consultants and time-consuming if you do it yourself. If you need to undertake this kind of research, take a look at Chapters 18 and 26.)

Bright idea

The way you deal with correspondence can either enhance or damage your image. If you have a backlog of mail just now, issue holding letters. In future, respond to all mail promptly so your correspondents know they are not forgotten.

Eight easy ways to assess your image

1. 'Audit' your printed material. Gather all promotional material – leaflets, annual report, letterheads, direct mail packages, brochures, advertisements – and see what image they promote. Look closely at design, at copy and at the photographs and the illustrations. What would you think about your company if you received these things and had no other knowledge on which to base your view?
2. Listen to the message on your office answering machine. What does this say about you? (Could you improve it? Re-record the message to make it more friendly and informative. If you don't have an answering machine, get one.)
3. A good image starts at your own front door. What do your premises look like from outside and what assumptions will customers make before they get through your door? Perhaps they won't get that far if they don't like what they see.
4. Try to look at your reception area as a stranger would see it. A grubby area filled with half-dead plants and out-of-date magazines will impress no one. What impression does yours convey? Is that the image you want?

Bright idea

Visitors will eye up your premises and use what they see to form an impression of your company. Perhaps you cannot afford luxury offices, but don't use that as an excuse for working in a flea-pit. With a bit of imagination you can create an attractive workspace on a shoestring. Invest in a tin of bright paint, some stencils, a few framed prints and some pot plants. It will do wonders for your image.

---

5. Examine your offices. Clean and tidy offices create a professional image. Disorganised and dirty workspaces do not inspire confidence and may cause customers to question your competence. (Tidy your offices and keep them that way.)
6. Dig out your company's job application form and the other blurb you send to would-be employees. What image does it convey about you? Would people actually want to work for you, based on what you send prospective staff?

True story

I was interested in applying for a job a few years ago. The application form asked so many irrelevant personal questions about marital status, medical history and dependants that I decided this was not the sort of outfit I would like to work for. The position itself sounded great, but the application form let the organisation down. How many good candidates failed to apply because of it?

7. Here's a good test of how well known you are and what sort of an image you have. Stand 500 metres from your premises and ask passers-by for directions to your office or shop. Have people heard of you, or do you just get blank expressions? Are people's comments favourable or disparaging?
8. Finally your staff. Do visitors always receive a warm welcome from a friendly receptionist? Ask a friend to make a telephone enquiry to your company. What's their assessment of your image? Were your staff helpful and knowledgeable? The role of front-line staff – receptionists, telephonists, sales assistants – is often overlooked, yet they are fundamental to a good image. Often they are the only contact customers have with your company, so the image they convey can be all-important. Your entire company may be judged on their performance. (Greet visitors warmly, even if you are not pleased to see them! Smile when you answer the telephone – it will make a difference.)

Bright idea

If your office, shop, factory or hotel is difficult to find, produce a map showing where it is and how to get there. Show useful information such as bus stops, train stations and car parks. Mark local landmarks to help orientate people. This way your visitors will not arrive late, flustered, harassed and blaming you!

Be realistic

Consider the image you have, then turn your attention to the image you would *like* to have. Compare the two, then see how PR and marketing techniques can help you bring them into line. Aim for a realistic and achievable image for your business. Once you know what you want, write it down. This is a good way of focusing your mind and clarifying your thoughts. It also provides a useful check that you share the same understanding as your partners or colleagues.

Once you have written down and agreed your ideal image, come up with an action plan to improve any shortcomings in your current image. Now focus on new ideas to make your work reflect your target image. For example, if you want to be seen to be child-friendly, ensure that you have toys, comics and sweets at your premises to occupy children while you do business with their parents.

True story

The shoe shops near my home are not at all child-friendly, making it a nightmare to shop there. By contrast, my out-of-town superstore has tiny seating for children, Disney videos to keep them occupied, and helpful staff. It's worth the extra travel. Many companies work on their family-friendly image because it makes good business sense.

Mind the gap

Image and reality must coincide; if they don't, you have an image gap. You will raise expectations which you will then fail to meet. Everyone will be left feeling disappointed, let down, even cheated. This is one of the best ways to lose customers. The image gap once landed Body Shop in trouble. After years spent promoting their environmentally friendly and cruelty-free image, the public regarded Body Shop as an ethical company they could trust. When a damaging magazine article undermined many of the company's ethical claims, immense bad press followed. Many other cosmetic companies were guilty of far worse things, but they had not promoted an ethical image. In their case there was no image gap. Once you have earned a good image, promote it! There's no room for modesty, so get your trumpet out and start blowing:

- Issue a news release if you are commended or win an award (if you don't know what a news release is, read Chapter 8).
- Frame award certificates and hang them where they can be seen.
- Leave a file of 'thank you' letters in reception for visitors to read.
- Keep a book of favourable press coverage on show.

Branding

'Branding' – the way goods and services from one producer are distinguished from those of another – can help build a positive image. What are the ingredients of a brand? Branding involves the many elements that go into creating an overall impression: the product (or service) itself; package design and presentation; product name; the way the product's benefits are presented; and its advertising and promotion. A brand encompasses physical attributes (taste and smell), aesthetic (how good it looks), rational elements (value for money, usefulness) and emotional elements (perhaps your product makes the buyer feel better about themselves). Combine these factors to create a brand.

Two cricket bats may be indistinguishable in looks, performance, durability and materials, yet effective branding could help one outsell the other by 100–1. Perfume costing £9.99 might be outsold by another similarly smelling scent retailing at £50. Skilful branding can persuade customers to part with five times as much for an almost identical product! Those who buy expensive perfume are buying more than just a pleasant smell. They are influenced by the sophisticated images used to sell the scent. Wearing an expensive fragrance makes them feel good; a £9.99 perfume from a cut-price chemist does not.

True story

Pepsi wanted to differentiate itself from Coca-Cola. Both brands, and many others, came in red cans. Pepsi decided that rather than attempt to be the same as the leading brand, it would be different. Although the drink itself did not change, the packaging went from red to blue. This was backed up with extensive fun advertising which showed red things (tomato ketchup, a strawberry, a pillar box) as blue. Massive media coverage followed. The *Daily Mirror* even published on blue paper on relaunch day. A simple change in packaging (albeit backed up by an £8 million celebrity-studded launch, part of a £200 million worldwide rebranding exercise) resulted in a clearer identity that helped it stand out from the other types of cola.

Even products that you might imagine to be non-brandable, such as bananas, are branded. Labels are stuck on fruit and vegetables in supermarkets and greengrocers, and point-of-sale material is developed to attract customers to the produce. Glamorous TV advertising campaigns reinforce the brand's attributes. People may opt for Fyffes bananas because they have confidence in that brand, even though non-branded bananas alongside taste the same, look the same and cost a lot less.

True story

A test was carried out to establish the influence of brand names. Shoppers were asked which brand they used – consumers who said they used brand A exclusively were given a blind test where they tried both brand A (their supposed favourite) and brand B. Many preferred brand B! Some respondents were given brand B marked as brand A. Thinking it to be their favourite, they said that they preferred it over their actual favourite. The test shows just how powerful branding can be.

Branding as shorthand

Branding is a shorthand; your aim is to ensure that the name of your company, product or service comes to represent a host of associations for your customers. With a successful brand, customers feel confident about the whole product range. People trust the Marks & Spencer brand despite the company's poor performance in recent years, and this confidence extends from their shops to their home delivery service, their financial products, and so on. Having established the brand, Marks & Spencer do not have to start from scratch with new products, which benefit from their association with the 'brand' company. If a new retailer, Marx and Spender, set up shop, it would be regarded with suspicion. It would need to establish its credentials before gaining trust.

True story

Virgin have skilfully promoted Richard Branson as a brand. A survey revealed that 34 per cent of the population were more likely to buy a Virgin product because they like Richard Branson. (Ninety-seven per cent of people actually knew who he was. Few people could name other captains of industry.) Headlines such as 'Branson goes into trains' as opposed to 'Virgin go into trains' are not uncommon. Few companies, large or small, have such charismatic or popular figureheads at the helm; those that do should make the most of it.

Beware of copycats

Strong, successful new brands attract imitators hoping to cash in by copying. If you create a fantastic product, do everything possible (using patents, trade marks, etc) to protect it. Also, promote your product in a way that closely associates it with your company. That way theft will be more difficult.

True story

Some companies, in their efforts to stop imitators, are copyrighting the hues they use to colour their packaging.

A strong brand is an asset, but not a guarantee of success. All it can do is tip the balance in your favour. Although computer A might be the stronger brand, you might opt for next-day delivery on computer B if the best you can get on Brand A is six-week delivery. Imagine you are the strongest brand in the world of, say, catering. All things being equal you will probably attract more business. But if a lesser rival offers free pudding with every savoury buffet ordered, this may put you at a disadvantage.

Once you have developed a brand, establish its standing and then work very hard to maintain the brand value. If most other caterers start giving away free puddings or extras, you could be seen as poor value. On the other hand, your USP could be that you never offer sales gimmicks in order to attract business. You always offer quality and value, so there is no need for gimmicks which, after all, the customer ends up paying for. Such an image would be an integral part of your branding and promotion.

Invest effort in keeping the brand alive and well. If you have established your company as a top-notch service-oriented business, keep it that way. Otherwise competitors will overtake you and your image will be worthless. Maintain your position as the biggest, the best, the smallest, the most high tech, the most efficient, the cheapest... You've heard of Coca-Cola, Kodak, Del Monte, *Woman's Own* and Weetabix. Brand leaders in the 1920s and 1930s, they still lead the field today. Why? Because they put time, effort and money into maintaining the brand.

True story

Although you cannot change your image overnight, you can damage your reputation. Mercedes-Benz introduced a new car to its range in 1997, but the vehicle had potentially fatal design flaws which were revealed by the motoring press. The halt in production cost the company an estimated £70 million – that was on top of the cost of a product recall, and the damage to a prestige brand, with its consequent adverse effect on sales. Work hard to protect your brand and its reputation.

Brand extensions

An established brand can sometimes successfully extend its product lines into related new products. For example, many big name chocolate manufacturers now make ice cream. You can buy a Bounty chocolate bar to cheer you up in winter, and a Bounty ice cream to cool you down in summer. Because the name and the product are already known, establishing a product extension is not as difficult or expensive as launching a totally new and unfamiliar product. The brand name is used as an endorsement of the quality, origin and value of the new product.

The risk of a strategy of brand extension is that the value of the brand can become diluted. Furthermore, if one of your products goes under, attracts negative publicity, or is adversely affected in some other way, the rest of your brands could suffer.

The company as the brand

Usually brands relate to products; a company has its own identity as well as a range of products each with its own branding. But some companies use their corporate brand to sell their products. For example Sainsbury's, where the company brand is used to sell everything from nappies to nuts. For many small businesses, their brand is the company as a whole (which is more distinctive than the services and products it provides). A company's unique personality can differentiate it from the many other businesses working in the same field.

Branding services

Branding can also be applied to services. Service industries can create a perception in the marketplace of their individual personality, setting themselves apart from the competition. They can use such factors as efficiency, friendliness, cost-effectiveness, speed, courtesy, etc to differentiate themselves.

Manufacturers use product packaging as an element of their branding. A tin of Heinz baked beans is instantly recognisable, even from a distance. Service-orientated companies can also make use of visual elements in building their brand. Leading airlines, for example, use their visual identity on flight timetables, tickets, bag tags, staff uniforms, condiments supplied with in-flight meals, even the upholstery in the plane. Unity of design, combined with good service, can help service companies build a strong brand. (You can read more about visual identity later in this chapter.)

Bright idea

Sound can also play a part in branding. It is an underused yet easily introduced element. Why not use music to make you distinctive? You don't have to go down the deafeningly ubiquitous pop music route. For example, the waiting room in an up-market lawyer's office could be made more memorable if Vivaldi were quietly playing in the background. Such music would reinforce the visual image presented by the wood panelling, leather chesterfield sofa and crystal chandelier. Can sound be used to advantage in your business?

Repositioning the brand

Stuck with an outdated or inappropriate brand image? Don't worry. Many companies have successfully repositioned their brand to attract new and different customers. Lucozade is the most quoted example. When I was small, Lucozade was positioned as a glucose drink for sick children. It came in a large bottle wrapped in mustard-coloured Cellophane and was ministered almost like medicine. I was told to drink up my Lucozade to help me get better. In 1983 a dramatic repositioning exercise was launched. British Olympic decathlon gold medallist Daley Thompson promoted Lucozade as a dynamic sports drink. Gone was the image of ill health. Lucozade was for the super-fit. The big bottles and the Cellophane disappeared. In came cans and one-drink mini bottles. Brand extensions – Lucozade glucose tablets and isotonic sports Lucozade – also came along. The composition of the drink is unchanged, but thanks to its radical repositioning, today's teenagers have quite a different perception of the product. Instead of drinking it once or twice a year when they are ill, it is downed once or twice a day. Imagine the impact of that change on the balance sheet! You can follow Lucozade's example and use rebranding to take an existing product to a new and more profitable market.

What's in a name

Your company name and your product names are central components of your branding. Pick the wrong name and your customers might make the wrong assumptions. I don't want to do battle with the Bard, but I think Shakespeare got it wrong (as far as marketing is concerned!) when he wrote those immortal lines for Romeo:

> What's in a name? That which we call a rose
> By any other name would smell as sweet.

Just think about your own name and how it affects your image. Pop stars and actors use assumed names because they know name and image go hand in hand. Reginald Dwight wisely adopted the stage name Elton John. Would John Wayne have had the same image if he had kept his real name, Marion Morrison? How many tough guys do you know called Marion! Names can often give clues to gender, age, social class and ethnicity. Conjure up a mental picture of Charlotte Perciville-Grainger. Now imagine what Parminder Kumar looks like. We all make assumptions about people; their name is one of the factors we use to assess them. Our judgements may be completely wrong but we may never get to find out, if our prejudices prevent us from getting to know that person. The same goes for your business. People will form a view about your company based on its name.

Which company is run by one man and his dog – Joseph Goldberg Market Research or Research-a-Market? Joseph Goldberg's business sounds small; companies containing the proprietor's name generally do sound like one-person bands. This could put people off. Some larger companies using consultancy services prefer to use a fair-sized consultancy. Your name might prevent them from getting in touch with you in the first place.

In the old days of rail travel there were three classes: first, second and third. 'Third class' has negative connotations, being the most inferior choice, with overtones of being a third-class citizen. Now we have just two classes on our trains: first class and standard class. Sometimes it is better not to call a spade a spade!

Naming names

Great thought goes into naming children, pets, pop groups, even hurricanes. Give the same care to the selection of names for your products. Good brand names are short, memorable, and meaningful, evocative or descriptive.

While some product names have become household brands, the meaning or derivation of the name is unknown by the public. For example, we have all heard of nylon. But did you know that it takes its name from 'NY' for New York, and 'LON' from London? Or that *the* brand name condom, launched in the 1930s, got its name from 'DU'rability, 'RE'liability and 'EX'cellence.

There are specialist consultancies that devise brand names. They use a mix of brainstorming and focus groups to create potential names. These are reduced to a short list from which one is selected, which must be:

- *Available*   some names are already spoken for, are too close to already-registered names, or are rejected because the Web name has already been taken.
- *Pronounceable*   if a product is for a worldwide market, its name must be easy to pronounce in all languages.
- *Suitable*   a product name must not translate into a rude or negative word abroad.

True story

If you are planning an international product, make sure the product name you select will not cause offence or hilarity in other languages. I came across an ice lolly called Bum Bum when I visited Hungary. That's one I'd definitely prefer not to lick! Other foodstuffs available abroad include: Slag, Plopp, Krapp, Dribly, Zit and Sweat. With names like that, they are unlikely to do well over here, harmless though they may be in their own lands. Even innocent-looking number/letter combinations can be dangerous. Toyota's MR2 sports car, pronounced 'M-er-deux' in French, sounds too much like the French slang for 'shit'. Then there are the foreign names that sound so sophisticated, except in their country of origin. Would you buy 'Kevin' aftershave, 'Keith' cigarettes, or 'Colin' tuna fish? They are all available abroad.

A name must be apt and concise, while at the same time conveying the right kind of image. Charlie S. Miller and Sons Building and Timber Yard Limited is descriptive, but it's not snappy. It implies a small, family-run business, which might be the image you want. By contrast, the Timber Depot sounds larger and

---

Bright idea

The most uncommon letters in the English language are X, Q, Z, J and K. (They are also the higher scoring letters in the word game Scrabble.) Because they are unusual, they tend to leap out from the page. That's why so many product names include them, particularly the letter 'X'. Look through your cupboards for Andrex, Dettox, Dulux, Durex, Tipp-Ex, Kleenex, Weetabix, Rolex, Radox, Biotex, Copydex, OXO, Sandtex, Moulinex, Exlax, Pipex, Zovirax... Can you use these letters to effect?

---

more contemporary. A shop called Krazy Kutz sounds cheap, cheerful and definitely down-market. One called Sloane's of Piccadilly sounds quite the reverse.

Name dropping

While it has been argued that a well-known business should stick with an established name, the big accountancy and management consultancy firms are forever changing their names following frequent mega-mergers. A number of household names, too, have successfully changed their names to keep up with the times and appeal to a new generation. You may need to consider a name change if you fear your name is turning away potential customers.

True story

There are always quirky exceptions to the rules about product names. There is a New Zealand Sauvignon Blanc wine called Cat's Pee on a Goosebury (sic) Bush. Part of the wine's appeal is its name, which has become an in-joke among wine connoisseurs. It is so popular that demand outstrips supply. The bizarre product name has been complemented by equally eccentric packaging. While most wine labels look pretty similar, Cat's Pee shows a cartoon cat grinning on the front label, and the back label shows the same cat urinating on the bar code.

Visual identity

Branding encompasses visual identity. People are often judged by how they look. Your company will be judged on its letterhead, its product packaging, its annual report... the list goes on. Your logo is one of the key elements of your visual identity; its colours and design set the style for everything else.

Logo low-down

A logo is such an important part of your visual identity that you should avoid doing it yourself; invest in a professional designer. It need not break the bank; you should be able to get a new logo for around £400 if you shop around. (See Chapter 24 for advice on how to choose and use a designer.)

Before you start talking to designers, think about the sort of logo you want:

- What do you want your logo to say about you? What sort of image should it portray? (Fashionable? Welcoming? Stylish?)
- Does the logo need to reflect your area of work? (eg if you build ships, does the logo need to show a ship?)
- How could this image be achieved? Sketch your ideas if you like. (Don't worry if you don't have strong ideas of your own. That's what you are paying a designer for, though it will be a help if they have something to go on.)
- Does the logo need to incorporate any words? (eg the company name)
- Will it incorporate a strapline (a brief statement or description of your work)?
- Will your logo be a design in its own right (such as the logo for Shell, the petrol company) or will it be 'typographical' (a stylised version of your name, like Harrods, Coca-Cola or Kellogg's)?
- How many colours will you want? (Do you want particular colours? Are there any colours that should be avoided?)

Once you know what you are looking for, find and brief a designer.

Your designer will produce rough drawings of their ideas. Keep the sketches for a few days, get them out from time to time to look at them, and share them with others whose opinion you value. Take your time; if you choose the wrong one it might prove a costly mistake. You could even end up living with it for years. (Logos have a long shelf-life so avoid anything that will date quickly.)

After careful consideration and consultation, have another meeting with your designer. Outline your reaction, thoughts and comments on the designs. If necessary, don't be shy about commissioning further sketches. After all, it's your logo so it's important that you like it. Don't accept a design you are unhappy with. Sometimes a designer will produce a rather obscure design accompanied by some fancy explanation of its inner meaning. Don't accept any pretentious nonsense. Your designer might claim that a blob with lines emanating from it is a visualisation symbolising honesty. If it looks like a stripy blob to you, chances are that it will look like a stripy blob to your customers. Don't get taken in; trust your instincts.

Bright idea

The test of a good logo is its 'sizeability'. Will it look good really large? Or really small? Blow it up and reduce it using a copier to test it out. It should be able to be reduced to just one or two centimetres across and still be clear. If you plan to use it as a decorative element on cartons and packaging, make sure your chosen design will work well for this purpose.

What colour?

Don't get carried away with colours; too many and your logo will be expensive to print. A talented designer will be able to produce an attractive and creative design with just one or two colours plus tints. If you opt for a two-colour logo that uses soft pastels or light shades, you may still end up having to use a third colour for printing text, as you will find that the colours used in your logo are too light to work effectively for text in leaflets and other publicity materials, or even on your letterhead. You will probably need to add black for text.

Bright idea

Select a design that will photocopy and fax well, and that will look effective in black as well as in colour. If you use computers and desktop publishing, consider a logo that will scan and print out well, so that you can drop it into documents, on to typed invoices, and use it in other ways via your computer, thus giving everything that you produce your corporate identity.

When choosing colours, remember that certain colours carry obvious connotations (red – Labour, left wing; blue – Conservative; pink – gay; green – environmental; yellow – cowardly), while others have subconscious meaning. The use of colour can alter perceptions. An experiment showed that women offered coffee in a brown pot felt it was far too strong, while coffee served from a yellow pot was considered too weak. In fact the coffee in both pots was of the same strength! If you are having a new corporate identity developed, think how your main colour will look on packaging, labelling and other materials you produce and consider the effect it will have on the consumer.

The colours you select for your logo are known as your 'corporate colours'. Take every opportunity to use them to reinforce your visual identity. Applying your identity can be fun, so don't limit yourself to your letterhead! Be imaginative. For example, dream up original ideas like planting window-boxes with flowers which bloom in your corporate colours.

> ### *Bright idea*
> *Ask to see your shortlisted logos on letterheads, compliments slips,*
> *etc, to get a proper feel for how they will look in use.*

True story

My business is called Pink Anglia, so I use pink on my letterhead, sign my name in pink ink, use pink staples and paper-clips, and have pink flowers on my desk. Perhaps it is gimmicky, but it is memorable too. And that's what it's all about. One of my clients spotted a pink Anglia (a car) when holidaying in New Zealand. It made him think of my company, so he took a photo of it which now hangs on my office wall. Do your customers have cause to think about you when they are on the other side of the world?

Straplines

Many logos incorporate a strapline – a statement or description which is used in conjunction with a company's name and/or logo. Here are some examples:

- Dick's Diner: great food, great prices.
- The Handmade Cabinet Company: where quality counts.
- CrackAttack: the windscreen repair people.
- Jeremy's Furniture Emporium: the best furniture for less.
- Aitken, James and Company: putting you first.

Use a strapline to explain a business name that is not self-explanatory, or to emphasise a feature or benefit. Incorporate it into the design of your stationery, adverts and publicity material.

There are benefits in a coherent corporate identity. A revamp can freshen up and update your image, helping you appeal more to your target customer. Having a strong visual identity need not be monotonous, and it is undoubtedly a good way of reinforcing your presence and encouraging quick recognition among customers and the public. The more they are exposed to it, the sooner they will come to associate your colours with your company, and to recognise your logo.

True story

At the tender age of three, before my son could read or write, he was able to spot Pizza Huts and McDonald's in towns he had never before visited. His recognition must have been based on visual identity.

Most large companies produce design guidelines on the implementation of their corporate image (see Figure 5.1). Unless you are a biggish business, or have more than one person producing publicity material, there is probably no need for you to worry about this.

Figure 5.1 Design guidelines

Design Guidelines for Bert's Bistros

INTRODUCTION
This design guide illustrates the main elements of our visual image and style. The aim of having a coherent design is not to create dull conformity, but to present a strong and instantly recognised image. A customer walking into Bert's Bistro in Aberdeen will be greeted with the same detailing as a customer using our Luton outlet.

COLOUR
Our logo is printed in red and black on white paper. To ensure that you get the right shade of red, you should tell printers that the red we use is 'PMS 032'. (PMS stands for pantone matching system, an international system used by printers for ensuring colour match.)

Tempting though it is to introduce new colours, it is important that you stick to the official colours, so that all our menus and other material have a unified look. If you are printing in black only, you will find that the logo reproduces well in black and white.

TYPEFACE
We use a typeface called Marker Felt Thin. If you are reproducing in colour, the words 'Bert's Bistro' should always appear in red. Body text should appear in black in a typeface called Palatino. You can use bold, regular or italicised text as appropriate.

LOGO
Our logo is an extremely versatile image and it's tempting to be creative with it, changing it to make it more interesting. Please don't. The logo should always appear as it does in this guide. Please use it on all publicity you produce.

POSITION
The logo should appear on the top right-hand side of the page, with our name centred beneath it.

BROMIDES
The bromides (master artwork) enclosed with this contain some words and images that you might find useful. We have provided a limited number of sizes, but these can be enlarged or reduced as required.

FURTHER APPLICATIONS
Our logo should be used on all stationery, menus, posters and other publicity materials and on our vehicles and staff uniforms.

Remember that image is not the icing on the cake. Without a good image you might find that you no longer have a cake! So take good care of your image and constantly strive to improve it.

6

The price is right: pricing for profit

Everything has its price, but do you know how to use price to your advantage? This chapter will explain how discounts, promotions and special deals can boost sales. It warns of the pitfalls of poor pricing policy and shows how you might even be able to sell your products for more.

'Price' is the most flexible of the marketing mix's 'four Ps' (product, place and promotion being the other three). It takes time to implement a new promotional strategy, to change distribution networks, or to develop a new product altogether. But price can be changed instantly and frequently is. How often have you seen petrol prices change overnight?

What if your products are making you a nice profit? Can you ignore price and concentrate on the other 'Ps'? Maybe. Maybe not. If you are in a business where your price is affected by competitors' activities, price monitoring should be a constant part of your marketing research. If a competitor reduces prices, you will need to consider why they are doing it, what their strategy is, and what your response should be. Remember that in price wars there are casualties on both sides. So before the knee-jerk reaction to cut prices to match, step back and take a considered view. But even if your business is not prone to competitor-provoked cost-cutting, price is still a factor you must consider.

Bright idea

If you sell through direct mail, why not do a test mailing to see the effect price has on sales? You can send out a batch of direct mail literature featuring your product at a lower price, a batch featuring a medium price and one priced on the high side. (See Chapter 18 for full information on how to do a test mailing.)

Don't go cheap cheap: six reasons not to undersell

Some companies believe that they must sell cheaply in order to shift their products. It can be a dangerous strategy.

1. *It may put you out of business*   Companies offering knock-down prices are working on very tight margins and relying on a high volume of sales. All it takes is a downturn in your market, even just a slight one, to threaten the life of the business. You can then either put prices up (which makes it even less likely that you will regain your previous sales volume), or cut quality. Once you mess with quality, you are doomed. You will lose credibility, lose customers and lose your business. The moral? Don't sell too cheaply.
2. *It may give you a bad name*   Low price is often equated with low quality, so pricing cheap can work against you. Customers might actually pay more for an identical product because they think it must be better.
3. *People buy through need*   It isn't cost that gets people to buy; we buy through need. Your aim is to meet the need at the right cost. A cheap car radio is no good if it is too big to fit the slot in your car. An expensive car radio is no good if you can't afford it. A medium-priced one that does the job is just what you need. Aim for Goldilocks pricing – not too cheap, not too expensive, but just right.
4. *It may be unnecessary*   You may be more 'price aware' than your customers. If they are very price conscious and do a lot of shopping around, you have to pay attention to your price. If they don't, you would be a fool to sell too cheaply.
5. *You might spark a price war*   If you enter the market with cheap goods, or sharply cut your prices, you could start World War III in your market sector! You might find that your bigger rivals are better placed to undercut you and drive you out of business.
6. *The cheapest does not always win*   In tendering, there may be many factors at work, and one of them will inevitably be price. But being the cheapest may not guarantee you the work. The other benefits you offer may give you an edge. By cutting costs to the bone in order to produce the lowest tender, you might lose out to a company charging a little more, but offering a lot more.

True story

Research has shown that people often find it impossible to distinguish cheaper and more expensive products in 'blind' tests; one butter tastes very much like another. But if you let testers catch sight of prices during the blind test, they tend to say they prefer the one with the pricier tag. Because they know it is more expensive, they actually think it tastes, smells or sounds better! In one test, people were given three samples of the same whisky, but told each was different: one cheap, one medium-priced and one expensive. The higher the supposed price, the higher the perceived quality!

Creative discounts

Sometimes a business finds that it must offer discounts from time to time. Perhaps they need to fill up slack demand, shift excess stock, or get rid of some poor-selling lines. Never discount just because others are. Only do it if you must and only if you know what you hope to achieve by so doing. If you must discount, use your discounting creatively:

- Don't just offer 20 per cent off, combine it with a time limit to force the sale.
- Use discounts to sell more. For example, offer the discount only if a sale is for more than a certain amount, or only if the customer buys two.
- Rather than offer cash off, give away something extra free. For example, offer the customer something that has a high perceived value, but which actually costs you very little.

If falling sales are tempting you to discount, first look into the cause for the fall. If it is internal (eg poor quality control, poor customer care), tackle that problem first.

Sometimes you can build a permanently cheaper rate into your pricing structure as a conscious marketing ploy. It can be really effective if you do it well. For example, a restaurant might offer a discount to diners eating in the slack period before 7.30 pm. Such a policy would help recoup some fixed costs and entice people in who might subsequently come back at peak times and pay premium rates. Many nightclubs offer free or half price entry before 11 pm as a way of making a profit by selling expensive drinks at times when the club is normally quiet. Everyone gains with such offers. You help cover your fixed costs, while your customers benefit from a discount. Can you develop a price structure based on market segmentation that suits you and your customers? A health club swimming pool may normally be empty during the day. By launching a cheaper off-peak membership targeted at people who are free to swim then, you can make money out of your slack times. Peak times such as after work could attract higher prices. What is important with such offers is that they are branded or differen-tiated. For example, in the case of the health club, it could market its discount as the 'Mother and Baby Swim Club'. Restaurants could offer pre-theatre dinners; shops could offer early bird prices, and so on.

Bright idea

If you charge differently according to your own workload (eg if your printing presses are lying idle, you might charge less just to secure some work), make sure you never appear desperate for business. Package your price deal so it looks like a special offer the punters can't refuse. Or perhaps offer the normal price, but with a guaranteed 25 per cent discount off the next three orders. At least that way you will get some repeat business.

Don't round up

There is one discounting technique that really works and is highly recommended – you will have seen it in action thousands of times. How often have you seen goods offered at £9.99 or £119.95? By knocking a penny, or 5p, off the natural round price, you can sell more. It's silly, but it's psychological too. It does work. Look at your own prices and see if it can work for you. Your aim is to ensure that the first digit your customer sees is one lower than it would be if you rounded off your prices. So 40p becomes 39p and £1,000 becomes £995. It is a powerful way of making your prices appear more affordable without having to offer a significant discount.

Six ways to charge more

1. *Offer added extras* You may be able to charge more than your competitors if you offer something extra to justify your higher price. This might include better guarantees, more flexibility, better delivery times, easy payment, technical or after-sales support, 'free' gift-wrapping or some other benefit that gives you the edge. Look at your products and list their strengths and weaknesses. Now look at the main competition. How do they measure up? Don't just look at their product, look at their after-sales support, their customer service, delivery details, and so on. Now do a list of what your customers are looking for. See how well you can meet their needs, and how you compare with your rivals. This exercise should show you clearly what makes your product or service distinctive. If you can find nothing, look at what features you can build in that will allow you to justify charging more. Be sure your customers will value the extras you can provide and are willing and able to afford the extra cost. (Better still, try to add value to any offer without adding too much to cost.)

2. *Get them to invest, not buy* If you are selling a product, you are offering something tangible. Buyers can see what you offer, and compare it with what else is available for the same price. Selling an intangible, like consultancy, is so much more difficult. If you are in this game, and you charge a higher hourly rate than competitors, customers will rightly want to know what makes you better. If they are shopping on price, perhaps you need to change their way of thinking. Get them to think about expenditure as an investment that yields a return. Let's say you run an advertising agency and you will produce a company's adverts for £5,000. They can get Dodgy Advertising down the road to do the same job for half the price. You know Dodgy's reputation; their adverts will not do the job. You are confident that your £5,000 will reap £100,000 in extra sales. You wonder whether Dodgy's work will bring in enough sales even to cover the promotional costs. £5,000 bait used to net £100,000 is cheap. £2,500 netting £2,000 is expensive.

3. *Sell on value, not on price* Look both at the cost of providing your service, and the value of that service to your client. To run a profitable business the cost to you must be a great deal less than the value to your customer. Customers' perceptions of value are important. Understand the value of your service to your customer, and be sure to promote that value vigorously. Let's say your business is to stuff envelopes and undertake large mailings for companies. If you promote your service on price alone, you will sell only to price-sensitive companies already interested in using such a service, who may already have shopped around, and will select you because you are cheaper. A better strategy would be to sell on value. Such a strategy involves promoting the benefits for the customer (see Chapter 10 on selling) and creates a sense of worth in their minds. For example, instead of saying 'Mail house offers a collating and mailing service that is fast and affordable', say instead: 'Save staff time and hassle by letting us take care of your big mailings. We can do it in a fraction of the time, allowing you to get on with your business…' Once you have conveyed the value of the service, in terms of hassle-free mailings and stress-free staff, you can then get on to cost-effectiveness. It does not matter that other mailing houses charge less than you. If the value of what you are offering is great enough, your wares will be bought.

4. *Alter perceptions* The perceived value of your product is not fixed. You can influence it, even add to it, with good branding (see Chapter 5). If, through branding, you have positioned your product as a luxury item, people will perceive it as luxury and be willing to pay more for it. Luxury, gift-wrapped soap with an exotic name may cost 20 per cent more to make and package than household toilet soap, yet sell for ten times as much. Price and product positioning are inevitably related. A magazine that is positioned for a down-market readership cannot charge the same price as an up-market glossy. Equally, readers of *Exclusive Interiors* might not like their magazine quite so much if it costs the same as *Budget Home Weekly*. Branding, and with it customer perceptions, are important.

5. *Charge a premium*   Sometimes you can charge different prices for the same product. Obvious examples of this are first-class post, peak rate travel or phone calls, and high-season holidays. If your customers need to catch a commuter train, get their mail to its destination by the following day, or take their vacation in July or August, they will have to pay a premium. The product is the same, but their need is greater and they are willing (or obliged) to cough up.
6. *Launch something new*   Companies can sometimes charge a very high price for a new product in a deliberate attempt to put it beyond the reach of the mass market. People who see themselves as trend-setters are prepared to buy at inflated prices. Once you have exhausted the trend-setter market, your prices can be lowered to appeal to the less fashion-conscious.

Bright idea

If you are planning a price increase, use it to your advantage by turning the bad news into good news. Tell your customers that prices will go up in four weeks and send them an order form so they can buy up stocks at the old price. It's a clever way of attracting sales and making people feel they are getting a bargain.

Presenting your price

If you sell goods with a price tag stuck on them, or you publish a price list, presenting the price is straightforward. But many businesses are asked to quote for a piece of work. The way you present your price in the quote could make or break the deal for you. See the following two Figures 6.1(a) and 6.1(b) for redecorating a room and repairing a flood-damaged ceiling.

Figure 6.1(a)   Quotation for room repair and redecoration

Dan Dosey and Son Decorators

QUOTATION

Repair to ceiling and redecoration of master bedroom	£715 (PLUS VAT)

Compare it with this:

Figure 6.1(b) Quotation for room repair and redecoration

The Efficient Decorating Company

QUOTATION

Rake out old plaster and remove all debris
Apply plasterboard and two coats of skim
Strip walls and rub down skirtings and door
Apply lining paper and wallpaper to walls
Apply lining paper to ceiling and paint with two coats of emulsion
Apply undercoat and two coats of gloss paint to all woodwork
Clean up all mess and remove all rubbish

£735 plus £137.37 VAT = £872.37
(includes all supplies except wallpaper)

Which would you choose? I would select the Efficient Decorating Company, even though they want £20 more. Perhaps both companies are offering the same service to the same standard, in which case I would be better off with Dan Dosey. The point is, I know what I'm getting with the Efficient Decorating Company and it looks to me as though it's better value than Dan Dosey, who hasn't bothered to spell it out to me. The lesson? Itemise and explain in detail what is included in the price. Use the quotation as an opportunity to get your prospect excited about the purchase rather than depressed about the cost.

Price setting

Many companies undertake research among potential customers to assess what price they are willing to pay for a particular product. If you ask customers: 'What would you pay for this?' people will find it very difficult to answer. It is far better to ask a series of questions, such as:

1. 'If you were about to buy product X, what price would you consider so low that you would have doubts about its quality?'
2. 'If you were about to buy product X, what price would you consider to be affordable or good value, but not so low that you would have doubts about its quality?'
3. 'If you were about to buy product X, what price would you consider to be expensive, but at which you'd still consider buying it?'

4. 'If you were about to buy product X, what price would you consider to be so expensive that you would not consider buying it?'

Using this data you can get a good feel for an acceptable price range. (You can read more about surveys and questionnaires in Chapter 18.)

Do not overlook the role of price in your marketing mix. Really get it working for you – your profits depend on it!

7 How to produce a PR and marketing strategy

To be good at PR and marketing you need to know what you are doing, when you are doing it and why you are doing it. In other words, you need a PR and marketing strategy. This chapter will show you how to go about developing one that is tailor-made for your company.

If you want your business to really benefit from PR and marketing, you will need to be strategic in your approach. 'Doing a bit of marketing' is not an option. Effective public relations and marketing require a systematic, sustained and strategic approach. *Ad hoc* or casual attitudes to marketing result in failure. PR and marketing are time-consuming, requiring in-depth research, detailed planning and long-term commitment.

The only way to achieve real and measurable benefits from marketing is to produce a PR and marketing strategy. A marketing strategy has been likened to a road map. A good one will show you the place you want to be and the route you will need to follow to get there. If you lose the way, like a road map, your strategy will show you where you went wrong and how to get back on course.

Teamwork

Unfortunately I cannot give you an off-the-peg marketing strategy for your company. Every strategy needs to be tailor-made. Developing one from scratch is a daunting prospect, and getting started can be the hardest part, particularly if you try to do it all by yourself. Involve others if you can, perhaps your partners or others whose judgement or views you trust and respect. This group will be your marketing team and it will be responsible for devising your marketing strategy.

Your team must be clear on its role and everyone in it must understand what marketing is. Hold a briefing meeting to make sure that you all share an understanding of marketing and its benefits for your company. It will help if you make sure everyone involved in your marketing reads this book first.

Begin by reviewing where you are as a company. Your aim is a thorough understanding of how you currently work and of the factors that affect that work. This involves:

- looking critically and objectively at how you operate;
- understanding why you take the decisions you do;
- examining what influences your work.

Now is a good time to undertake a 'SWOT analysis'. SWOT is an acronym that stands for:

- *Strengths*   What are you good at as a company? What do you do better than others?
- *Weaknesses*   What are you poor at? Where is there room for improvement?
- *Opportunities*   What opportunities are there for you externally, either now or in the future?
- *Threats*   What threats exist externally, now or in the future? Who are your competitors and what threats do they pose?

Your SWOT analysis will help you understand your company and your market a little better. When you come to write your strategy you will need to find ways to build upon your strengths, strengthen your weak areas, take action to minimize threats and ensure that you grasp opportunities.

During your SWOT analysis you will have looked at the threats from competition. You will also need to examine other external factors over which you have no control. (Look at Chapter 4 again if you need a reminder of what to consider.) Also focus on the internal variables over which you have complete control (for example, the set-up/structure of your company). This will show you which factors you can influence, and which will inevitably limit you.

Your strategy will focus on your customers, so build up a clear picture of them before you set to work on it. List who they are. Group them into categories, for example frequent buyers, bulk buyers, loyal customers, older women, families. (Categorise them in any way that makes sense.) Examine what they want from you and take a realistic look at what you can offer. When you finally get started on your strategy, you may need to examine ways of better meeting customer needs. Perhaps you will have to change your company in order to give customers what they want (ie altering internal variables). For example, you may need to alter your set-up so that you can offer a round-the-clock ordering facility, an overnight dispatch of goods or room service after 10 pm.

For each customer type establish their three main needs. (Research may be required to find out what your customers would like from you and what their needs/priorities are. What is really important to your customers when they buy? Price? Quality? Guarantees? Convenience? Flexibility? Choice? Find out. Chapter 18 will help guide you through the research maze. Chapter 2 will help you get to know your customers.)

Set your targets

Your review should have highlighted any problems. Perhaps it showed that you are not doing a good job of reaching potential customers, or that your customer service is poor. Tackle any identified weaknesses and shortcomings. This is where your objectives come in. Objectives state what you are trying to achieve, and enable you to keep a check on progress (or lack of it!). Come up with objectives aimed at improving performance in weak areas. For example, one of your objectives might be 'to reduce customer complaints by 40 per cent in six months'.

You have already looked at where your company is just now. Next focus on where you want it to be in, say, five years' time. Draw up some short- and long-term objectives. Your objectives should state clearly and measurably what you hope to achieve. For example:

- to introduce a vegetarian range of frozen meals for pubs by the end of the year;
- to have a 10 per cent larger share of the pub catering trade in Leicestershire within five years.

Once you have agreed objectives, you can begin on your strategy. 'Strategy' is an overused business buzz-word. Everyone talks about being strategic but few know how to be. It is not difficult. All you need to do to produce a strategy is to write down the action required to achieve your objectives.

Timetable

Once you know what PR and marketing activity is required you will need to sort out when it is to get done. Set out your intended actions in the form of a timetable. This will enable you to pace yourself properly. For example:

1 July	Launch new gloss paint
	Hold news conference for trade press
	First adverts for new paint appear in trade press
	Direct mail campaign begins. Mail samples to key suppliers
July–August	Follow up direct mail with visits to companies by sales reps

20 August	Start research on favourite colours. Use results as a media opportunity to get some positive coverage for company
25 August	Copy deadline for customer newsletter
30 September	Issue quarterly newsletter. Send copies to media with a news release highlighting newsworthy story
1 October	Start work on annual report. Prepare outline and production schedule
	Begin research to find out what extra sales support we can offer retailers
	Start planning annual sales conference
16 December	Assess PR and marketing successes and review strategy for next year

Ensure that any events you plan will help you meet your marketing objectives, reach your target groups and promote your key messages. Set a date at the outset for reviewing your PR and marketing activity and evaluating its success.

Evaluation

Some companies joke, 'Half our marketing works, but we don't know which half!' It might be a funny joke, but it's not an amusing position for a company to be in. It is vital you know whether or not your marketing activity is working. It's not enough to *feel* it is working, you need to *know* that it is. If parts of your marketing strategy are letting you down, being able to pinpoint which parts will save you money and wasted effort. Your marketing strategy should contain details on evaluation, that is how you will measure the impact of your marketing activity. Clearly you will need to ensure that you have achieved your objectives. You will also need to consider whether you can measure the success of your marketing in other ways, such as:

- increased sales/improved profits;
- reduced costs;
- customer compliments;
- fewer customer complaints;
- effective advertising;
- more visitors to your outlets;
- more hits on your Web site;
- increased positive media coverage;
- more requests for your sales brochure.

There are many ways to measure effectiveness. Set down how you will measure yours.

Not a one-off

The problem with documents is that they have a tendency to sit on shelves gathering dust. Marketing strategies are no different. Producing a strategy is the start of the marketing process, not the end of it! Your job hasn't finished when the strategy rolls off the photocopier. You must action it, keep it under review, evaluate it and amend it over time. The task of marketing your company is ongoing. There will never come a stage when you can sit back and announce: 'Right. That's our marketing dealt with. What shall we do next?' Marketing is like breathing; you have to do it all the time. Stop and you will die.

Budget

How much you should spend will depend on your turnover, size, staff resources, and how high a priority you give PR and marketing. Time spent on marketing is an investment in the business's survival and development, and therefore an integral part of your everyday work. You make time and money available to do the payroll, the annual accounts, for staff training, and so on, so set some aside for marketing. Your investment may not lead to riches overnight, but it should ensure your long-term survival.

Before launching headlong into developing a marketing strategy, read through the rest of this book. Let it fire your imagination and inspire you with good ideas that will help you achieve your marketing goals. Best of luck!

Part 2

The practice

Introduction

If you have been working through this book from the beginning, you will now have a good theoretical grounding in marketing and will hopefully be raring to go. Here's where you get to try out some of the main marketing methods using the simple step-by-step instructions and helpful tips and hints.

If, like me, you prefer to steer clear of too much theory, you may have skipped some of Part 1. The chapters in this section will give you plenty of hands-on advice, but you may occasionally need to refer to the first part for an explanation of some key concept. Largely, though, you will find that this section is fairly stand-alone.

The ideas, information and advice given here are tailored specifically for small businesses. However, as every business is unique, you may need to personalise it a little to fit your own company.

8

Read all about it: using the media

In this chapter you can find out how to attract valuable publicity in news-papers and trade magazines, how to come across well on radio and TV, and how to monitor and evaluate news coverage. There's also helpful advice on how to cope with the media in a crisis. And lots more beside.

An essential ingredient of any marketing strategy is publicity; you must promote your products and your company. The media can help you. You can buy space in newspapers or airtime on the radio (see Chapter 15 on advertising), but you can also secure coverage for free – if you know how.

If you are launching a new product or service, enhancing an existing one, or have some other news, you have an opportunity of gaining some media coverage. Using the media in this way can be a cheap and powerful alternative to media advertising.

Not everyone is clear about the difference between media coverage secured by advertising, and editorial that results from public relations' efforts. Essentially, editorial coverage secured by PR is not paid for, while advertisements are.

Pros of PR over advertising

- Generally it is cheaper.
- Potentially you can gain coverage in lots of publications for little more than the cost of a stamp.
- Editorial comments are more likely to be believed than statements made in adverts, so it can be very persuasive. Glowing statements about your product or company in editorials are more likely to be seen as true, having been written by an impartial reporter.

- An article is more likely to be read, less likely to be ignored than an advert.
- It is the only really affordable way of getting on TV and radio.

Pros of advertising over PR

- Advertising is much more controllable and precise than PR.
- Coverage is guaranteed; it is not left to chance.
- You define the message – you choose the words.
- You decide who you want to say it to – by selecting the right publication.
- You decide what photographs or illustrations to use.
- You decide when you want to say it – the timing.
- You decide on the position in the publication (eg front page, top of page 4).
- You decide on the size (eg full page, quarter page).
- You decide whether to go for full colour, spot colour or black and white.

Cons of PR

- You cannot guarantee coverage.
- You have no control over where or when your coverage appears.
- Your news release may be edited or distorted.
- You have no control over the wording of the story that finally appears; it might take a very different line to the one you had hoped for, perhaps leading to damaging or negative coverage.

Cons of advertising as against PR

- Cost is a major drawback. Usually a PR campaign is cheaper than advertising.
- Editorial coverage carries more weight than advertising because it is regarded as more impartial.

Five ways to get editorial coverage

You can get media coverage for your company, your services and products, in five main ways:

1. by sending a 'news release';
2. by holding a news conference or media event;
3. by setting up a feature;
4. by setting up a photocall;

5. by talking to media contacts.

Each of these five areas is explained in this chapter.

The term 'media' covers radio, TV, newspapers and trade publications. Since most small businesses most of the time will be dealing with local newspapers or the trade press, that's the emphasis here.

What the papers say

A large proportion of what local newspapers and trade magazines write is based on information contained in news releases issued to them by companies and PR consultancies. A news release is a news story written and laid out in a particular style. (You may have heard of 'press releases'. A news release is the same thing, but you may risk irritating the broadcast media if you call it a press release.)

News releases

Understaffing is a problem in the media, so news releases can be a real help for busy reporters. A good release could secure you some valuable free publicity.

Bright idea

Send a relevant photograph with your release (suitably captioned). If it is used, you will have gained editorial coverage that has higher impact on the page than a news story without a photograph. (Don't send photos to radio, for obvious reasons!)

In order to achieve your ends – media coverage promoting your company – and to meet the needs of the press, your release must be a 'good read'. Journalists hate receiving what they dismissively term 'PR puffery' – releases overselling a product and using exaggerated claims and hyperbole. These releases don't end up in the newspaper; their final resting place is the waste-paper basket. To stand a chance of your release being used, you need to find a newsworthy angle. Anything blatantly commercial is a no-no; the media is not in the game of free advertising.

Where you can, send your release to a named person. With the exception of free papers and some trade publications, most newspapers have reporters who specialise in a particular area, for example business, finance, industry, health or features. Get the name of the correspondent who specialises in your field. Unnamed releases go to the news editor, who will do no more than glance at the first paragraph, reading on only if it looks interesting.

The majority of releases are rejected because they have no news angle, are too commercial, are irrelevant for the readership, arrive too late or because the publication has too much news already. Assuming yours is selected for use:

- it will be used verbatim in the paper/magazine; or
- it will be edited and then used; or
- a reporter will call you for further information and then write their own story.

Get your looks right

National newspapers receive hundreds of releases daily; even local papers get more than they can use. With such stiff competition you must do everything to ensure that your release is not among the many rejects. Maximize your chances of getting into print by making sure your release looks right:

- Use *double spacing* so your release is easier to read and edit.
- Use *wide margins* to allow for easy editing and so the reporter can write notes.
- Type *single-sided*, never on both sides of a sheet of paper.
- Use your A4 *headed notepaper* for the top sheet, but plain paper for continuation sheets.
- Avoid too much *formatting* such as underlining, italicising, capitalising, emboldening, and so on.
- Do not *split* a sentence from one page to the next and ideally don't let a paragraph continue over the page.

Bright idea

Try to keep your release to one sheet of paper. Newsrooms are busy places and news editors don't have time to read over-long releases. If you need to include a lot of information, see if you can put it on a separate sheet as background briefing material. Always staple sheets together – it is easy for paper-clipped pages to get separated.

Getting started

Include all the relevant information early on in your release, by covering the 'five Ws'. These stand for:

Who   – who will be doing it? (eg your company, a celebrity)
What   – what will they be doing? (launching a new product, making a major donation to charity)
When   – when will they be doing it? (Thursday, 25 May)
Where – where will they be doing it? (at your HQ, up the Eiffel Tower, on Blackpool Pleasure Beach)
Why   – why will they be doing it? (to satisfy customer demand, to become a market leader, to put something back into the local community).

Bright idea

Write your release so that it can be chopped paragraph by paragraph from the bottom up, and still make sense. This is what often happens to releases and news stories if there is not enough space in the paper – they are brutally hacked at the end! So next time you are reading a news report that ends rather abruptly, you'll know why.

Textbooks will tell you that the five Ws should come in the first sentence, but don't be too rigid about this; it can make for a boring release. Instead, aim for something newsworthy in the first sentence to capture the news editor's attention; continue with the five Ws in the second one. The following example, Figure 8.1(a), shows an opening paragraph that follows the five Ws formula:

Figure 8.1(a)   The 'Five Ws' formula

NEW HQ FOR LOCAL COMPANY

Buffy Butterworth, Managing Director of Buffy's Biscuits, will be opening the company's new HQ and biscuit museum in the High Street, Crumbleigh, at 10.30 am on Wednesday, 21 June.

It has all the facts, but it's boring. How can you turn a dull story like this into a more exciting one? By thinking about the story and its novel aspects. The same story, turned on its head, reads:

Figure 8.1(b)   The 'Five Ws' formula.

CUSTARD CREAM QUEEN OPENS BISCUIT MUSEUM

Next week Crumbleigh will make history by becoming home to Britain's first biscuit museum. It will be officially opened by Buffy Butterworth, Managing Director of Buffy's Biscuits, who is known locally as the Crumbleigh Custard Cream Queen…

The story leads with a strong and newsworthy angle that would hold more appeal for local papers than a new HQ for a biscuit manufacturer. Always lead with a newsworthy angle. To find your angle, ask yourself:

- Is what we are doing the biggest?
- Is it a first?
- Is it special in some way?
- What will it mean for our customers?
- What will it mean for the town?
- Is there a more interesting angle?
- Is there something different or unique about it?
- Are we breaking new ground in doing this?

Here are some more examples of news angles showing how to do it (and how not to do it):

WRONG:
Warm as Toast, the draught-proofing company, has conducted a survey of 2,500 homes in the south of England and the findings are published today.

RIGHT:
Householders in the south of England are losing up to £150 every year through poor insulation, according to the findings of a survey published today by Warm as Toast. Across the whole country this amounts to around £3 billion.

WRONG:
SUPERMARKET STAFF FUNDRAISE
Staff at Steve's Superstore in Anytown hope to raise around £200 for the town's Dogs' Home by being sponsored to skip their Christmas dinner.

RIGHT:
DOGS' DINNER
A group of kind-hearted dog-lovers in Anytown have pledged to give up their festive meal so that over 100 strays can enjoy a slap-up Christmas dinner. More than 20 staff at Steve's Superstore are being sponsored to forfeit their Christmas dinner in a bid to raise around £200 for the town's Dogs' Home.

WRONG:
Yesterday the Felix Flea Collar Factory welcomed a delegation of foreign dignitaries on a tour of the premises.

RIGHT:
Businessmen from across the globe descended on Anytown yesterday on a fact-finding mission. Visitors from as far afield as Africa, America and China came to see how our top companies work. Their first port of call was the Felix Flea Collar Factory.

A useful device for introductory paragraphs is to use statistics in a thought-provoking way. For example, don't write 'Nearly 5,000 people are burgled each year in Potterston, and 80 per cent of them do not have a burglar alarm or security system fitted...' Write instead 'Every two hours someone in Potterston is burgled...' Other useful comparisons are:

- The equivalent of a jumbo jet crashing every day.
- For £5.20 – just 10p a week...
- Equivalent to a town the size of Tunbridge Wells.

See Figure 8.2 (overleaf) for an example of a complete news release, illustrating layout as well as presenting an interesting storyline. Note that real news releases should be set out with double spacing between lines.

You can see that a 'Note to editors' has been included. This is where background information that is useful or interesting, but not vital to the story, is included. It helps keep your release short, while ensuring that you don't leave out something that could be useful to the reporter. The additional information about Wilson's Breweries is a good example. You might find it beneficial to include a similar note about your own company, dropping it once you are sure that your local or trade papers know who you are and what you do.

Bright idea

Try not to send the same release to all publications. The needs and interests of your local newspaper will be different from those of national or trade papers. There's no need to send a different release to each publication, just to each group of publications. Major rewriting is generally not required, just topping and tailing.

Figure 8.2 News release

Wilson's Breweries
Hops House, The High Street, Ponton
Tel. 01993 123456

NEWS RELEASE

For immediate use
Friday, 6 November 2002

**CORONATION STREET
COMES TO ANTHORPE**

The Rover's Return in Anthorpe, which has been derelict for nearly 20 years, is to get an £80,000 transformation into a traditional public house modelled on its more famous Weatherfield namesake.

Wilson's Breweries have bought the pub and plan to restore its original features and sympathetically upgrade its facilities, turning it into a faithful reproduction of an old-fashioned public house.

Kevin Colgan, Managing Director of Wilson's Breweries, explained: 'The traditional public house is an endangered species. So many have closed down and been replaced with theme pubs, wine bars, bistros and the like. We believe people hark back to the days of the traditional pubs, where real ale was on tap, and fruit machines, computer games and juke boxes unheard of. That's the atmosphere we hope to create at the Rover's Return. It won't be a million miles different from its more famous namesake and, who knows, we may even persuade Bet Gilroy out of retirement to pull the first pint!'

The refurbishment will begin next week and the pub will open for business in February 2003.

ends

Note to editors:
Ponton-based Wilson's Breweries has been brewing beer for nearly 100 years. It operates 50 public houses across the north of England, including the Black Bird in Anthorpe and the Spotty Cat in nearby Cortown. A full list can be found on www.wilsonbreweries.com

For further information contact:

Kevin Colgan, Managing Director	Andrew Granton, Marketing Manager
Office 01993 123456	Office 01993 123456
Mobile 077 676794	Mobile 077 686143

Nine necessities for release-writing

1. Avoid jargon, hype, clichés and unexplained abbreviations.
2. Date your release. If you don't, the news editor might think it is old news.
3. Keep your release snappy, with clear, positive language, and short words and sentences.
4. Stick to the essentials.
5. Include at least one contact name and number – someone who is available, easy to get hold of, and fully briefed.
6. Include a home or mobile telephone number, as journalists keep strange hours and they can be extremely impatient. If they want to follow up your release, they will soon drop your story if no one answers the telephone after a couple of attempts.
7. Don't try to write witty or clever headlines for the national press – they will be rewritten by the newspaper. (Free newspapers and many trade publications don't mind headlines with good puns.)
8. Use embargoes only if you really must – they can be an irritation. There is a place for embargoes; if you use them properly, you will be doing reporters and yourself a service. They are valuable for complicated stories when a reporter might wish to do some advance work on the story. They are also good if you are sending material to Forward Planning Departments in radio and TV. Remember that there is always the danger that your embargo may be broken, although they are generally respected.
9. Include a quote in it from a named person. Newspapers like this, as it makes their readers believe that they actually interviewed you, when really they just used your release!

Now over to you

Time to test your knowledge. Rewrite the following Figure 8.3(a) of a news release to make it more likely to be used by a local newspaper.

Figure 8.3(a)   News release

Embargo. Not for use until
Sunday, 26 July 2002

NEW INTUMESCENT PAINT

A new intumescent coating is now available. It has been subjected to a rigorous fire resistance test (BS476 Parts 20 and 22). Just one coating of 30 microns DOT of FireCracker Lifesaver basecoat, followed by 30 microns DOT of topcoat, renders a door fire-safe for twice the necessary 30 minutes required by building regulations. FireCracker Lifesaver is not solvent-based, unlike many other intumescent coatings on the market.

Patsy Khan, FireCracker's Sales Manager, said: 'We are delighted with our new product, which places our company at the cutting edge of fire safety. We are confident that householders will wish to use our product to enhance the fire-resistant qualities of their doors. It could save their life.'

ends

For further information contact:
Patsy Khan, Sales Manager, on 01961 67115

Discussion

What was wrong with that release?

- The newsworthy bit – the fact that this new paint could save lives – is buried in the very last sentence.
- The release lacks news value.
- It is full of completely unnecessary jargon.
- The opening paragraph, which must catch a news editor's attention, has no local angle.
- The release lacks a local flavour.
- The quote is too inward-looking, focusing on the company rather than on what might appeal to the reader.
- The quote is from a sales manager, which makes the release sound a bit too commercial.
- An unnecessary embargo has been placed on the release.
- There is no after-hours contact number.

So how should the release have looked? Compare yours with Figure 8.3(b):

Figure 8.3(b)   News release

For immediate use
Sunday, 26 July 2002

**NEW LIFE-SAVING PAINT
GOES ON SALE IN LITTLETON**

A new fire-resistant paint that could save lives goes on sale in Littleton tomorrow (Monday). It is estimated that around 50 lives in Littleton alone could be saved if families switch to this new paint, FireCracker Lifesaver. That means potentially up to 10,000 lives saved across the whole country.

Humphrey Lewis, FireCracker's Director of Safety, said; 'This paint really can save lives. A simple two-coat process, applied in the same way as conventional paint, can make a standard domestic door fire-resistant for up to one hour. Just close the door on a fire and you have an hour's protection from the flames, which is more than enough to safeguard a family until the fire brigade arrive. If everyone in Littleton were to apply this paint to their doors, we would see the death toll from fires fall by around 50 every year in this town alone. Think of the number of lives that could be saved on a national scale.'

Hardware shops and DIY stores across the town will stock FireCracker Lifesaver.

ends

A full list of stockists, plus technical information, can be found at www.firecracker.co.uk

For further information contact:

Humphrey Lewis	Patsy Khan
Director of Safety	Sales Manager
01961 67115 (office) or	01961 67115 (office) or
01961 11212 (home)	077 891891 (mobile)

Discussion

What makes this one better?

- It has a local angle right at the start of the release and in the headline.
- It has a quote that is thought-provoking.
- Quoting the Director of Safety gives the quote an air of authority and re-inforces the safety message.
- It contains local statistics.
- It contains no unnecessary product information.
- There is a home contact number and a second contact person.
- There are details of where to buy the product.
- It has been sent at the weekend so the newspaper can use it on a Monday, the day the paint goes on sale (which also happens to be a light news day).
- Journalists are directed to the Web site for background information.

Fifteen ways to hit the headlines

What sort of things in your everyday work merit a news release? Here are just a few of the many things you probably already do that might be worth publicising:

1. *Landmarks* – such as your 10,000th customer through the door, your 50th boat off the production line, your 5,000th house sold.
2. *Anniversaries* – your 50th birthday, your centenary.
3. *New products or services* – particularly if unusual, such as a low-calorie chip shop, a poodle parlour for disabled dogs, a dress service for colour-blind people.
4. *Appointments* – announce the appointment of new members of staff, eg 'Top French chef Anton Blanc has joined Ruskin's, Anytown's only five-star restaurant...'
5. *Jobs* – the creation of a significant number of jobs locally.
6. *Results* – if you have had a profitable and successful year.
7. *Research and surveys* – both when you commission it and when the findings are ready, assuming it is on a subject of interest. (Some companies commission research purely to hit the headlines, eg Durex carried out research to discover the most unpopular day of the week for love-making. It released its findings on Valentine's Day in order to maximise coverage. Sex is always a hot subject and the regular surveys commissioned by Durex do very well in terms of column inches.)
8. *New premises* – if interesting, eg 'Buffy's Biscuits have bought the derelict church in the High Street and plan to develop it into their new head office and biscuit museum...'
9. *Predictions* – what you believe future trends in your field will be, eg 'It has been predicted that by 2020, 90 per cent of shopping will be done via a computer, leaving the shopping mall, the High Street and out-of-town superstore obsolete. This is the view of Davies and Hall Chartered Surveyors, who...'
10. *Announcements* – importing some new piece of machinery, offering Balkan cuisine for the first time, opening a new store.
11. *Issues* – pedestrian zones and their effects on businesses, business rates, food labelling, greenhouse gases.
12. *Investment* – in new machinery, equipment, premises.
13. *Events* – open days, exhibitions, charity events, sales.
14. *Topical comment* – budget increases, January sales, summer holidays, cold snaps.
15. *Action* – eg, 'Traders in Anytown are calling on the council planning department to veto the proposed out-of-town superstore that threatens to put them out of business...'

Send a release to your local and trade papers whenever you have something newsworthy to say. Table PR as an item at every partners/directors' meeting, so that you regularly focus on what you are doing, how newsworthy it is, and whether it could be publicised by a news release.

> ### *Bright idea*
>
> *If your company is large enough or specialised enough, you can try to become known experts in your field, so that the media contact you when they are looking for spokespeople on your subject. Put together a list of people in your business who are expert in their subject, include their home telephone numbers, and send your list to newsrooms.*

Send it to who?

Whether you should issue your release just locally or whether you should aim regionally, nationally or even internationally depends on how important the story is and on the kind of business you are in. If you export, perhaps international trade journals will be interested in your news. For small, local companies, contact will generally be with the local media, especially newspapers, and possibly with the trade press.

Achieving coverage in the local media is easier than hitting the headlines nationally but don't rule out the national media for something really newsworthy. Some small businesses do make national news, though perhaps only once in their lifetime.

True story

Don't feel that because you run a small business, you can never make national headlines. I run a small, unfunded pressure group in my spare time. In our first 12 months I secured coverage for the campaign on *Newsnight*, *Kilroy*, Radio 1, Radio 4, Radio 5 Live, local TV, all the national and many local newspapers, local radio, women's magazines and specialist publications. All of this was achieved on a zero budget. If you have a good story to tell, and you know how to tell it, you can make the big time.

With a big story, or a very specialised one, it can be difficult to know where to send your releases. You probably know your local and trade media, but what about other publications? How do you find out what exists and where they are based? Thanks to various specialist directories it is a simple task. There are directories listing trade, technical and consumer titles, local papers, TV and radio, national media, European media and business publications. Entries include:

- the title of the publication (or name of radio/TV programme);
- the names of the editor and any special correspondents;
- mail and e-mail addresses, telephone and fax numbers;
- circulation details;

- frequency of publication/broadcast;
- advertising rates.

They can be organised alphabetically by title, under subject headings, or geographically. All of them are easy to use; many are available at reference libraries. The best known include *PR Planner*, *Editors* and *Benn's*.

Bright idea

Read the papers you send your releases to, get familiar with the type of stories they run and the sorts of photographs they use.

You can also get directories on CD ROM. Subscription is not cheap. The advantages, however, are that you can do searches of the entire UK media in seconds, you can de-duplicate the lists you generate, you can easily print out personalised mailing lists, and you can produce labels to make distribution of news releases easier. You can also get updates via a modem – at a price.

Bright idea

To cut the subscription cost, why not club together with other (non-competing) local businesses to subscribe to one of these directories, or ask your local Chamber of Commerce to get a subscription?

Tabloid versus broadsheet

If you are aiming for national coverage, you need to assess whether your story is best suited to a tabloid or a broadsheet. You may be able to get coverage in both, but remember that tabloids and broadsheets have very different readerships, styles and interests. Generally, the tabloids will love anything to do with animals, children, personalities (especially TV and sport) and human interest. The 'qualities' will be more interested in current trends, policies, politics and issues. The news release on page 66 is a good example of a story with both tabloid and broadsheet appeal. Tabloids would love pictures of Bet pulling pints at the Rovers. Broadsheets might be interested in a more serious social trends-type feature on the traditional pub as a dying breed or an urban myth.

Tabloids have a mass readership which you may want to reach, though remember that the treatment your story will get will be quite different from a broadsheet.

Why send a release?

- It may generate free, positive publicity. Even if it is not used, it will let local journalists know what you are up to and keep your company's name in their memory.
- It can be better, initially, than a potentially irritating or ill-timed phone call.
- It puts into journalists' hands the information you want them to have, so it puts you in control.
- Local and trade papers are often badly understaffed, so good releases are welcome time-savers for busy reporters.
- You can keep a copy, and if a journalist badly misquotes you or twists your story, you have got proof.
- They are easier to read and more logically ordered than a reporter's scribbled and often illegible shorthand notes.
- There's less chance that they will get your or your company's name wrong from a release, or give your story the wrong emphasis.

Bright idea

If you send a release embargoed for midnight, the daily press will be happy to use it (assuming it is newsworthy enough). However, evening papers and evening news programmes on TV and radio will be less keen if it has been covered in the morning papers. So if you want to get on TV, don't go for a midnight embargo.

Follow-up

Having posted, faxed or e-mailed your releases you sit back and wait for news-hungry journalists to call you. The phones are silent. What do you do? It might be worth phoning a couple of days later to establish personal contact and to 'sell' your story, but be careful not to be a nuisance – some journalists are easily irritated, and even the easy-going ones will get annoyed if you keep pestering them or you catch them as their copy deadline approaches.

The best time to call a daily paper is between 10.30 am and 11.30 am, as this is the least busy period and reporters will have more time to talk and will be more receptive to news. Never call between 4 pm and 7 pm, when journalists are writing and checking their copy, or you will get short shrift. And another tip: don't bother to call Sunday newspaper journalists on a Monday – it's their day off.

Bright idea

*Find out the deadlines of your local papers. Bear these in mind when
sending releases and planning events.*

Getting in the picture

When seeking editorial coverage, do not limit yourself to words. Think pictures
too, if you really want to make an impact. There are three ways of getting photographic coverage:

1. Arrange a stand-alone photocall and invite press photographers.
2. Ensure that you have a photo-opportunity as part of your press conference or
   event, and invite photographers to that.
3. Send your own photographs to a newspaper with a news release, but make
   sure that the quality is really good (by using a freelance press photographer
   who knows what is expected). National papers rarely use submitted
   photographs, although local and trade papers frequently do.

If you have something photogenic on offer, send out a media invitation to picture
desks (and TV), headed PHOTOCALL NOTICE. Explain briefly what you are
planning, and invite them to turn up at a certain time to film or photograph it. Set
out your invitation like the example included on page 78.

What makes a good picture?

- cute babies and children;
- animals;
- costumes and funny/strange outfits;
- props and giant things;
- celebrities.

What makes a poor picture?

- product shots;
- people sitting round tables or in meetings;
- 'grip 'n' grins' (people clutching flowers/certificates/awards, etc and
  grinning manically);
- men in grey suits;
- large group shots;
- the backs of heads.

These dull ideas will not be considered by a newspaper, so be creative and go for a photo-opportunity with flair. Here are a couple of ideas.

- A house builder is opening a new development on the site of a former railway station. Instead of getting the chief executive to cut a ribbon, he decides to exploit the site's railway history by getting Thomas the Tank Engine and the Fat Controller along instead. It makes a far better photo, a more interesting event, and is more likely to attract the press.
- A restaurant is celebrating 40 years of trading. It's tricky to turn something like this into a photocall, unless you find a good angle. It offers customers 1960s prices if they turn up in 1960s clothing. All staff are in period dress, 1960s music is playing and it has been arranged that the 1960s group Wayne Fontana and the Mindbenders will be there to enjoy a meal. Now you have a picture that works.

You can telephone the picture desk the day before your photocall to ask if they hope to send a photographer. If the paper is not sending anyone, you might decide to employ your own photographer to take some prints for you to send to your local paper, but don't spend your money on this unless you have a good photo-story.

Bright idea

Use a freelance photographer, ideally one who works for your local paper, as they will have the right contacts and they are generally no more expensive than other photographers. Telephone the picture editor and ask for a recommendation.

A picture editor of a national daily will have viewed 400 images by midday, so bear this in mind if you are targeting the nationals. The competition is fierce and you need a really good, relevant and topical photo if you are to make it here.

Five tips for greater success

Here are five ways in which you can increase, sometimes quite dramatically, your chances of success in attracting media attention.

1. If you can, time your events or releases for a Sunday, as little news happens then. You might have noticed how Monday's papers are often quite thin, and this is why. Newspapers have staff working on Sundays in order to produce Monday's paper, although the day tends to be a fairly quiet one in the newsroom.

2. Along the same lines, plan events or releases for slack times such as the period between Christmas and New Year, or Bank Holidays. By having less to compete with, you increase your chances of success.
3. When dealing with weekly or monthly papers, find out what day they go to press, for the day following press day is a flat one, compared to the business of the day before. This can be the best time to make contact, for it is the least busy period, and it is when reporters are thinking about material for the next issue.
4. Remember the Press Association. They look over the news releases they are sent, and those that merit it are edited and issued as items available to newsrooms via telex and computer links. If the Press Association think your release is of interest, the chances are that it will be picked up by a national newspaper too, even if it just makes one or two paragraphs. The Press Association have offices in various cities, so find out the address of the one nearest you by looking in *Yellow Pages* under 'News and Photo Agencies'.
5. Friday can be a poor day for an event because it will be covered in Saturday's paper, which has fewer news pages and is taken up with entertainment information, TV listings, etc. Try to avoid it.

Bright idea

If you are inviting a photographer to your premises, tidy up first! Get the place looking good, clear out junk and rubbish, and make sure there is no extraneous matter in the background.

News conferences

Releases are the easiest and most cost-effective way of using the media to promote a new service or product, although there may be times when it is preferable to talk to them face to face. On such occasions (such as when your story is fairly complex or especially newsworthy), you can hold a 'news conference'.

Only have one if you have something really important to say. They are hard work to organise, and the media won't thank you for dragging them out to hear some news that does not merit the effort they have made. Journalists claim that up to nine out of ten news conferences they attend are a waste of their time, either because there is no newsworthy story on offer, or because they could get the same information in a news release, thereby saving themselves the hassle of leaving their desk. If you are considering a news conference, ask yourself: 'Would a release be just as effective?' If the answer is 'Yes', send one and save everyone unnecessary effort.

Be realistic about who will attend. Don't expect the sort of attendance that you see on TV, where there are photographers' flashguns going off, packed rooms full of reporters, and TV microphones everywhere. Even if you get several national newspapers plus radio and television – which is unlikely – you will only have half a dozen or so people!

Nine golden rules

1. *Start and finish on time*   Journalists are busy, under pressure, and working to tight deadlines. They have better things to do than sit around waiting for you to get started (or finished!).
2. *Get to the point*   Say what you have to say, keep it to a minimum, and then shut up. If there's something you haven't covered, you can be sure that a reporter will ask you about it.
3. *Select the right time*   The best starting time is around 10.30–11.00 am. This allows TV and evening papers to cover the event, as well as the dailies. It also enables radio to attend and to get back in time to broadcast your news on the lunchtime bulletin.
4. *Use name plates*   Speakers at the top table should have name plates in front of them which can be seen from a distance.
5. *Issue guests with name badges*   Keep a note of who attended by asking attendees to sign a guest book. It's useful if you want to monitor coverage or to fax releases to those who could not make it.
6. *Set aside a quiet room*   You may need it for radio interviews to take place.
7. *Clear your diary*   You will need to be available both before and after the news conference and possibly even the day before. Sometimes radio or TV reporters cannot attend at the time you have scheduled, and they might ring to ask you if they can do an early interview; perhaps that morning, or even the day before. Try to be as helpful as you can at accommodating this, as ultimately it's your company that will benefit from the coverage.
8. *Try to find a central venue*   If you must have your conference off the beaten track, send out maps with the invitation.
9. *Check your venue*   TV will want an attractive or appropriate backdrop for filming against.

Bright idea

Promote your company by giving reporters a press pack – an A4 folder containing your news release plus any background briefing material. Also enclose leaflets about your company, your annual report (if you have one), relevant captioned photographs and illustrations, and product samples (if appropriate). If your press pack is a useful one, it will be held on file for future reference.

Whether you are planning a news conference or organising a photocall, you will need to let the media know in advance of your plans so that they can slot it into their schedule. Send them a media invitation (see Figure 8.4).

Figure 8.4 Media invitation

Wilson's Breweries
Hops House, The High Street, Ponton
Tel. 01993 123456

INVITATION TO NEWS AND PICTURE EDITORS

For operational use only:
not for publication or broadcast

**TV BARMAID BET GILROY PULLS A
PINT AT ANTHORPE'S ROVER'S RETURN**

TV's most famous barmaid, former Coronation Street star Bet Gilroy, will be in Anthorpe next week to pull the first pint at the town's very own Rover's Return in Pitvale Street.

Anthorpe's Rover's Return, which was derelict for over 20 years, has been given an £80,000 facelift by Wilson's Breweries. Barmaid Bet will don her famous low-cut leopard-skin dress, stilettos and larger-than-life earrings as she poses for photographers.

You are invited to send a representative

Time: 10.30 am
Date: Thursday, 4 February 2003
Venue: The Rover's Return, Pitvale Street, Anthorpe

For further information contact:
Kevin Colgan, Managing Director
Office: 01993 123456
Mobile: 077 676794

Media invitations

A media invitation invites the media to attend an event, a photocall or a news conference, enabling them to cover a story for themselves. It is best to send an invitation out about a week before your event. Include:

- a paragraph explaining the purpose of the event;
- a description of what will happen at it;
- a list of all the necessary information (start times, venue, who will be there, and so on).

Remember that media invitations are designed to attract reporters to your event, not to take the place of a news release. Don't give too much away in your invitation, just enough to get people there.

When a news desk receives an invitation, the news editor will make a decision about the newsworthiness of your event. If it looks interesting, it will be entered into the diary and a reporter sent along. Events with picture potential will be passed to the picture editor, who will arrange for a photographer to attend. (It is sensible to send an invitation to the news desk and a separate one to the picture editor; internal communication is not always as effective as it should be.) Boring events will not be attended, but don't assume your event was dull just because no media turned up. It could be that they were short-staffed that day, or that there was a more important event on at the same time.

Keep a list of who you invited and ring to see if they are coming. If they can't make it, offer to send the news desk a news release.

Make sure you assign someone the task of meeting the media at the event, and checking on their needs. If you are helpful to reporters and photographers, they are more likely to be well disposed towards your company, and to attend future events, but if you see them as an irritation, you would be better off not inviting them at all.

Features

Sometimes you can promote a new product or service by arranging for a feature in the press or on TV or radio. The example given above would work well as feature material. A reporter could talk to pub-goers to find out what amenities and ambience they look for in a pub. Archive material (photos for newspapers, footage for TV) could be used to show how pubs have changed over time, and an interview could be done with Kevin Colgan from Wilson's Breweries to see why they want to reintroduce traditional pubs. It would also be a good radio feature, thanks to pub sound effects such as juke boxes, fruit machines and general banter. If you are launching a service or product that lends itself well to a feature, start by deciding on the best place for it. Radio or TV? Or the press? (Or all three.) Which paper? Local, national or trade? When? Sometimes it is easier to approach just one publication (or programme) and to offer them an exclusive feature which they can run on the day of the launch or opening. Write briefly to the features editor (or to the Forward Planning Department for TV) in the first instance, outlining your ideas. Follow this up a week later with a call to assess interest.

If you can't get a feature of your own, why not try for a mention in an existing feature in a relevant trade or professional publication. There are services you can subscribe to which tell you about forthcoming features, though they are expensive. Why not just phone your target publications and ask for a features list. This sets out what subjects they will be covering and when. Usually the features list will cover a 6- or 12-month period.

Once you find a feature that is relevant to your company, write to the features editor explaining how you can help/contribute, perhaps by supplying some facts and figures, being interviewed, providing photographs, or sending the reporter some useful background material or product samples. You might end up getting valuable publicity, but even if you don't, you will have made a useful contact as well as making yourself known to the publication. They might well get back to you in the future.

If you have in mind a topical feature, remember that magazines have a very long lead-in time, often more than three months. So if your proposed feature is a Christmas one, you'll need to make your approach no later than August, as that's when they will be putting the magazine together.

Another way of getting a feature on your company is to write it yourself. If you are able to write a lively, informative and interesting article, you might be able to persuade a local newspaper or a trade magazine to accept it. I have had great success with this. Remember, though, that no self-respecting publication will accept blatant advertising.

How to write your own feature

Journalists are professional writers; you cannot expect to be able to churn out a story the way they do. If you are unused to writing anything but business correspondence, you might find feature-writing a real challenge but one that you are willing to take on, and win! Consider the following points before you set pen to paper. You might also find it useful to refer to the section on copywriting in Chapter 11.

- Look at the publication and see what length the average feature is – it's easier to write to a target figure than to try to edit later on.
- Make sure you are familiar with the publication and its style – try to use the same style when you come to write.
- Before you start, jot down the key points that you want to get across in your article. Tick them off your list as you write about them.
- Get an angle. You need a theme or a storyline – preferably something unusual. What makes your company or your product different? Are you doing anything innovative or unique? Do you offer a special approach?
- Don't save your best line for the end – the reader might never get that far. Lead with it! You must capture the reader's attention in the first paragraph.

- Use short subheadings to help you break up the text into readable chunks and to link different themes.
- If you are writing for a local newspaper, remember to emphasise local connections, even if you operate nationally. Readers of a Plymouth paper will not be interested in your services or offices in Aberdeen!
- Think about your audience – are they professionals who will understand the jargon, or are you writing for people who will be unfamiliar with your particular terminology? Use appropriate language.
- Try to make your article appear independent. Quote people from other companies and use facts and figures to support your case.

The following Figure 8.5 shows an extract from an article I wrote for a client of mine, a small business selling fire-retardant paint. They found that many of their customers were churches, so they decided to try for some editorial coverage in the publications read by those responsible for the maintenance of old churches (amazingly, there are such specialist publications!). I wrote the article with the aim of promoting them and their products in a way that was informative and relevant for readers.

Figure 8.5   Extract from an article on fire-retardant paint

PROTECTION FROM FIRE ON EARTH

The Great Fire of London, which destroyed so many churches, would not have spread as rapidly as it did had not so many buildings been made of wood. With the recent revival of interest in the aesthetic qualities of fine timber, many interiors in all sorts of structures – from the latest style of the executive villa to the giant shopping mall – make extensive use of wood. But of course the modern age is, thankfully, much more safety-conscious than were our ancestors. Anyone responsible for the construction or refurbishment of a building today has to comply with stringent and detailed building regulations. It can be very easy for those professionally involved to overlook the implications of this for any work affecting interior timber surfaces.

For many years the usual method of protecting timber against fire, and, even more important, preventing it from feeding the flames and perhaps trapping those struggling to escape, was to remove the wood from the site and subject it to pressure impregnation. This was costly, inconvenient, indeed often impossible, as for example with the roof bosses in an early Gothic church. Furthermore, any varnishing or painting had to be done after treatment was finished. Not surprisingly, the owners of many buildings and their architects took the view that such a disruptive operation could not be justified.

However, tougher rules sometimes leave no option but to treat timber. For example, even the refitting of the kitchen in the crypt will have consequences for the whole church. Not only will any new or refurbished timber have to conform to regulations, so will all the wood finishes throughout the building. Fortunately, there is a straightforward solution to these often unanticipated problems – intumescent coatings. There are many available on the market which have been specially designed to protect timber. However, only one of these products – Aquafire FRC – is a water-based coating system. If fire starts, a carbonaceous layer forms on the wood, protecting it and at the same time greatly delaying the fire's spread. Aquafire has been used in a very wide variety of settings – hospitals and nursing homes, schools, prisons, museums, hotels, leisure centres, shops and, not least, in churches and other religious buildings. Caledonian UK, who developed Aquafire, have done a great deal of work helping ecclesiastical authorities to avoid having to choose between safety and preservation.

Alan King, Director of Caledonian UK, says that one of the projects he is most proud of was for King's College in Wimbledon. By using Aquafire FRC, the architects were able to upgrade the sixteenth-century hammerbeam roof just by washing down the existing timber with clear water. 'The beauty of it is that you can apply it just as you would any water-based paint, and it is available in any colour,' he says. 'It doesn't even smell like paint.' Aquafire was also used recently as part of the reordering of St Luke's, Leek…

As a controversial Church of England report reminded us recently, not many active Christians believe any longer in the fiery torments of that everlasting hell whose existence few of our Victorian ancestors doubted. What is quite certain, however, is that church-goers would always have been glad to count on having the best available protection against fire on earth!

My article was accepted because it was:

- not a blatant plug for the paint company;
- informative for the intended audience;
- relevant to their needs and interests;
- contained examples and case studies relating to churches (I submitted similar articles to other specialist publications, using different examples – hospitals, schools, etc – depending on the specialism of the publication).

Using contacts

Build good working relationships with journalists. Then, rather than going through the formality of issuing a news release, you might find it easier and quicker to pick up the phone and chat to a friendly reporter about your new product or service.

Creating contacts

Start by being nice to the journalists you meet. Being a journalist can be a lonely job, interviewing unknown people in unfamiliar places. That's why journalists appreciate it when someone is there to meet them, greet them, give them a cup of coffee and introduce them to the people they need to talk to. This is all part of building up a good relationship with them. You need to be helpful and professional, always to meet their deadlines, and available to keep them informed of newsworthy developments. Do this and they will soon come to realize that you are an important source of information. Hopefully, the closer you get, the more you will be able to trust them not to misrepresent you. You need each other, so aim for a reciprocal relationship and you will both gain.

Reporters keep a contacts book and refer to it when they need a comment on a particular issue. If you are regarded as especially helpful by a reporter, they will favour you over another spokesperson, thus giving you the chance to get valuable publicity and to be seen as an authority in your field. So when reporters start ringing you out of the blue for comment on an issue, or because they have a gap in the paper and wonder if you can help them fill it, you know that you have achieved that all-important relationship.

Off the record

Only tell a journalist something if you are willing for it to be reported. There are occasions when 'off-the-record' briefings are useful; very experienced PR practitioners can use them skilfully, but if you are fairly new to the game they are best avoided.

Radio and TV

Newspapers will be your main source of coverage, but don't overlook radio and TV for important stories. TV can be difficult to get on to, though do send releases to TV news if it's a big story. The sample news release on the Rover's Return reopening is the sort of quirky story that could easily find itself a slot at the end of the news. Local radio is easier to get airtime on, although it is becoming harder as stations reduce their staff. If the broadcast media wish to cover your story, they will:

- invite you into the studio for a live or recorded interview or;
- do a recorded or live interview down the telephone or;
- do their own news report based on your release, possibly following a brief, informal chat with you on the telephone, or;

- send a reporter to you for a live broadcast or a recorded interview.

Sometimes you will get asked on to TV or radio as a direct result of your news release. Or you may get a call out of the blue, because a researcher is looking for an expert to provide comment or opinion, and you have been recommended, or are already known to them. Or, horror of horrors, because your company has been accused of wrongdoing.

A proactive way of getting on TV is to find out what programmes are being made and to try and influence the producers. Finding out about programmes in the pipeline is too big a job for any small business to take on, for there are over 1,000 independent production companies, in addition to the BBC, ITV, cable and satellite stations. The only feasible way of keeping up to date is to subscribe to a service that will tell you who is making what and when. A publication called *Programme News* (Tel: 020 7405 4455 for details) provides an early warning of programmes in production or currently being planned. It gives a brief synopsis of the content, contact, and details of support the programme-makers would welcome. However, this is not an area that will be of interest to the vast majority of small – and even large – businesses.

On the box

If your company is invited on to radio or TV, ask if the interview will be live or recorded and find out who else will be appearing. Always pick the best spokesperson – who may not be you! Whoever goes on TV representing your company must be articulate, and able to speak clearly in plain, everyday language. They must come across well with the audience that particular programme is likely to attract. Your business will be judged on their performance.

Preparation

Prepare as well as you can in advance of an appearance:

- know what you want to say;
- be clear on what you are not willing to discuss;
- be familiar with all the facts and figures (but don't quote too many statistics on air – it's a real turn-off for listeners).

Bright idea

If you are likely to have to do radio and TV interviews, practise with a tape-recorder or camcorder first. Watch/listen to the tapes and be alert to any irritating mannerisms. Try to avoid them when you do interviews for real.

Twelve TV dos and don'ts

1. *Don't* rush out and buy a whole new outfit; people rarely feel comfortable and relaxed in brand new clothes. Think carefully about what to wear. TV is a visual medium and you will be assessed according to how you look.
2. *Do* wear something that makes you feel confident and that is suitable for the occasion.
3. *Don't* wear large, dangly earrings that will distract viewers, or glinty jewellery that will catch the light too much.
4. *Do* make sure your socks are long enough to cover your hairy ankles!
5. *Don't* wear strapless dresses, or you will appear to be naked in head and shoulders shots!
6. *Do* avoid jackets, shirts and ties where the stripes are too close together; they appear to 'jump' or move on TV screens. The same goes for very small checks.
7. *Don't* fidget, or fiddle with your hair or clothing, as this is really irritating for viewers.
8. *Do* sit still. If you swivel about on your chair, rock to and fro or wave your hands in a manic way you will not look your best.
9. *Don't* point your finger on TV – it is definitely a no-no; you'll either look aggressive or mad.
10. *Do* look at the interviewer, not at the camera or monitor.
11. *Don't* be distracted by what's going on behind the camera.
12. *Do* remember that you might be on camera even when you are not talking – so don't choose a silent moment to scratch your ear or pick your nose!

Bright idea

Before an interview take a very deep breath and then relax. If you don't, the listener or viewer will hear your nervousness. Forget the thousands (or millions!) of people listening and watching, and just concentrate on the interviewer. Imagine it's just the two of you, and you will be far less nervous.

What will happen?

Before you are put in front of a camera or microphone, you will get a chance to have an informal chat with the interviewer or researcher. They might ask you a few questions, or get you to fill them in on the background to the story. This is the time to ask questions yourself, if there is anything you are unsure about. Some interviewees like to know in advance what questions they will be asked. If the interviewer is reluctant to reveal them, it is simply because they don't want you to rehearse the answers, making you sound wooden and unnatural.

Unless you are asked on to TV to address your company's alleged wrong-doing, your interviewer will not be trying to catch you out. They will be as keen as you are for the interview to go smoothly; if it runs badly, it will not reflect well on them. If they ask a strange-sounding question, it's simply to get you to speak, so don't be worried. Their aim is to get you talking, not tongue-tied.

Making your point

The average TV interview lasts 2.4 minutes, up to half of which may be taken up with the interviewer talking. That leaves very little time for you, so be clear from the outset on the main points you want to get across (no more than three), and stick to these. Keep your key messages simple, as you will be addressing an uninformed audience through, in all probability, an uninformed interviewer.

Getting your points across can be difficult; the interviewer will not always ask you the right questions. It's up to you to turn questions around to enable you to get your message across. For example, say you are spokesperson for a local traders' campaign against a bypass and you want to get over the following three points:

- A bypass will have a major effect on trade and will cause many local shops to close.
- Closure of local shops will result in a loss of amenity for local people.
- If local shops close, the vitality and character of the town will be lost forever.

This is how you do it:

Interviewer: Some would say that local traders are selfish, putting their own profits above the safety of local people. Many children have been knocked down by the heavy traffic that will be diverted on to the proposed bypass.
You: Naturally we are very concerned about local safety and have been working on a series of measures that would improve it. However, it is important to remember that without a passing trade, many local shops are simply not viable. If they close, everyone loses out.
Interviewer: So it's back to the profits of local businesses again?
You: No. Naturally we must earn a living, like anyone else, but the real issue for this community is that the building of a bypass will change the whole character of the town. Yes, there will be less traffic, and that's a good thing. But there will also be far fewer shops. Where will old people go to buy their groceries? What about people who do not own a car? If passing trade goes, the shops will close. If the shops close, the heart will be knocked right out of this town. We will all lose.

Do not get drawn into answering questions that will detract from the main points you want to get across.

Using a self-operate studio

When it comes to radio programmes, whether you are doing an interview live or recorded, you may come across a self-operate studio. You will have to use one of these if your contribution is coming from one city and the programme is being broadcast from another. Essentially, a 'self-op' is a small studio containing a table, chair, microphone, small control panel and telephone. You will be called on the phone by the programme-maker, who will explain what happens next and which buttons to press. It can be nerve-wracking sitting alone in the studio waiting for the phone to ring, but keep calm and you'll do OK.

Bright idea

If you are doing a radio interview and you need notes, don't have them on paper, as the rustling will be picked up by the microphone. Write your prompts on small pieces of card instead.

Keeping tabs

If media exposure is important to your company, you will want to monitor the media to see what is being said about you and by whom. You will want to know whether your news releases are being used. You will also want to know whether or not the coverage is positive and beneficial for the company.

Keep good in-house records, including a copy of all your releases and a list of who you sent them to. This makes it easier for you to monitor your proactive press coverage and to build up a picture of which papers, and indeed which reporters, are interested in your work. (See Figure 8.6 for a distribution list form.)

Figure 8.6   Distribution list form

NEWS RELEASE DISTRIBUTION LIST

Title of release: . . . .

Date of issue: . . . .

Method of issue:

    Mail (1st/2nd class). . . . .

    Fax . . . .

    Courier. . . . .

    E-mail . . . .

Issued to: . . . .

. . . .

. . . .

. . . .

Also prepare a media enquiry form (see Figure 8.7 – amend the example form to your own needs) to record any reactive dealings you have with reporters. Keep the forms filed in a ringbinder – your media log. By completing the proforma each time you are contacted by the media you can:

- ensure that enquiries from the media are recorded properly;
- be sure that all enquiries are dealt with efficiently;
- make sure a record exists of any response you make. If you are misquoted, you have a copy on file as evidence;
- build up a picture of media interest in your company.

Give supplies of the proforma to anyone who might have to take calls from the media.

Bright idea

Start a scrapbook of press cuttings, with details of the date of the cutting and the publication in which it appeared, as it's nice to be able to look back over old clippings. It can give your company a sense of history, and your new staff an insight into your work over the years. Leave a copy in your reception area for customers to look at.

Figure 8.7 Media enquiry form

MEDIA ENQUIRY FORM

Name of reporter: ....

Publication/TV or radio programme:............................

Telephone number: ....

Call received on (date): .... at (time) .... am/pm

Message taken by: ....

Nature of enquiry:

Deadline: ....

Response:

Issued by: ....

Date and time: ....

Using a clip joint

In addition to your own monitoring, you can – if you have the money – use a press cuttings agency to give you details of the media coverage your company is attracting. A cuttings agency is a company which specialises in reading practically every publication – from the national press to obscure publications such as *Pig World* and *Pigeon Racers' Gazette*. They read trade and technical press, consumer publications, and other specialist magazines, as well as national, local and regional papers. All articles which refer to your company are cut out and sent to you with a note of where and when they appeared. You can also get the agency to monitor competitors, or send you cuttings relating generally to your field of work.

If you use an agency, they will charge you a monthly reading fee (around £100 will cover you for all publications). On top of that you need to pay a set price for each cutting (usually in the region of 80p). You might wish to use the service only when you have a really big media push on and monitoring is vital. (Try to negotiate a special deal – never accept the first price you are quoted.) Even then, it can be possible to do it yourself – unless you are sending material to a very large number of publications.

The Newspaper Licensing Agency, which is owned by nearly all of the national newspapers, charges companies for photocopying (or even faxing) newspaper articles and cuttings. You can produce original press cuttings and circulate these free of charge, but as soon as you make a photocopy, you are breaching the Copyright Act. Technically you can go to prison for up to two years for this offence, though I think that would be extremely unlikely. You must obtain (and pay for) a licence. For further information and a free explanatory booklet, contact the NLA at Wellington Gate, 7 & 9 Church Road, Tunbridge Wells TN1 1NL, tel: 01892 525273, fax: 01892 525275, e-mail: copy@nla.co.uk, Web site: www.nla.co.uk. Not surprisingly, many PR practitioners feel very resentful. They write news releases that are used verbatim by newspapers, and then the original author has to pay a fee to copy work they wrote in the first place!

It's also possible to get verbatim transcripts of radio and TV interviews from monitoring companies, although again it's very expensive (around £40 for a transcript of an interview lasting up to two minutes). You can also get copies of interviews on video (around £60) or cassette tape (around £30). Always ask the price before using one of these companies, or you could be in for a shock when you get the invoice. Requesting something for urgent delivery (eg the same day or overnight) adds a premium of up to 50 per cent. There is no need to subscribe to these companies in order to use the service, although if you are a subscriber, they will ring you up to let you know about mentions; you don't need to call them.

How good was it?

Don't just monitor your coverage; you should also try to evaluate it too. An unsophisticated approach to press evaluation (still used by many) is the advertising value equivalent measurement. Here you simply measure the column inches of coverage you receive, then work out what the exposure would have cost had you paid for it as advertising space. This approach is too simplistic as:

- It tells you nothing of the quality of the coverage.
- It does not tell you the value to your company of keeping negative stories out of the press.

- It assumes that the sort of coverage you received was of similar value to paid-for advertising. In reality, a favourable restaurant review is a great deal more persuasive than a similarly sized advert for the same restaurant; people are more influenced by editorial.
- It does not take into account the number of releases issued as a ratio of the number of news items secured (ie you cannot view a media campaign as successful if you issued 200 releases and only secured two mentions in the press).

See Figure 8.8 for a media evaluation form that has been created to help you assess whether the coverage you received, including broadcast coverage, was a help or a hindrance, and whether it conveyed the messages you hoped it would. You can develop your own form based on the one here, adding questions relevant to your own company. For example, you might attempt to measure whether increased media coverage has led to an increase in sales or requests for your sales information, or more visitors to your shop or warehouse.

Media evaluation is increasingly becoming a science. You can buy evaluation software that will help you assess the value of your press coverage, both financially and in terms of its effect on your image. The software will produce graphs and charts that will show you how much the coverage would have cost had you had to pay for it, whether it has communicated the key messages, and whether the editorial was in a prominent position in the publication.

Evaluation is more important than many companies realise. It is pointless issuing releases and trying to attract coverage if you do not stop to assess whether your releases are doing any good. If they only result in bad coverage, pitiful coverage, or no coverage at all, perhaps you are wasting your time and money. Perhaps you need a new approach. Unless you evaluate, you will never know.

Don't be a headless chicken

However well run your enterprise is, you cannot be sure that there isn't a crisis lurking around the corner. There is considerable scope for companies to get negative and highly damaging media coverage:

- A customer might go to the media with their complaint about poor goods or services.
- You might have to manage a product recall.
- One of your goods might injure someone.
- You might be accused of dodgy practices.
- Your staff might go on strike.
- You might be taken to an industrial tribunal or to court.

Figure 8.8 Media evaluation form

MEDIA EVALUATION

Publication/programme: ....

Date: ....

Subject: ....

Did the coverage convey any of the key messages we wanted to promote? If so, which ones?

....

....

....

....

Did it get anything wrong? If so, was the error(s) damaging?

....

....

....

....

Was the news item favourable/helpful, unhelpful/damaging or neutral? In what way?

....

....

Has there been a noticeable increase in calls/visitors/enquiries following publication/broadcast?

....

Dealing promptly and efficiently with a crisis can help you preserve – or even enhance – the good image you have worked hard to establish. Keep a cool head. This is no time to run around like a headless chicken.

Journalists say that real news is not what you want to get into the media; it's what you want to keep out! If something happens that results in bad coverage, or that you fear might do so, take the following steps immediately:

The six-point crisis action plan

1. Don't panic. Remain calm and keep a sense of perspective.
2. Brief staff who need to know about it.
3. Don't forget to tell switchboard – they are the first line of contact for journalists, so they need to know how to react and who to put calls through to.
4. Sit down and list the facts that you are prepared to release – share these with other staff who need to know, so you are all clear on what you can and can't say.
5. Prepare a press statement (a short quote or outline of your views) or news release to put forward your side of the story if necessary.
6. Keep your own staff informed, to stem unhelpful gossip and rumour.

Bright idea

Prepare in advance for a crisis and have plans in place. If the real thing happens, you will be better able to cope. Identify potential crises and ensure that everyone knows what to do.

If a journalist gets hold of a damaging story and phones you, play for time if you need to. You don't have to answer questions there and then. Simply make a note of the questions and promise to get back to the reporter in, say, half an hour, explaining that you are in a meeting and there are one or two facts you need to check. This will give you time to think about your response and to discuss it with colleagues if necessary, but always make sure that you ring the reporter back within the agreed time.

You might find that reporters you have previously had a good relationship with become aggressive and pushy in pursuing their line of enquiry. Don't take it personally; they are paid to investigate stories. However hard they push you, remain polite and helpful; you'll need their support again once everything blows over.

It might be that your company was in the wrong, and often it is best to admit this openly, and to explain what you intend to do to rectify the situation.

Bright idea

Don't always be too forthcoming with information. First of all find out what the reporter knows – it might be much less than you think.

Don't be surprised if you are phoned at home. Journalists are good at tracking people down. The same rules apply – take a note of the questions and then ring back once you have got your facts together. Make sure you have a note at your home of the home or mobile telephone numbers of relevant staff who you might need to talk to.

You might find yourself embroiled in a tricky situation that is going from bad to worse. If you get invited on to TV or radio in such a situation, remember:

- The aim of the interview may be confrontation, so make sure you are not being set up. Find out in advance who else will be appearing and then decide whether or not you want to take part.
- Be prepared to say no to the interview if you believe that it will do more harm than good. You don't have to accept – be clear on what you want to get out of it. (Consider carefully the signal that will be sent out if you refuse to participate.)
- Be clear about what you are not willing to say, but never say 'No comment'. Find another way of avoiding a difficult question. Practise this before the interview, and watch news and current affairs programmes to see how politicians avoid tricky questions without loss of face.
- Don't let the interviewer make you lose your temper – always keep calm, whatever you are accused of, but do make sure that you firmly but politely rebut anything that is incorrect or untrue. If you lose your temper, you will lose the argument, because the viewer or listener will side with the interviewer and you will come across as aggressive and unprofessional.
- Be as positive as you can be.

Complaining about the media

Sometimes the media will get it wrong and publish or broadcast inaccurate or damaging material. This may be done deliberately (though this is unlikely), carelessly (by not being thorough and checking their material) or quite innocently. There are a number of things you can do when the media makes a mistake. If it's something small (perhaps they spelt your name wrong or said that you employ five staff when you actually have eight) it's best forgotten. It might matter to you, but it won't bother the reader or listener and a complaint would be petty and pointless.

Newspapers

If the matter merits complaint you can, depending on the circumstances:

- Make an informal call to the editor to discuss the matter (always have in mind what outcome you would like).

- Request the publication of a correction, apology or full retraction.
- Request that a letter of complaint is published in the letters page.
- Do a deal whereby the paper agrees to do a more sympathetic article in a month or so (this will only work with local papers; nationals would never agree to this).
- Suggest that the reporter responsible visits your company for a couple of hours to find out more about what you do, so that errors will not occur in the future.
- Make a formal complaint to the Press Complaints Commission, 1 Salisbury Square, London EC4Y 8JB, tel: 020 7353 1248. It's best to do this only as a last resort, if you've been unable to rectify matters with the paper concerned. Write in with your complaint and all necessary material, such as a copy of the offending article, copies of correspondence between you and the paper, etc.

Before you fire off an angry letter, stop and think. Will you damage a relationship that is important to you? Will you achieve anything by complaining? If so, what? Is it worth it? Is there a better way of dealing with it? Do you have the energy and time to go to the Press Complaints Commission?

TV and radio

Contact the producer of the programme first. If that gets you nowhere, you can get in touch with the Broadcasting Standards Commission, the equivalent of the Press Complaints Commission. They will only consider complaints which fall into at least one of the following categories:

- unfair or unjust treatment in broadcast radio or TV programmes (including satellite and cable services);
- unwarranted infringement of privacy in programmes or in their making.

You should write to the Secretary of the Commission giving the title of the programme and the date and channel on which it was broadcast. Explain your complaint and supply any relevant information to back up your complaint. The Commission can be contacted at 7 The Sanctuary, London SW1P 3JS, tel: 020 7233 0544, e-mail: bsc@bsc.org.uk.

Now over to you

Lock & Key make window locks to keep burglars out and to keep children in (by preventing them falling from upstairs windows). The managing director is called one evening by the local paper. The reporter tells him a child has fallen from a second floor window and is in hospital. A Lock & Key window catch was fitted; it must have failed. She wants to have a response on the accident. The reporter also asks the MD whether he will advise the local authority to replace the 10,000 Lock & Key catches recently fitted to council properties, and whether he plans to recall the product.

The MD knows nothing about the incident, explains that he needs to look into it, and promises to fax a statement to the newspaper first thing in the morning. He sends the following statement as set out in Figure 8.9(a). Read through it, list what is wrong with it, then draft a better response.

Figure 8.9(a)   Press statement

STATEMENT TO THE CORRINGTON COURIER FROM LOCK & KEY

We regard the incident of a child falling from a second floor window as most regrettable. However, we should stress that we have sold 150,000 locks over the last 10 years, and this is only the second time that one of our locks has failed. Thankfully, in this case, the child has suffered no serious injury.

Although the very thought of a child falling to its death is hard to contemplate, we want to stress that there is no need for alarm. We will not be suggesting to the council that they replace Lock & Key catches in the 10,000 rented properties that have recently had them fitted. It is unlikely that any of those catches will fail.

Our window locks are manufactured to BS 5750 (ISO 9000) standards and have enjoyed a very good reputation among professional locksmiths. We hope this rare incident will not jeopardise that reputation.

Discussion

- The first error the MD makes is in answering all of the questions. Answer questions put to you if you think they will not damage your image or reputation, otherwise avoid them if you can. Often a newspaper will settle for a statement, and might not contact you again for further answers.
- It was foolish of the MD to mention the previous incident. It does nothing for the public's confidence in the company. He would be wise to prepare himself to answer questions should the previous incident be exposed, but it is madness to raise it first.
- Mentioning the possible death of a child is a terrible mistake. It is emotive and leaves the reader feeling that the company is uncaring.
- Saying that 'Thankfully, in this case, the child has suffered no serious injury' suggests that the first child did.

- He says that the lock failed. Presumably he does not know this yet and should therefore not comment on it.
- Using jargon such as BS 5750 is off-putting.
- Showing more concern for their reputation among locksmiths than for child safety will win them no votes.

So what should he have said (see Figure 8.9(b))?

Figure 8.9(b)   Press statement

STATEMENT TO THE CORRINGTON COURIER FROM LOCK & KEY

First of all we want to convey our sympathy to Jamie Clough's family for what we can imagine must have been a frightening ordeal. We are delighted that Jamie has only minor injuries and has been discharged from hospital. We have sent a box of toys to Jamie by way of a 'get well soon' present.

As for our window catches, they are made to safety standards that exceed the rigorous requirements of European law. It is not possible to buy a safer catch. That said, we are aware that one of our catches may have failed. We take this very seriously and will be sending an independent inspector to examine the catch and report to us. If it is found to be a manufacturing fault, we will take full responsibility and we will publish the inspector's findings.

We must stress that anyone with a Lock & Key window catch need not worry. They are the very safest catches on the market. However, anyone with a concern may telephone us on 0116 123 9887 for advice.

Discussion

This is better because:

- it is a more confident, positive, upbeat response;
- it shows genuine concern for the injured boy and his family;
- it does not acknowledge liability, but comes across as open and responsible;
- it does not answer irrelevant or potentially damaging questions;
- it stresses how safe these catches are and goes a long way towards reassuring people who might have them fitted in their homes;
- the telephone line is a good ploy; it appears that you are doing something proactive.

9 *A day to remember: organising PR events*

Any busy business is likely to have the occasional event. Whether it is a seminar or conference, dinner or buffet, party or product launch, making it a success is a must. This chapter will show you how to plan and coordinate the perfect event.

Big companies spend copious amounts on corporate entertainment. Even if you do not entertain on the same lavish scale as the multinationals, there should still be countless opportunities to plan affordable events that can be used to help build your business:

- you might lay on a special dinner for your best customers;
- organise an opening event for a new store;
- put on a seminar for potential clients;
- plan a product launch;
- take clients to a football or rugby match;
- hold a media lunch;
- arrange an open day;
- organize a drinks or cocktail party;
- hold a company birthday party.

The opportunities for events are limited only by your own imagination. Your efficiency as a business may be judged partly on the basis of your ability to put on a good, enjoyable or informative, well-organised event. If you cock up, you might lose some valuable business. Do it well and the investment should pay off in pound notes.

Even small events are time-consuming, diverting your attention from the important task of running your business. Always double the amount of time you think you will need to arrange an event, because planning will take longer than you imagine and it will involve more work than you expect. Last minute or rushed events are the ones that are most likely to go wrong, so do allow the time you need for planning and preparation. Set up a small planning group to ensure everything gets done. Your team will carry its responsibility right through to an after-the-event evaluation.

The concept

Begin by deciding on the type of event you want. In some cases it's obvious. You might already have in mind a seminar or a conference. For other types of event there can be a bit more scope for creativity. Perhaps you are having a party or a product launch and want something with a bit of a twist, to make it more memorable. When it comes to creativity, two heads are better than one. Why not involve your event planning group in the search for ideas? Hold a brainstorming session to see what ideas you can generate between you.

The dos and don'ts

There are no hard and fast rules about the type of event that your customers will expect. However, there are some guiding dos and don'ts. Try to avoid:

- *The overdone* – your prized clients may not turn up for a drinks party (having already attended three that week!), but offer them a morning's go-kart racing and you might get a better response – and you'll have a more memorable event. Aim for originality.
- *The predictable* - everyone holds a ribbon-cutting ceremony to mark an opening. See if you can think of something with a bit more flair.
- *The boring* – how many presentation ceremonies have you attended where flowers, crystal and other unimaginative gifts were presented? Make your gift one to remember.
- *Sleep-inducing speeches* – I have heard many a speech that would have had an insomniac snoring. If a speech is to be part of your event, make sure the speaker is a good one.

Choose something that will enhance your image and reinforce any corporate branding and positioning. You can do this by ensuring that your chosen event is appropriate – taking into account venue, speaker/personality and subject:

- If you work in the motor trade industry, drag-car racing might be appropriate, or a drinks party at Silverstone, or an opening event performed by a Formula 1 winner.

- If you run a business selling art, you might choose a talk by an art historian, a private view to mark your sponsorship of an exhibition of up-and-coming painters, or a workshop on the painting techniques of the old masters.
- If you run an upmarket travel company, the Egyptian Room at the Victoria and Albert Museum might be the ideal venue for your talk on Egyptian holidays. Perhaps you could get the Egyptology curator to say a few words of welcome. It all adds cachet to the event.

Objective setting

Approach event organising in a businesslike way. Be clear at the outset what you hope to achieve by setting objectives. Consider whether there is a less time-consuming or more cost-effective way of achieving the same outcome. Here are some examples of events, along with some possible objectives:

Event	Business seminar
Objectives	• to bring key potential clients into our premises;
	• to demonstrate our expertise and establish our company as an authority;
	• long term, to develop relationships that will lead to new business.
Event	Restaurant opening with celebrity chef
Objectives	• to get potential diners into the restaurant to see how pleasant it is, to sample the food and look at the extensive menu and wine list;
	• to get a mailing list of potential diners;
	• to attract media coverage for the new restaurant, especially in the food pages;
	• to gain by association with the top chef.
Event	Exhibition at trade fair
Objectives	• to show our products to key trade buyers;
	• to attract new customers;
	• to see what the competition is doing.
Event	Annual general meeting
Objectives	• to fulfil our legal requirements;
	• to bring together key stakeholders and to enthuse them;
	• to present the highlights of the year and to explain our plans for next year.

By having objectives you are clear on the desired outcome, you can design an event to help you achieve your aims, and you can measure success afterwards. With objectives set you can, at last, make a start on the detailed planning.

Six steps to a successful event

1. In the form of a checklist, itemise everything you need to do. (If you are having a ceremonial cake-cutting, someone must remember the knife. For a balloon release, someone will need to order helium and get clearance from the airport. These items of detail – often overlooked – can ruin an otherwise well planned event.)
2. You already have an event planning group. Put someone reliable in overall charge and give that person the authority to get things done.
3. Brief your event coordinator on their duties and responsibilities. The golden rule is that they must never assume. Make sure the coordinator always knows who is doing what, and that the doer knows they are doing it too!
4. Ensure the coordinator assigns each task, however small, to someone.
5. Set a deadline for the completion of each task and write the details of this on the checklist you have prepared.
6. Circulate the checklist and get your event coordinator to keep a check on progress, and to remind everyone about their tasks.

To ease event-planning, create your own checklist proforma which can be amended according to the event. It will save time and effort, and help ensure that nothing important is overlooked. Look at the checklist in Figure 9.1 and use it as the basis for your own.

Figure 9.1   Events checklist

EVENTS CHECKLIST

Name of event: . . . .

Date of event: . . . .

Update as at (date): . . . .

ACTIVITY	DEADLINE	ACTION BY	COMMENTS
Decide on type of event			
Set a date for the event			
Select speakers/ participants/celebrities			
Check on their availability			

Draw up programme and timetable			
Select a venue			
Check venue for suitability			
List props needed (eg red ribbon, giant scissors)			
Check to see if any licences or permissions are required			
Apply for any necessary permission and licence			
Arrange any necessary insurance			
Arrange for the supply of props			
Draw up list of people to invite			
Draw up media list			
Book photographer and write confirming details of job			
Write to speakers to confirm details and to brief them			
Book caterers and don't forget special requirements (eg Kosher)			
Get invitations printed			
Draft and agree news release			
Organise name badges			
Organise the venue – top table, exhibition, signing-in book, etc			
Mail invitations to guests			
Mail invitations to media			
Prepare press packs			
Check on final numbers			
Confirm final numbers with caterers			

Bright idea

Consider computerising your guest lists according to event type with one list for seminars, another for media events, and yet another for official functions or dinners.

Making it legal

You might like to include sections on your checklist for permissions, licences and insurance.

Permission

Some events, or aspects of your event, may require permission from the police, local authority or another body. Anything likely to disrupt traffic flow, for example, will need to be cleared with the relevant authority.

Licences

If you plan to sell alcohol at your event you must have a liquor licence. Dancing and musical events will require an entertainment licence. Other licences may be necessary too, depending on your plans, and laws and by-laws to comply with. (Ask the police and your local authority for details.)

Insurance

It is a good idea to take out public liability insurance. It is not expensive and gives peace of mind to event organisers.

For large public events (such as an open-air concert or a market), here's some of the items you will need to consider:

- *First aid* Get the St John Ambulance or Red Cross to attend (and budget for a donation in return for their help).
- *Stewarding* Have sufficient stewards who know how to cope with accidents and crowd control.
- *Contingency plans* These are essential for outdoor events. (You can get rainfall insurance. It's not a weather guarantee, just a policy to cover costs such as equipment hire if you are rained off. Contact an insurance broker for details.)
- *Other matters* Don't forget loos, parking, litter, food hygiene regulations, consultation with neighbours...

In the right place at the right time

Choose your venue with care:

1. *Facilities* Select your venue with the needs of attendees in mind. For example, if you are holding a children's fashion show, you may need to arrange baby change facilities or a crèche for parents bringing children. An antiques fair would require a large venue with easy parking and preferably

good public transport links too. Something aimed at elderly people, such as a talk on the holiday options for the over-75s, might benefit from being held in a venue with an induction loop system for people with hearing aids… the list goes on. Think what your customers will need and make sure your venue measures up.

2. *Image*   Your chosen venue should reinforce your company's image. An event held in a cheap and seedy backstreet hotel will reflect badly on you.

3. *Themes*   Try to select a venue to suit the occasion. If you are launching a new range of outerwear for sailing enthusiasts, the National Maritime Museum, the Cutty Sark, or some other venue connected with water would suit. Kew Gardens would be a good place to unveil a revolutionary new lawn-mower or a new range of seeds. Ascot, Aintree or York Racecourses might be perfect for a new equestrian product. Be creative when selecting a venue for such events.

Bright idea

If attendees are likely to be unfamiliar with your venue, send them a map and make sure that you have lots of signs and directional arrows to help them find their way to the right place. There's nothing more frustrating than getting lost trying to find the right building, or the right room within it.

Good timing

The right time is as important as the right place. A drinks party at around 6.30 pm is far from ideal, being too late for people to come straight from work, but too early to give them time to go home first. Consider season too. A business event in Edinburgh during the International Festival will attract premium rates from hotels and venues, assuming you get rooms. However, you might find that your event is a great success because everyone wants to come in order to enjoy the Festival too. Events during school holidays might be poorly attended if aimed at working people; they will be taking time off to spend with their children. However, events aimed at schoolchildren will be a sell out during these times.

Famous faces

Many events incorporate a famous face as a way of pulling the crowds and maximising media coverage. Unless you have megabucks to spend, you will not be able to afford a chart-topping band or TV super-hero. Stars are expensive, but specialist agencies will find you a famous face – for a price.

Look for a link

If you plan to use a celebrity, select someone who is in some way linked with your event. For example, if you were opening a sports hypermarket, you could do worse than opt for a famous sportsperson or sports presenter. A high-powered business conference could be addressed by Sir John Harvey-Jones or Charles Handy. A pub in the East End of London could be opened by one of the regulars at the Queen Vic from the BBC's *EastEnders*. New stables could be opened by a well-known jockey or trainer. Look for a link.

True story

A woman opened a Scotch pie shop in Blackpool just before the Labour Party's conference in that town. As business was slow, she wrote to Labour's Deputy Leader asking him to give her shop a plug. He did so during the conference, later dropping in for a pie with newspapers and TV crews in tow. What a business boost that was! It's worth asking a famous face for a favour because they might just say yes!

Taking serious events seriously

Social events should be enjoyable. The odd glitch may be forgiven by your guests (though don't take that as an excuse for slack planning!). But if you are organising something more serious, such as a talk or presentation, you are in effect putting on show your business ability. It is vital that such events run hitch-free.

- If equipment is required – a video recorder or overhead projector, for example – check it is working.
- Check the presenter knows how to use it.
- Have contingency plans for equipment failure, such as spare bulbs and fuses.
- Prepare the room in advance. Place, plug-in and test equipment to check that your leads are long enough, that sockets are in the right place, etc. (This is especially important if you are hiring a venue with which you are unfamiliar.)
- Don't forget the small items, like Blu-Tack and flipchart pens. They might be minor bits of equipment, but it makes a very bad impression if they are overlooked.

Bright idea

Try to identify possible events well in advance, for example anniversaries and AGMs, and schedule them into your events calendar and your PR and marketing strategy, where they can be used to support your general marketing aims.

Giving a briefing

If you are inviting a guest speaker, or even just getting a partner or director along to say a few words, issue a written brief outlining:

- why the event is taking place and what you hope to achieve;
- who else will be participating;
- what you expect of your speaker (eg a witty warm-up lasting no more than eight minutes);
- what your speaker can expect (eg they will be required to address an audience of 200 using a PA system and speaking from a lectern on a podium);
- who will be in the audience.

Also enclose:

- a programme of the event/a timetable;
- details of when to arrive and who to report to;
- practical information (eg parking, whether lunch is provided);
- for a speaker who is unfamiliar with your company, include background information too.

Without a good brief your speakers will not know what to expect. They will have a poor view of your company and its ability to organise, and you will not get the best out of them. A well-briefed speaker will make the biggest impact on your audience and help create the most impressive and memorable event for your guests.

Open days

Many companies hold open days; they are often a great flop. Most of us have attended events where visitors shuffle about nervously and escape at the first opportunity. Usually there is little to see, certainly nothing that compensates the visitor for the effort spent getting there. If that's what happens at your open days, you are defeating the object and damaging your reputation. Open days can and should promote your company, enhance its reputation and attract new custom. To do this you must:

- Offer something to visitors to make their attendance worth while (eg a genuinely interesting look behind the scenes, practical demonstrations, an interesting and informative interactive exhibition, free samples and publicity material, free advice).
- Attract the right target audience (you don't want any Tom, Dick or Harry popping in and freeloading, you want potential and existing customers/ clients).
- Have an appropriate staff:visitor ratio.
- Follow up on new contacts after the event. (The open day is not an event in its own right, it is a means to an end – increased business – so follow up those leads.)
- Be clear on what you want to achieve, who you want to attend, and what you want them to go away with (a product sample, perhaps, or a better understanding of your work).

Roadshows

Many large businesses go on the road with their promotional message. I saw a roadshow recently where the British School of Motoring had a promotional caravan and a driving simulator machine. Hordes of would-be drivers queued to have a go and left clutching their BSM blurb, eager to get behind the wheel for real.

Roadshows like this can be great for business. Unfortunately, too many road-shows are a waste of time and money. Cost your roadshow carefully and ensure that the benefits, in terms of enhanced reputation or new business, outweigh the not inconsiderable cost. You may need to produce new or special promotional literature and exhibition boards, to hire a caravan or pay for a venue, organise extra insurance, hire a generator, pay staff overtime… The costs soon mount up. Would an advertising trailer achieve the same objective at a fraction of the cost?

If you are sure the roadshow route is the one for you, make sure you have something good on offer. It is not easy to get people inside your caravan or venue. So whether you are wanting to attract the passing trade, or hoping to entice the invited guest, think about what is going to be a big enough pull to get them off their backsides and into your roadshow. You'll have queues of people if you are giving away free product samples, but how many of those people will become loyal customers afterwards? You will need to find a way of weeding out the freeloaders and targeting those who really matter – not an easy task! Many of the issues you will need to consider when planning an open day (see above) also apply for roadshows.

Talks and seminars

How better to promote your work than face to face? Talks and seminars offer you a perfect opportunity to build your business, so take full advantage of them. Here are some examples of how you can win new business this way:

- Let's say you are an independent financial adviser (IFA). A free seminar exploring the pros and cons of IFAs versus 'tied agents' should attract an audience of people who need financial advice and are unsure where to turn.
- If you are a graphic designer, offering a free design surgery and inviting local companies to attend could be a good way of getting new business.
- An interior designer could hold an illustrated talk showing rooms before and after transformation. This would be a real magnet for people contemplating using an interior designer.

When hosting a talk or seminar, take on board the points on pages 105 and 106 relating to using equipment, preparing a room and briefing participants.

Bright idea

Often companies get asked to present a talk or workshop at a conference or seminar. It could provide you with a valuable promotional platform. But don't be reactive all the time. Try to get yourself invited to talk at relevant events, and make this part of your promotional strategy.

After-the-event evaluation

Once the big day is over, it is tempting to sit back and relax. Don't – not until you have carried out a post mortem to assess the success of your event. Did you achieve your objectives? No? Where did you go wrong? What lessons can you learn? Could you do it better next time? Learn from your evaluation and make your next event one that is unforgettable.

10

Money, money, money: successful selling

There are better ways to sell than using aggressive salespeople to pressure unwilling customers to sign on the dotted line. This chapter will show you how to sell more for little or no extra effort. There are powerful tips for successful sales letters, advice on how to sell yourself, and pointers on how to sell your company at formal presentations.

Many businesspeople are remarkably bad at selling. Some are good at setting out their wares and hoping people will buy, but that's not the same as selling. Selling is active; hoping people will buy is passive.

Bright idea

Set yourself or your staff sales goals and targets. Work out what the annual target should be, then break it down into monthly or weekly chunks to make it more manageable.

Imagine you run a greengrocer's shop. Mrs Antrobus calls in one day and asks for 1lb of apples and 2lb of bananas. What have you sold her? Answer: nothing. She has bought apples and bananas; all you have done is serve her. But suppose you said to her: 'Here are your apples and bananas. And by the way, we've just got in a few punnets of early strawberries. They're lovely and sweet and make a fantastic fruit salad.' If your tantalising description of the strawberries persuades Mrs Antrobus to ask for a punnet (as well as some grapes to add to the fruit salad), you can now claim to have sold her something.

Some pizza chains try this tack. You order a pizza and they ask if you want any garlic bread. Most people say yes. You end up *buying* a pizza and being *sold* some garlic bread. Be careful with this approach. Many customers, myself included, resent this way of selling. Far better is the method of selling that brings in sales for you and acts as a service for your customers. Here's an example. I recently bought an antique hand-painted table. A few weeks later I got a letter from the shop telling me that they had just acquired some beautiful German hand-painted pieces and that, being a valued customer, they would give me 10 per cent off any item I chose so long as I acted before the end of the month. I called at the shop intending to browse and came out £800 poorer. Had they not written to me, I would probably not have visited the shop for months. I was delighted with my furniture and with the 10 per cent saving; they were delighted with their £800 sale! Combine selling with good customer care, as in this example, and you are on to a winner.

True story

Some months after a visit to the theatre I received the following letter: 'Recently you came to see the Citizens' Company's production of *The Milk Train Doesn't Stop Here Anymore* by Tennessee Williams. The production, directed and designed by Philip Prowse, played to great acclaim. I am delighted to tell you that Philip Prowse will direct the British première of Tennessee Williams' *In the Bar of a Tokyo Hotel*... next month...' The letter went on to tell me how wonderful the play is, how much tickets cost and how to book them. Presumably they got my name and address from the details of my credit card booking. Their mailer worked; I bought two tickets.

Letters of this sort are a simple and cheap yet effective way of making further sales. Why do so few businesses use the technique? Fewer still use it to effect. The examples in the following exercise show both a good and a bad follow-up letter.

Bright idea

One good ploy for selling more is to present the price in a more affordable way. So instead of offering a building insurance policy for £182.50 per year, say: 'For just 50p a day you can have real peace of mind . . .' or 'You could drive a brand new Mercedes for just £99 a month'.

Now over to you

The following letter (see Figure 10.1(a)) is a classic 'how not to' letter. It is dreadful, yet it is based on real sales letters I have received. List everything that is wrong with it.

Figure 10.1(a) 'How not to' sales letter

Shady Motors, High Street, Dellingville

Dear Customer,

We thank you for calling at our showroom, where you viewed our extensive and comprehensive range of quality vehicles, and had your own vehicle valued. Shady Motors would be delighted to see you again so that myself and my work colleagues may be of assistance to you in selecting your new car.

Trusting we may be of service to you in the very near future.

Yours faithfully,

Gary Bonnet

Gary Bonnet
Sales Executive

Discussion

- It has not been personalised and it reads like a standard, impersonal letter.
- It is obsequious.
- It is full of clichés.
- The letter seems to be pointless; it is not telling the reader anything they do not already know and is more likely to irritate the customer than get them rushing back for a trade-in.
- It is from a sales executive, which might make the reader a little sceptical about why the letter is being sent.

By contrast, compare it with Figure 10.1(b) showing how it should be done:

Figure 10.1(b) 'How it should be done' sales letter

The Caring Car Company, 101 Limpets Lane, Lillingworth

Dear Mrs Smith,

£200 OFF YOUR NEW CAR – FOR ONE WEEK ONLY

When you called in to see us last week we gave you the very best trade-in price on your old car, and an incredibly competitive price on the new Rover you were looking at. Obviously it was not enough to tempt you. Perhaps a £200 discount on your new car, whatever make or model, is enough to tip the balance and entice you back to the Caring Car Company? But hurry – this offer lasts for just one week.

I hope to see you within the next few days (we're open seven days a week until 8 pm), but if there's a problem getting in to see us this week, please let me know and I'll see if we can hold open our special offer for you.

Yours sincerely,

Douglas Jarvie

Douglas Jarvie
Managing Director

PS I have enclosed a brochure showing the entire Rover series, and a copy of the special finance plan I mentioned to you.

Discussion

This one is so much better:

- Even though it could well be based on a standard letter, it has been personalised.
- A subheading flags up the special offer, making it more likely that Mrs Smith will read on.
- It offers money off – in reality Mrs Smith could easily have negotiated £200 off the list price of a new car, but it is presented to her like a gift.
- The time limit on the offer is likely to prompt early action.
- The letter is less trite than the other example.
- A brochure is enclosed to feed Mrs Smith's dreams of a new car, and an easy pay finance plan to show her that she can afford it.
- If Mrs Smith is unable to get to the showroom within a week, there is still scope for making a sale; by asking her to call in, you're getting her part-way to making a commitment.
- The letter is from the managing director, which hopefully makes the recipient feel more valued.

Ten time-tested tactics to boost sales letter response

There is no magic formula that can assure success for every sales letter you write. But there are time-tested tactics that can make success more likely:

1. *Start with the punchline* Too many sales letters fail to grab the reader's attention right at the outset. This terminal failure results in many letters being binned well before your reader has reached the exciting and relevant part. If you start with the background, cover some detail, then end with the offer, you will lose too many readers on the way. Start with the offer, then explain the detail. Hook them first. They need to know upfront that your letter contains important information that will help them make money, save money, be more attractive to the opposite sex, get ahead at work, give their children a head start in life, lose weight... or whatever. Use a bold headline to attract attention.

2. *Sell a solution* Remember that people don't buy products or services *per se*, they buy solutions to problems. Letters that sell are letters that address a problem head on and offer the solution. For example; 'Balding? Hudson 100 will give you a full head of hair again' or 'Feeling cold? Make your home snug and cosy for under £100'. Put the solution in your headline. Then address any objections or questions.

3. *Don't be a feature freak* Only bores of the train-spotter variety are interested in features; normal people want to know about benefits. I don't care that my computer comes with 32Mb EDO RAM, or that it has a Pentium 166 processor, Intel Triton 2 chipset and 512K pipeline burst cache (even if I knew what these things meant!). What does interest me is that it is easy to use, even for technophobes, that it comes ready to plug in, that it is powerful enough to multitask, and that the pre-installed software will save me loads of time previously spent on administration.

4. *Make them an offer they can't refuse* A good 'offer' can be a real clincher. You have addressed the reader's problem, offered a solution – now clinch the deal with a great offer. Don't just state the price, say: 'Just £18 when you buy direct – so cut out the middle man and save pounds'. Wording it like this makes people feel they are getting a special deal. Simply stating the price is a missed opportunity to sell.

True story

The way you phrase your offer is all-important. A book club offered 'Two books for the price of one'. Then they discovered that 'Buy one, get one free' was more effective! Research shows that 'Buy one, get one free' produces a significantly better response than '50 per cent off'. 'Free' is a powerful sales word, so use it if you can – preferably in larger letters or bold type, so it stands out.

5. *Give a 'get-out' clause*   Many people are suspicious of sales letters. They might be tempted by the offer, yet fear being ripped off. Eliminate fear with a 'get-out' clause. It is unlikely that it will actually be used, but it does offer that all-important reassurance. For example, 'Just return your package to us within 10 days if you are not completely satisfied and we will give you a full refund' or 'We will not invoice you until you are satisfied with the work'.

Bright idea

Use a choice of offers. This makes customers feel in control of the transaction by exercising their choice.

---

6. *Offer guarantees*   You should be satisfied with the quality of your product or service. Show your confidence by offering a guarantee. Again, this gives apprehensive potential customers the necessary reassurance they need before taking the plunge and buying from you.
7. *Ask for the order*   Spell out very clearly to people what they need to do in order to take up your offer, for example 'Call into the showroom before the end of March' or 'Return the tear-off slip within the next 14 days'.
8. *Set a deadline*   This increases the sense of urgency and prompts an immediate response. If you let readers delay, they might never get round to it. 'Hurry. Offer ends this Saturday' is better than 'Take advantage of this special offer now'.

True story

Urgency sells. I saw an advert by Wimpey homes that was a clever example of how to use urgency effectively. They had a number of part-exchange homes to sell. Their newspaper advert showed each property, but across some the word 'sold' had been stamped. This clever ploy gave the reader a feeling of urgency. It looked as if the homes were being snapped up fast and thus prompted action. See if you can use urgency to sell.

9. *Make it easy to say 'yes'*   If you've got this far with a customer, you are doing well. They have read the sales letter, considered the offer and want to say 'Yes please, I'll order two dozen'. But you could still lose them. Make it as easy as possible for them to say yes, for example by including a return stamped envelope, including your telephone number, and printing an easy-to-complete coupon. (Some ideas on making it easy to respond can be found in Chapter 16.)

10. *Give payment options*   Make buying easy. The more options you offer (eg credit card, monthly instalments, boxes to tick requesting an invoice, the option to enclose payment, direct debit) the easier it is for readers to respond.

True story

Some companies use limited edition goods as a sales technique. It adds a certain cachet and air of exclusivity, and urges buyers to act quickly before the limit is reached. Some most unlikely goods are being sold with a limited edition tag. Kit Kat, for example, brought out a limited edition orange flavour bar. Walkers, the crisp-makers, brought out a limited edition 'Salt & Lineker' flavour, linking up with its series of adverts featuring footballer Gary Lineker. Sales of Walkers salt and vinegar crisps went up by 60 per cent during the promotion.

Lead-generating letters

A sales letter should generate sales as a result of the letter. A lead-generating letter helps you get a list of strong leads. It should weed out those who are not serious buyers, leaving you with genuine prospects to concentrate your efforts on. Lead-generating letters are step one. They need to be followed up by other letters, further information, samples, a telephone call or some other method. When you write a letter, ask yourself: 'Is this a sales letter or a lead-generating one?' If it is the latter, keep it fairly short and don't get bogged down in too much detail. All you are doing is asking someone to show an interest; you are not trying to sell at this stage. There are three ways to generate leads:

1. Ask prospects to seek further information, offering some free gift as an incentive. This will produce lots of leads, though many will have replied merely to get the gift.
2. Ask people to arrange a no-commitment meeting/sales presentation. Only those seriously interested will take this step (you will therefore generate fewer leads). You will be sacrificing quantity for quality.
3. Offer a 'gift' that is relevant to your product. For example, if you sell bathroom suites, offer a guide on how to plan a new bathroom. If you manufacture hi-fi, offer an information pack on how to select a new hi-fi, what to look out for and what to avoid. Offer your information free and stress that responders are under no obligation. This way you can attract mainly those interested in your product while simultaneously showing the expertise of your company by producing such a helpful guide.

Bright idea

You need not offer something costly in order to make an appealing offer. For example, 'Buy two and get a £10 voucher off your next order' is an offer that encourages customers to buy two rather than one, and gives them an excuse (a £10 voucher) to buy from you again, thus becoming a regular customer.

Unlock their 'motivating key'

We all buy for a purpose and you need to discover it. Behind every purchase there is a motivating key. One company might consider buying a scanner for their computer to save them the effort of keying in text. Another company might buy the same scanner, but for a very different reason; to scan images for in-house design. If selling to company A, you would emphasise very different benefits for the scanner than if selling to company B. Each has a different motivating key. The obvious way to find the motivating key is to ask! 'Why are you thinking about buying a scanner?' or 'How would you plan to use the scanner?' are good starter questions that allow you to probe.

True story

My local wine bar has the following notice on a blackboard: 'Try a dish of olives with your wine. Only £1 at the bar'. I have never seen so many olives being eaten outside Spain! Without that tempting notice, who on earth would think to ask for a dish of olives?

Building customer loyalty

It is easier to sell to an existing customer than to a new one, and it is cheaper to keep an old customer than to attract a new one. One company did its sums and found that to increase its profits by £500,000 over five years, it had a choice; either find 22 per cent more customers, or increase customer retention by just 2 per cent! So if you want to sell, hang on to those customers. Good customer care (see Chapter 19) will help you keep your customers. Look for ways of building customer loyalty and ensuring that your customers come back again and again. Rewards for regular customers work well. My favourite café gives regulars a card. Each time they buy a coffee their card is stamped. Complete cards can be exchanged for a free drink. It costs the café next to nothing, yet it keeps the customers coming back.

Bright idea

When advertising include a price. The same goes if you sell through a retail outlet; always display a clear price. People like to know what they will need to pay, many hate asking, and most feel that if a price is not displayed, the reason is that the goods are too expensive.

Cement customer/client relationships

Companies which view selling as a series of one-offs soon go bust. Successful companies aim to develop a relationship with their customers that continues well after the sale. Think of ways you can extend your relationship beyond the sale, as this is the best way of increasing customer loyalty. For example:

- invite customers to sales and special events;
- send them details of special offers;
- produce a customer newsletter;
- send them a Christmas card;
- send money-off vouchers;
- remind them, for example, that their car needs a service, that their insurance renewal date is approaching, or that term starts soon and they need to buy new school clothes for their children.

What suitable excuses can you think of for writing to your customers?

Bright idea

Treat every customer as if they are really important to you. After all, they are! No customers means no business. No business means no money.

Developing a relationship with customers involves building up a picture of who they are, what they buy from you, how often, what is important to them, and so on. You might find it useful to keep notes on your prized customers that will help you sell to them. Figures 10.2 and 10.3 can be amended to suit your needs.

Then you can adopt the sales approach that produces the best results. If you find that customers have stopped buying, or changed their buying patterns, take action. Keep a note of enquirers too. If someone makes two or three enquiries without even making a purchase, see if you can find out why.

Figure 10.2 Customer-buying history record

Name:	Suzanne Smith
Address:	27 Cottage Gardens, Sweeny Street, Cambington
Tel.:	012332 122123

BUYING HISTORY

Date	Purchase	Cost	Payment method
11/12/01	New lawn mower	£110.99	Visa
1/2/02	Aluminium greenhouse	£500	£100 deposit followed by £33.33 per month

OTHER COMMENTS:
Has a big garden. May be interested in sprinkler system.

Figure 10.3 Customer contact log

| Name: | Dil Patel |
| Address: | 122 Acacia Avenue, Peterston |

Date	Contact	Outcome
1/12/01	Sent customer newsletter	visited store on 12/12/01 and redeemed coupon
6/3/02	Sent invitation to spring sale preview	Attended and spent £100 on jewellery

OTHER COMMENTS:

True story

Instead of using salespeople on its stall at the Motor Show, one company used real satisfied customers to sell its cars. Cheap and neat ideas like this can have a major impact on sales, so think creatively when it comes to selling.

Selling yourself

In manufacturing and retailing, companies sell goods; their aim is to get the right goods, at the right price in the right outlets. Those involved in consultancy and certain service sectors are often selling themselves. In a way their sales job is harder, and there is little room for modesty.

Bright idea

Some sales are made by chance; being in the right place at the right time. Don't trust to luck. Be proactive in getting your name in front of prospects so that, when they need a plumber, an architect, a photocopier – they are reminded of you. Give-aways such as key-rings, calendars and coasters put your name (and contact details) before your customer. Make sure that free gifts are relevant and appropriate, for example key-rings for car sellers, pens or pads for office suppliers, mouse mats for computer suppliers.

True story

A company selling baby care products gives prospective parents a free car roller blind to protect their new infant from the sun when travelling. Needless to say, the roller blind is emblazoned with the company's logo. It's a good give-away because it is useful to parents and valued by them, while at the same time being cheap for the company to produce and effective in terms of the exposure it generates for them.

You cannot sell yourself until you feel confident about who and what you are. There's no need to be cocky or arrogant, ultra-confident and excessively self-assured. If that's not your nature, no problem – so long as you are not a shrinking violet. You need to be comfortable with others and able to put them at ease. You must be satisfied with how you look and how you come across. Dress for the part and have the right attitude. Be keen, enthusiastic, knowledgeable about your product and service, and personable. First impressions are important because you might not get a second chance. Research shows that first impressions are

Bright idea

Boost your confidence while making the most profitable use of your time. Buy self-improvement tapes and listen to them during what would otherwise be dead time, for example in the car to and from home or meetings.

formed in the first two minutes, based 55 per cent on how you look, 38 per cent on how you say what you say, and only 7 per cent on what you actually say.

Work at developing the right skills. Think carefully about your weak points and start to tackle them. Emphasise your strong points and make the best of them. Think about good salespeople you know. What are their attributes? Can you learn anything from them and adapt it to suit you? Here are some of the traits of top salespeople.

- *Ambition* – they are determined to get on.
- *Fearlessness* – they work hard to challenge the fears that hold the rest of us back.
- *Belief* – they really believe in themselves, their companies and their products.
- *Planning* – before setting foot in any sales situation they prepare, gather their facts, do their research and, as a result, walk in confident.
- *Eager* – they are keen to learn and they avidly read, go on courses and do what they can to be better at what they do.
- *Responsible* – they don't believe that life owes them a living. They take responsibility for their own situation.
- *Enthusiasm* – they are keen to work, positive about themselves and their work and optimistic about the future.
- *Professional* – they are thoroughly professional, returning calls, taking their work seriously, taking a long-term view.
- *Good listeners* – they listen to what their customers are saying and can put themselves in their customers' shoes.

Bright idea

When you attend a conference, always wear noticeable clothes, and when you get up to speak – which you should always make yourself do – start by saying 'I'm from Widgets & Didgets, which is the largest widget manufacturer in the Black Country...' and then go on to make your point. Read the delegate list and make sure you meet everyone there who it's important to meet. Then later you can ring them up and say 'I'm from Widgets & Didgets. We spoke at the conference. I was the one in the bright red dress/fluorescent bow tie...'

Pitches and presentations

If you are in the sort of business that requires you to stand up and make a presentation, or to pitch against others to win new business, you will certainly need to be able to sell yourself. After all, your success will depend as much on you personally and how you come across as on your price and what you are offering. Some people describe this as chemistry or rapport.

When making a presentation, apply the KISS principle: **K**eep **I**t **S**hort and **S**imple. Drone on and you will bore the pants off your audience. Get too technical or try to make too many points and you will lose them.

Do your homework before making a sales presentation. Know as much as you can about the company, what it is looking for from you, who will be at the presentation, and so on. As they say in the Boy Scouts, 'Be prepared'. Rehearse, anticipate any problems or issues they might raise, and go in there ready and able to take whatever they throw at you. (You can pick up tips for preparing presentation material by reading Chapter 12.) Take with you any visual aids that will enhance your presentation. You can choose from:

- *Flipchart* This low-tech visual aid can be a bit tacky. You also risk appearing as if you are running a training event rather than pitching for new business.
- *Overhead transparencies* They are cheap and easy to use. You do not need a fully darkened room.
- *Slides* They are more expensive, harder to update at the last minute, but they do look better than overheads. You do need a fairly dark room for slides to look effective.
- *Video* Unless you already have a company video, it will prove too expensive for you to produce one for a one-off pitch. They can, however, be good for regular sales presentations – so long as they are short (10 minutes maximum).
- *Computer presentations* Most laptop computers come with Powerpoint, enabling you to produce an impressive presentation in-house. Be careful not to let the technology take over. Visual aids should enhance your presentation, not replace it!

True story

An advertising agency was presenting its ideas for a TV commercial to a potential new client. Once the introductory talk was over, it was time to show the storyboard for the advert. Horror of horrors, they had forgotten it. Thankfully a spot of quick thinking and an outgoing personality saved the day. One of the account directors leapt on to the table and acted out the advert. The client was impressed and the agency won the work. A potential disaster was turned to advantage.

The seven deadly sins of sales presentations

1. Talking too much, listening too little.
2. Not preparing thoroughly and not having all the necessary information with you.

3. Not knowing what to say when the audience raises an objection. (You should have listed six likely objections beforehand and rehearsed answers.)
4. Not having a clear goal or objective.

Bright idea

After every sales presentation ask yourself: 'What did I do right? What would I do differently?' Learn from your successes and your mistakes. That way each presentation you make will be a little better than the one before.

---

5. Arriving late or not allowing enough time to catch your breath or set up the room.
6. Having poor selling aids (eg dog-eared product information, no samples, tatty overheads).
7. Making false promises. Overselling and under-delivering.

If after all that effort you don't get the business, don't leave it at that. You have two options:

1. Write and ask for feedback. Explain that you were disappointed not to win the business and that it would be useful to have some idea of the areas in which you failed, so that you can make the necessary improvements.
2. Write saying that you were naturally disappointed not to be selected, but that you hope their chosen supplier works well for them. Stress that should any other opportunities arise, you would be delighted to discuss them. This can lead to new business. I once pitched for a PR account and failed to win it. I followed it up with a pleasant letter and, months later, was contacted by the client. Their chosen PR consultant was not up to scratch and they wanted me to step in.

True story

Kogan Page, the publishers of this book, were the natural choice for me as an author, being both the biggest small business book publisher and the chosen publisher of the Institute of Public Relations. I approached them with the idea for this book and was rejected. Nearly two years later I was made an offer by Kogan Page and, as you can see, I accepted. Never give up hope! A rejection now need not mean a rejection later.

---

11 *Writing worth reading: planning and penning persuasive publicity*

Even the very smallest business produces promotional material of some description, whether it is a simple and cheap flyer or a glossy and expensive sales brochure. This chapter will show you how to write good copy, share with you cost-effective tips on improving your publicity and warn you what to avoid.

For many people, your publicity material will be the first point of contact they have with your company. Get it wrong and it will also be their last. It would be a great pity to lose customers even before you have found them, so work hard to ensure that your publicity material is powerful, punchy and persuasive.

Before producing any publicity, stop and ask yourself:

- *What* do we want to produce? For example, do you want a short flyer that can be quickly read, or a large poster with a clear message that needs to be viewed at some distance?
- *Why* do we want it? Is it necessary? (Too much publicity is produced because someone in the company felt that it would be a good idea 'to have some promotional blurb'. No one questioned its purpose and use.)
- *How* will we use it? For example, will we mail it, drop it through doors, hand it out in the street, put it in a leaflet dispenser?
- What is the *purpose* of the material? Do we want it to inform? To sell? To promote? To build an image? To persuade?
- *Who* is it for? Who will read it? Professionals? The general public? An informed audience? Shoppers in a hurry?

- *What* do we want in it? What are the main points we want to make?

Do all this *before* you put pen to paper. Only once you know what you are doing, and why, is it time to start writing. This is the bit many people dread. Thankfully you don't have to be a best-selling author or top journalist to use words well; a few top tips will put you on the copywriting straight and narrow, turning you instantly into a better writer.

True story

The French novelist Balzac could not write unless he had an unripe apple on his desk! Perhaps he was taking things a little too far, but he was far from alone in having strange foibles. Perhaps you find that you can write well only when the lights are dimmed, or with a radio playing in the background. Work out how you can create the best environment for getting your creative juices flowing.

Gobbledegook-free zone

Every piece of publicity you write must be in plain English. For your copy to qualify as plain English, it should:

- use short words – two short words are often better than one long one;
- comprise fairly short sentences;
- contain no jargon or unnecessary technical terms;
- contain no legalese or officialese;
- avoid padding or puffery;
- follow a clear and logical order;
- demonstrate an understanding of what the reader needs to know.

Bright idea

Never use jargon in anything written for the general public. Ask a friend who does not work in your field to read through your draft copy to test that it is comprehensible to a layperson and to spot anything unclear, such as unexplained acronyms.

Most companies and professions have their own jargon. This is really useful when talking to others who understand it, but use it with those outside your profession and you might as well be talking Greek to a Bolivian! If there is no alternative to jargon, at least explain in simple terms what it means.

True story: getting it wrong

Here is an extract from a letter I received from my solicitor about my new office: 'For the avoidance of doubt, the subjects comprise the subjects with several rights and under the several obligations more particularly described in the draft disposition annexed and executed as relative hereto'. I'm glad we got that clear! The Plain English Campaign (see below) stress that even legal documents can be gobbledegook-free.

True story: getting it right

I know a law firm that uses plain English as its unique selling point. Here's an extract from one of its press adverts:

'BEWARE OF THE GOBBLEDEGOOK

Jargon, heel! Goodness knows, corporate finance is complicated enough already without you wrestling with nasty legal terminology. But communicating in plain English is just one of the ways that we at McGrigor Donald are determined to make life as easy as possible for you... If you'd like to talk to a law firm you can actually understand...'

Bright idea

For more about clear, jargon-free copy, there are two main sources of help. The Plain English Campaign promote the advantages of clear communication: The Plain English Campaign, PO Box 3, New Mills, High Peak SK22 4QP, tel 01663 744409, e-mail info@plainenglish.co.uk Web site www.plainenglish.co.uk. They also produce an 'A–Z Guide of Alternative Words', which is also available on their Web site, and a pack on how to write letters in plain English. Investing in one could help you improve your image and win new customers!
The Plain Language Commission will, for a fee, edit text for adverts, mailings and any other material. They can also help ensure your design aids clarity. Both these organisations offer training and a plain English 'kitemark'. The Plain Language Commission can be contacted at The Castle, 29 Stoneheads, Whaley Bridge, Stockport SK23 7BB, tel 01663 733177, e-mail mail@clearest.co.uk, Web site www.clearest.co.uk

Write on

Writers are denied the intonation, stress and body language that add meaning to the spoken word. It is therefore all the more important that you choose your words carefully, so that they convey your message clearly, succinctly and unambiguously. Too much business material relies on striking design for impact. Design can help attract that all-important attention, it can even help make publicity material easier to read, but good design is no substitute for good copy. Good copy and attractive design should go hand in hand.

Bright idea

If you are having trouble getting started, just write the bits you can even if that means starting at the end and working backwards! That's fine. Just find a method that works for you.

Copywriting made easy: 12 simple steps to really readable copy

1. Always apply the ABC of good writing: accuracy, brevity and clarity.
2. Be natural when you write. Don't come across as too formal, pompous or stuffy.
3. Use contractions – I'm, don't, can't, etc – to add an informal, friendly air to your copy.
4. Use everyday words – the sort you would use if you were speaking to the reader.
5. Don't be afraid of the words 'you', 'we', 'our', etc. The 'first person' makes copy so much more personal and easier to identify with.
6. Avoid long words – they don't impress the reader. Well-written publicity is an easy read, not a struggle.
7. Use a mix of short, medium and longer sentences. Avoid too many sentences with more than 25 words, as they can start to get a little difficult to follow!
8. Use short paragraphs to create readable 'chunks'.
9. Check every sentence to make sure that the reader can understand it without having to read it twice.
10. Read your prose aloud; if it sounds stilted, rewrite it.
11. Don't be too inward-looking. Focus on your reader, not on yourself, because what excites you and your company may bore the outside world.
12. And finally, ignore what your English teacher told you. It's OK to start a sentence with 'And' or 'But', as I have just demonstrated!

Bright idea

Questions used as headlines and subheads are an excellent device for helping to break up the copy and guide your reader through your document in a user-friendly way. They also enable the reader to see at a glance which bits are relevant to them and which they can skip.

Don't contract hype-itis

Many copywriters suffer from hype-itis. How many times have you been promised 'The opportunity of a lifetime' or some other amazing offer that fails to live up to the description? Writing that overhypes a product is counter-productive, creating unhappy customers. It could even land you in trouble with Trading Standards if you are deemed to be providing misleading information. One holiday company offered a holiday it described as 'A peaceful alternative to livelier resorts'. Two women booked on the strength of this description, only to be plagued by disco music into the early hours of the morning. Their resultant court action awarded them £8,000. On the day of the verdict, a rival holiday operator, Thomson, launched a tell-it-like-it-is, 'warts and all' series of holiday brochures with down-to-earth descriptions of resorts. One Costa Brava resort, for example, is described thus: 'Charm is not a word that springs to mind when talking about Lloret'. Thomson believe that these frank descriptions will give them credibility. I for one agree.

Six ways to cut the crap

1. Only describe something as 'unique' if it really is.
2. Never say that something is a 'once in a lifetime' unless it has never happened before and never will again.
3. Don't say that something is 'an offer never to be repeated' unless it never will be repeated.
4. Avoid all hyperbole.
5. Use superlatives only if they accurately describe your product or service – if you are not the best, don't say you are.
6. Don't say something is 'An exquisite and beautifully hand-crafted...' if it is a cheap and shoddily-made Chinese import.

Accurate copy need not be dull copy. Indeed, accurate descriptions can be used as a unique selling point, differentiating you from your competitors. One mail order catalogue selling cheap novelties and curios prides itself on its correct descriptions of items. Its descriptions are amusing and readable yet very down-to-earth. For example, it sells a cheap polystyrene toy aeroplane which it says 'comes unadorned'. A butterfly fridge magnet is described as 'not an accurate representation of a specific butterfly'. The company goes so far as to describe its Christmas pudding charms (under £4 for a box of six!) as 'cheap and cheerful', adding: 'The manufacturer assures us that the metal used is at least 90 per cent pure silver and we believe him. But this is very much a cottage industry and inconsistencies are possible, so we do not guarantee it. Does it matter? Not at all, but consumer protection laws insist that we must tell you this.' As this company has been trading for over 22 years, it goes to show that you don't need hype or exaggerated claims to sell. Hype might get you an initial order but you won't get repeat sales if you create disappointed customers.

Now over to you

Get your red pen out and try your editing and copywriting skills on the following passage from a fictitious publicity brochure aimed at home-owners looking to move (see Figure 11.1(a)). Be as brutal as you like!

Figure 11.1(a) Editing and copywriting exercise

GOLDEN ACRES

Golden Acres is a quality housing development built by Wimp and Wally (Development) Limited. We saw a large number of architects eager to design this select development but we chose architect Alan Rike, a member of RIBA, author of a regular column in *Architect Weekly*, and expert in CAD. He has used a beautiful stone-effect finish on all façades, and project-managed the scheme from start to finish. A wide range of homes is available in this latest Wimp and Wally development for the most discerning purchaser, ranging from one-bedroom flats to five-bedroomed houses. All purchasers will receive a £1,000 voucher to carpet their new home in their choice of colour, as well as a decorating voucher. Those who have difficulty in planning and coordinating colours, styles and furnishings may have two free consultations with an interior designer as part of the purchase package.

Discussion

What was wrong with the passage above?

- It is too inward-looking. Why the developer chose the architect they did is of no interest to a house-buyer, whose main concern is the property, its features and any special offers.

- The use of jargon and abbreviations such as CAD and RIBA is unhelpful and irrelevant.
- The headline/title is unimaginative.
- The development might be really lovely, but the copy fails to paint an enticing picture of it.
- Referring to the readers as 'purchasers' is impersonal; it would sound better written in the first person.
- Clichés such as 'discerning purchaser' and 'select development' are best avoided.
- The special offer (free carpets, etc) is not worded in a very enticing way, and it is buried at the end.

Now that you've had a go at rewriting the passage above, compare what you have done with this version in Figure 11.1(b).

Figure 11.1(b) Editing and copywriting exercise (rewritten)

A COUNTRY HOME IN THE HEART OF TOWN – AND WE'LL EVEN HELP YOU PAY FOR IT

Imagine a home set in beautiful gardens edged by ancient bird-filled trees. Add a babbling brook, a pretty shingle pathway and row upon row of daffodils, bluebells and pretty country flowers. Imagine a place like this away from the noise, pollution and hustle and bustle of city life. Sounds great, doesn't it? But perhaps you would miss the convenience of local shops, restaurants and other facilities? How nice to be able to combine the benefits of city life with the tranquillity of country life. Well now you can. Golden Acres provides the best of both worlds. Designed by a leading architect, Golden Acres is an innovative development that creates a village feel right in the heart of the town. If you think it sounds good, there's more. Right now you can buy a home at Golden Acres and get it styled to your own specifications. We'll pay for you to see an interior designer, we'll pay for your decorating and we'll even give you £1,000 towards your new carpets. So whether you want a one-bedroom flat or a five-bedroomed family home, we think you'll find our offer too good to refuse. But please get moving – we can only hold this offer until 31 May.

Discussion

This is a great deal better, but why?

- Words are used to paint an attractive picture of Golden Acres. In this way, desire is created.
- The text is much more readable and more human.

- It contains no jargon.
- The headline/title is more appealing and the teaser about the offer is very effective.
- The deadline creates a sense of urgency designed to prompt readers into action.

Bright idea

If imitation is the sincerest form of flattery, flatter a few companies by copying their good ideas (suitably adapted to your own requirements). Get on company mailing lists and study their publicity for good ideas. Do the same with magazines. If you see anything you like, copy it!

A baker's dozen: better publicity for no extra dough!

For most small businesses, money is tight. These tips will help you to produce better publicity and they won't cost you a bean.

1. *Take your time* Allow plenty of time for a comfortable schedule. Rush and you might end up paying more for your suppliers, you will have insufficient time to write really good copy, you might not have time to check it for errors, the stress of rushing to meet the deadline might spark a heart attack – and you'll end up with poorer publicity that looks as if it was produced in a hurry.

2. *Keep 'mum' about your leeway* Prepare a production schedule and copy it to your designer, printer, etc. (and to staff involved in the process), but allow plenty of leeway in it for inevitable slippages. Don't tell anyone about the leeway – it's your own insurance policy! Always meet the deadlines you have set yourself, as it saves a mad rush at the end to make up for lost time.

3. *Don't let your printer pull the punches* Preparing a print specification could help save you money, by allowing you to compare like with like when you get print quotes. Get three or four quotes, as prices vary enormously. You will probably have to pay more for rush jobs, so try to get it booked in with the printer.

4. *Keep egos under control* You are not producing something to impress your managing director, you are aiming to sell a product. So keep control of big egos in the company, including your own. Appeal to customers. They don't want to see a picture of you in front of your new factory, they want to know what your products can do for them.

5. *Cut the mugshots* No photos are better than bad photos, so never use blurred mugshots, backs of heads, figures in the distance or sitting around a table, people shaking hands, dull and lifeless product shots. If you don't have good quality pictures, find other ways of making your material attractive.

6. *Don't forget that less is more* Stick to the key points and cut anything irrelevant.

7. *Use bite-size chunks*   Acres of unbroken text are off-putting. Offer relief to the eye with bullet points, headlines, subheadings, boxed text, and so on. Your publicity will be easier to read and more attractive.

8. *Use design trickery*   Tints and 'reversed out' text (see Chapter 24) will give the illusion of an extra colour, without the expense of using one for real.

9. *Get real*   Use real life stories to help bring your publicity to life. Show how your products have made a real difference to people. Use 'before' and 'after' photos. Get people to believe in what you are selling.

10. *Be upfront with the back page*   Many pieces of publicity material have a blank back page. Don't waste the opportunity to use the back page to full effect.

11. *Show off a smart jacket*   However interesting your leaflet or catalogue, if the cover is dull, it is less likely to be picked up, more likely to be tossed, unread, into the nearest bin. Publishers invest in good book jacket design because that's often what sells the book. Remember that it's as cheap to print a good cover as a bad one.

12. *Remember the reader*   Tailor copy, content and design to your reader's needs. 'Hip' words and funky design will go down a treat in material aimed at the young and trendy: it will sink like a lead goldfish in stuff aimed at the over-60s.

13. *Don't cut the captions*   Research shows that people read captions, so don't miss out on this opportunity of getting your message across. Caption photographs, ensuring your captions add to the photo rather than just state the obvious.

Bright idea

A cheap matt paper generally looks more classy than cheap glossy paper. If you can afford a more expensive, heavier paper for your publicity, check to make sure that it will not push your mailing into the next price band with the Royal Mail, thus giving you an additional cost to bear.

Special needs

Catering for customers with special needs is a nice thing to do. Banks and other large businesses, such as British Telecom, have come to realise that it also makes good business sense. They produce left-handed cheque books, Braille bank statements and large print telephone bills. Perhaps your blind or visually impaired customers would welcome information in large print or on a cassette tape. Use this service as your unique selling point. With an ageing population, poor eyesight is a growing problem and businesses catering for the 'grey' pound will find that they have a multiplying market.

Of the nearly two million people in the UK with a visual disability, most can read print if it is presented clearly. The Royal National Institute for the Blind recommends:

- a minimum point size of 14 for material aimed at partially sighted people;
- unjustified right margins (the text is aligned with the margin on the left, but ragged on the right-hand margin);
- matt paper – words on glossy paper can be hard to read;
- thickish paper – words can be difficult to read on thin, semi-transparent paper;
- spaces between paragraphs;
- minimal use of capital letters – some partially sighted people can recognise the shape of words, but words in upper case lose their distinctive shape;
- short line lengths – maximum 65 characters;
- good contrast – black type on white or yellow paper is ideal. Never use yellow ink on white paper; it is practically invisible to partially sighted people;
- dark inks (if black cannot be used) but never on dark paper;
- avoiding running text across photos or illustrations – it can look good from the design point of view but it is difficult to read;
- even word spacing.

Bright idea

It need not cost a fortune to cater for the needs of customers with a visual impairment. Simple steps, like using a large point size on your word processor when writing to them or billing them, costs the same yet gives your customers added value, gives you a competitive edge, and improves your customer care. Not bad for zero extra expenditure!

Publicity material

Now for a look at the main pieces of publicity you are likely to produce.

Leaflets

When producing a leaflet, start by being clear about its purpose. Most leaflets fall into one of the following four categories:

1. general promotional leaflets;
2. information leaflets;
3. sales leaflets;
4. booking leaflets.

Promotional leaflets

For such an important item, the promotional leaflet is frequently given inadequate attention during its preparation. Your leaflets need not be glossy and expensive, but they must be well-written, carefully thought through, and presented in a way that makes them easy to read and attractive to look at. Producing such a leaflet will take time and money, but it will also improve your chances of getting new business, keeping existing business and maintaining a positive image.

A general promotional leaflet can be difficult to put together; it can be hard to cover everything you do without getting too wordy. A good strategy is simply to try to present a flavour of what you do rather than go into the detail, leaving the reader feeling that they would like to do business with you. They don't need to know everything about you in order to feel good about you.

Information leaflets

Leaflets created to inform (eg 'All your double glazing questions answered' or 'The benefits of life insurance') are often the easiest to write. The 'questions and answers' format works best here. A question is also a good device for the front cover, for example 'Want to know more about home insulation?' (Never ask a question in a headline unless readers will answer it with a 'yes'.)

Sales leaflets

Sales leaflets must sell. Consider how readers can respond (ie buy), for example by incorporating an order form or reply device and by including your address, opening hours and directions, if appropriate. You might also want to list prices. If you often change your prices, why not produce a more expensive colour sales leaflet with a long shelf-life, and also a cheaper one-colour price list insert that can be easily and cheaply updated?

Booking leaflets

These are leaflets designed to publicise and encourage booking for a conference, training course, special event or similar. Make such leaflets as easy to reply to as possible. The tear-off slip is a good device here, but if you are using one make sure that you include the return address on it and don't put any essential information on the back of it.

Size and format

The majority of leaflets are A4 folded to either A5 (half A4) or to a third A4. Which to go for depends on three factors:

1. How you intend to distribute them. If by post, which size will fit most easily into your standard envelopes?

2. For leaflets which are to be displayed, will they be put into leaflet holders? If so, what size are they?
3. Some copy naturally fits a leaflet that is folded twice. Some fits better on an A5 leaflet. Take advice from your copywriter or designer (if you are using one).

Customer newsletters

Regard your customer newsletter as a sales tool, but be subtle. An aggressive sales newsletter will be ignored. Use your newsletter to:

- showcase innovative products and services;
- demonstrate how your products can and have helped your customers;
- remind your customers you are still there;
- attract new custom;
- maintain customer loyalty;
- inform in a way that is relevant and interesting;
- sell – softly.

Too many customer newsletters boast about how great the company is, how leading-edge its equipment is, how first class its procedures are, how efficient the staff are, how brilliant the customer service is. Customers take this corporate puffery with a pinch of salt – if they can be bothered reading it at all. Readers are not at all interested in you, only in what you can do for them. Newsletters written from a company perspective will never be read.

Nifty ideas for natty newsletters

These ideas will enliven your newsletter and, best of all, they won't cost you a penny!

- Make your cover page really attractive. A strong front-page photo and lead story will encourage readers to pick up your newsletter and start reading.
- Include a list of contents on the cover to entice readers to open up and delve inside.
- Use good headlines. Puns work well. For example, an article promoting special offers on new cars – 'Deals on Wheels'.
- Have regular features so that readers know what to expect, become familiar with the newsletter, and develop an attachment to it.
- Use a mix of long articles and short snippets.
- Number your newsletter and add the month or season of publication so readers know if they have missed an issue.
- Trailer one or two items that you will feature in the next issue.
- Include only what will appeal to the majority of readers.

- Publish the copy deadline for the next issue if you want to encourage contributions.
- Most articles will benefit from editing, so get the red pen out!

Bright idea

Find out what your readers think about your newsletter. Every year or two, do a readership questionnaire to discover which features are popular, which are not, whether readers like the style of writing, the design, the photos, etc. As an incentive to encourage readers to reply, consider a prize draw (but remember that feedback cannot then be anonymous).

If you have a newsletter that comes out frequently, it can be tricky finding enough information to fill it. Here are a few ideas:

Inspirational ideas for regular newsletter features

- *Hello/goodbye* – welcome new staff or prestigious/major new customers. Say bye-byè to departing staff.
- *Spotlight* – profile a member of staff or customer who is in some way interesting – interesting hobby, background or similar.
- *Focus* – take a closer look at the work of a relevant or related company, for example if you sell videos, you might want to focus each month on a different film director or movie production company.
- *Profile* – look at one of your departments or offices (but only if it will make interesting reading).
- *Fact file/Did you know?* – a different fact every month, for example 'We handle 100,000 enquiries each year' or 'Did you know that we sell one million eggs annually?'
- *Letters page* – to turn your newsletter from a one-way communication into a two-way one. (You can also pick up some valuable feedback this way.)
- *Soap box/what gets my goat* – a chance for readers to sound off about any issue.

Bright idea

If you can only afford to print your newsletter in one colour, it is usually best to opt for black print on white paper, as everyone is used to this combination from reading newspapers and books. It is also a good combination for readers who have a slight visual impairment, as it provides a clear colour contrast.

- *Helpful hints* – share useful or practical ideas with readers.
- *'How to' features* – give step-by-step guides on how to do a particular thing. Make sure it is relevant/connected with your area of business.
- *Calendar* – list forthcoming events, conferences, sales, talks…

Ten clever ideas for one-off features

1. *When I grow up* – ask a selection of staff or customers what they wanted to be when they were little.
2. *Crystal ball* – ask relevant people where they believe your business sector will be in 100 years' time.
3. *Bouncing babies* – get photos of staff when they were babies and run a competition to match the name to the baby.
4. *Seasonal* – for your January issue do a piece on people's New Year's resolutions. Follow up the following year to see if they kept them! Don't forget Christmas, Easter, spring, summer… There's plenty of scope for seasonal features.
5. *Pictures of the past* – publish photos from years back, of your work, premises, products or adverts.
6. *Pages from the past* – reproduce some front covers from newsletters you published years ago.
7. *Do a special themed issue* – for example a 'green' issue with tips on recycling, saving the planet, articles on the environment, etc. Print it in green ink on recycled paper.
8. *What the papers say* – run an occasional round-up of press coverage you have received.
9. *Do a special anniversary issue for a landmark year* – look back at the issues of the day, for example 'When we were founded back in 1973 the Rubettes were in the charts, a loaf of bread cost just 16p and…'
10. *Amusing or useful lists* – for example 'Ten things you didn't know about…' or 'Five uses for a… ' If you own a car showroom, your customers might respond to an article headed: 'Five reasons for buying a new car' or 'Seven ways to get the best deal on your next car'. Use an odd number if the list is long, for example 'Nineteen ways to get a good trade-in price'. It makes lists seem more genuine than a round number.

Annual reports

Not every company has to produce an annual report. If you do, perhaps you regard it as a yearly chore. Don't. It is a first rate opportunity to promote your company. Something that's going to last a whole year deserves special attention.

Bright idea

Newspapers and book publishers produce a 'house style' guide to ensure consistency. With so many different people writing for them, it is necessary to set down guidelines on how things should be done. You might find it useful to prepare one if you produce a lot of publications or have many people contributing to them. Here are some examples of what you might include:

- always spell out numbers from one to ten;
- use numerals for 11 onwards;
- express percentages in figures, that is 2 per cent (note – do not use the '%' sign);
- use full names at the first mention, but thereafter the first name only;
- commonly known abbreviations such as BBC or IBM are fine, but spell out at first mention any likely to be unfamiliar to the reader.

Bright idea

Get your previous reports and list what works well about each of them, as well as identifying the aspects of copy, design and format that are less successful. Translate these into a checklist of dos and don'ts. Do the same with other people's annual reports, making a careful note of anything that works particularly well.

Content

Plan and structure the content before you start to write your report. There is no need to follow the very rigid format of traditional reports – the usual directors' statements followed by several pages of financial information, more often than not presented in a boring way using dull pie charts. Dare to be different. Consider doing a themed report, writing your report around some appropriate theme. Don't put every last boring detail into your report (although there are certain statutory requirements that you will have to fulfil), just include the highlights or the bits that fit the theme. It's far better to give a readable flavour of your work than to pack the pages with stuff most of your readers will ignore.

Bright idea

Be imaginative with titles for publications. Don't just call your annual report 'Annual Report', for example. Think of something a bit catchier, such as 'Building Bridges: Anytown Construction Company's Annual Report 2002'.

Although strictly speaking the annual report is a review of the year, don't let that limit you. Use your report to promote your company, to discuss important issues that relate to your work/sector, to look to the future and flag up important new products or services planned for the coming years. Make it a really interesting and informative read.

If your report is written by half a dozen different contributors, that's how it will read. Connect the contributions to each other, integrate them around your chosen theme, delete any repetitions, and unify the style. Use a professional editor to do this, assign the job to a literate member of staff/director or – better still – employ a copywriter at the outset.

Focus on finance

Design should play a part in making your report stand out. It really comes into its own where the presentation of financial information is concerned. Old-style charts should be given the elbow. Use more imaginative graphic representations to present your financial information in a lively way that even innumerate people like me can understand!

True story

I received an annual report which looked really great but there was something not quite right about it. Then I realised – the year covered by the report was missing from the cover! It's easily done, so be careful not to make that mistake yourself.

You need not include your full audited accounts as part of your annual report; they can be produced as a separate insert, and many companies now opt to do this, sending the insert only to those who are actually interested in the financial nitty-gritty. The annual report then generally includes just a brief outline of the financial position, with a sentence to say that the full accounts are available on request.

> ### Bright idea
>
> Most reports contain lists. If a list is needed, at least make it interesting. For example, when listing your directors don't just state A J Baron, B Smith, P Singh, etc. Say something a bit more meaningful which gives an insight into why they are on your board. For example, Anthea Baron – Anthea has served on our board for three years, allowing us to benefit from her ten years' experience as a leading architect and award-winning designer.

You may have discovered, from bitter experience, that annual reports take much more time than you might have expected. For a comfortable schedule allow around six months from initial planning to final delivery.

Bright idea

Print an advert for your company on the back of your annual report, or include some kind of response form or money-off voucher as an insert in the report. That way you are using your report as a promotional tool, not just an information one.

Five ways to make your promotional material earn its keep

You have just spent a packet producing some great publicity material. Whatever you do, don't leave it gathering dust in a storeroom. Make your publicity material work for you:

1. Ensure that all your staff (if you employ any) know what publicity material you have and know when and how to use it.
2. Take copies of material to hand out at exhibitions, conferences, meetings and seminars.
3. Have supplies at reception and in any other outlets. Create opportunities for customers to see and pick up your material.
4. Send your publicity out to enquirers and with other mailings and correspondence.
5. See if you can leave supplies in places where they will reach your target customer, for example if you make designer dresses, place leaflets in local fabric shops; if you run a chauffeur and limousine service, leave leaflets at wedding dress shops.

If your promotional materials don't earn their keep, you might find yourself struggling to earn yours!

12 DIY design: how to produce stunning publicity in-house

Every business wants its publicity material to look good. You don't have to turn to a designer to achieve this. There are easy ways of producing good quality, affordable and attractive publicity in-house. This chapter will show you how. You don't have to be artistic, you don't need specialist equipment, and the end result can be highly professional.

Attractively designed material is a must for a business that cares about how it is perceived, but looking good need not be expensive. With a judicious mix of in-house and professionally designed material, you will be able to present the right image without breaking the bank. So if you can't always afford a designer, don't worry. There are some excellent (and cheaper) alternatives.

Tools of the trade

One design tool you already have is your computer. So why not use it? A basic understanding of computers, combined with a feel for good design, are all you need. You'll soon be turning out attractive material easily and cheaply.

Setting text to make it look attractive can be done by almost anyone, so long as you follow a few basic rules. Illustration is another matter. Unless you have an artistic bent, it is better not to attempt your own illustration though you can still include pictures in your publicity. Here are three ways:

1. *Clip art*   Computers come with a good library of clip art and you can buy additional CDs with a wide range of themes, such as sport, art and entertainment, music, countries, business and office, food, flags, flowers, animals or people. But do be careful when using clip art; it can be overdone. Some clip art images are really tacky and you see them cropping up everywhere. If you plan to use it, invest in some decent images and use them sparingly.
2. *Copyright-free books*   The low-tech answer to clip art is a copyright-free book, which allows you to add illustration without the need for a designer's fee. Most big bookshops sell these books, which contain images, cartoons, borders, logos and so on that you can reproduce without having to worry about copyright. They are really useful if you want to break up the copy with a few visuals. Scan the images into your computer, or photocopy them, cut them out and paste them down. Costing just a few pounds each, they are very affordable.
3. *Photographs*   You don't have to use illustrations, you can use photographs. Scan them into your computer, use a digital camera or give prints to your printer along with the rest of your artwork. You do not have to use the whole frame of the photograph; many photos benefit from cropping. Make yourself a useful tool to help you see how photos look when cropped. Cut two thick 'L'-shaped pieces of card and position them on your photo to form a frame. Move them closer together or further apart to see where it would be best to crop. If you are asking a printer to insert photos into your artwork, stick tracing paper across the photo and mark the crop lines on it.

DIY design alert

You do not have to be artistic to produce attractive material, but you must have an eye for layout and design. Being good at hanging wallpaper doesn't make you an interior designer; being competent at using a computer does not make you a graphic designer. DTP by the keen but untalented can be a disaster. So if you are new to DTP, try not to be overambitious. Going overboard with lots of different type styles and type sizes will make your publicity look messy. Your computer might be capable of producing 100 different fonts, but you don't have to use them all at once! The trick is to go for simplicity.

Twelve design tricks of the trade

1. Leave decent margins all around your page.
2. Use 'white space' – plan it into your design.
3. Create an 'eye path' which leads the reader round your text and draws their attention to the vital information.
4. Try not to cram too much in.
5. Avoid an overcluttered or bitty look.
6. Use clip art in moderation.

7. Stick to one or two fonts. Use too many and your publicity material will look fussy, messy and confusing.
8. Do not use too many capital letters; upper case words are more difficult to read than lower case.
9. Avoid too many point sizes – preferably stick to one for main text and one for headings.
10. Avoid putting large chunks of text in italics or bold.
11. Do not use text that is too small or too dense.
12. Break up the text as much as possible using boxes, bullet points and the like.

Don't create widows and orphans!

When designing page layouts, watch out for 'widows' and 'orphans'! A widow is when the last line of a paragraph appears on its own at the top of a page. An orphan is when the first line of a paragraph appears by itself at the bottom of a page. The result is an awkward and unattractive page break. Some DTP packages can be set to automatically avoid widows and orphans; if yours cannot, remember to look out for them and amend your design to avoid them.

Reach for inspiration

Starting the design process can be a bit daunting. Why not build up a file of inspirational, effective and eye-catching leaflets and other documents that you have come across? Put them in a big box file labelled 'inspiration'. Then next time you get stuck, reach for inspiration. Analyse successful designs and layouts and work out what you like about them. Is it the colours, the typefaces, the way the text has been laid out, the illustrations, the use of subheadings? Reproduce the techniques you like.

'Overprint' stationery

A number of companies offer attractively designed stationery items which you can overprint to create your own personalised leaflets, business cards, menus, posters, folders, certificates, notices, letterheads, envelopes, booklets, postcards, notecards, compliment slips, labels, newsletters and many other items. Choose your background design from a wide range available and then overprint it with text using your laser printer. Special software can help you with layouts.

For relatively small print runs this method is much cheaper than using a designer and commercial printer. It is a really cost-effective way of producing, say, 100 customer newsletters, or of doing menu cards, one-off notices and the like. The cost of small runs using a designer and printer is prohibitive. This way you get a professional and colourful product for a fraction of the price. The best

---

Bright idea

*If you produce a regular publication, such as a customer newsletter,
but you cannot afford the cost of a designer every time, there is a
halfway house. Find a friendly freelance who will design a masthead
for your newsletter and set up a template on your computer.
Thereafter you can do your newsletters in-house using the templates,
while retaining the air of a professionally designed publication.*

---

supplier I have come across for choice is Vista Papers, who produce a comprehensive mail order catalogue. (Telephone 0800 616244 for your free copy.)

The drawback of this method is that the copyright of the designs is owned by the company supplying them. You may, therefore, find it difficult or impossible to get permission to carry through your chosen design on to items they do not provide. For example, you would not be able to use it on company vehicles or staff uniforms.

Bright idea

*Ask to see samples before you order, as it can be difficult to make
your choice from a catalogue. Some companies will send you free
samples, others will make a charge which is reimbursed with your first
order.*

An alternative to ready-made overprint stationery is customized overprint stationery. Initially you will have to employ a designer to design 'blanks' specially for you. Get these printed up in quantity. You can then overprint them, as required, with your text (in the same way as with standard overprint stationery). This is a cost-effective way of producing lots of different leaflets, all with your corporate identity. It's also great for material you need to update frequently, such as price lists.

Getting a bit of colour

Bored with black and white? Introduce a bit of colour to your publicity. Use it to give your copy a lift, make your illustrations more appealing and your material more eye-catching. There are various ways you can produce colourful effects without having to turn to a commercial printer.

Five ways to use colour for maximum impact

- Use *coloured*, *textured* and *specialist* papers. A wide range of colours is available, from pastels to fluorescents. You can also buy see-through vellum paper, paper embedded with metallic flakes, fibres and confetti.
- Use a *colour printer*. Inkjet and bubblejet printers are now cheap. Use them for colourful documents in small print runs.
- Use *overprint* paper (see above).
- Use a *colour photocopier*. The price of colour copying has come down. Many offices already have a colour copier and every high street copy shop has one.
- Use *'lasercolor'*, a product that allows you to add colour to a document using a black and white laser printer or copier. Print the document, place the lasercolor over the area you want coloured, run it through your printer or copier again, then peel off the backing. The lasercolor will adhere to the toner, leaving spot colour just where you want it. This product is available in lots of beautiful metallic colours and in special effects such as prisms and glitter.

Presentations with flair

Making a presentation can be an important part of winning new business. The materials you use for your presentations can enable you to make the right impression on potential clients. Grubby, hand-scribbled overheads, will not win the business.

If you have a laptop computer with a presentation package (such as Microsoft's PowerPoint), you can ditch the overhead projector altogether. Use your computer to produce an impressive series of slides, which can be shown to a small audience on your laptop screen. Alternatively hitch up your PC to a larger screen using a special PC projector for a bigger audience. If projection equipment is not available, simply print off your slides on to transparencies for use with an overhead projector.

Bright idea

If you are planning on doing a lot of in-house design, invest in a decent training course. Find out what is available in your area and shop around before booking up. You might prefer to investigate the many computer training videos now available. They can be watched again and again, and enjoyed by more than just one person, unlike a course.

---

13   *Get out the placards: planning a local or trade campaign*

Our newspapers thrive on stories about local traders up in arms about parking restrictions that will affect their businesses or rent rises that may put them out of business. We frequently read about trade campaigns launched to counter consumer or pressure group campaigns. Many businesses find themselves involved in local or trade campaigns. This chapter will show you how to launch a successful campaign, how to build up support and how to avoid the pitfalls.

Campaigning is perhaps not an obvious aspect of marketing, but it can be a vital one. Many a business's life has been saved thanks to a successful campaign. High profile national campaigns are reported daily in the news: fishermen campaigning to protect quotas; the whisky industry lobbying to have excise duty reduced; pharmaceutical companies seeking to get certain drugs made available over the counter; farmers campaigning for an increase in subsidies. Our local newspapers are the stuff of small business campaigns. Many small businesses find themselves embroiled in a local issue that could threaten their livelihood, yet few know how to organize the kind of campaign that will see them on the winning side. Here are some typical small business campaign issues:

- the threat from out-of-town superstores;
- the threat from major players moving into your sector;
- the threat of increased rents/rates;
- the effect of proposed traffic restrictions near your business.

Big businesses employ professional campaigners, lobbyists and public affairs consultants to help them secure campaign victories. If your budget does not stretch to the high cost of external help, don't be disheartened; amateur campaigners can be effective. All you need is commitment combined with a professional approach and a big dollop of trade secrets.

Planning: your secret weapon

Underpinning every successful campaign is good planning. Campaigns that suddenly start up in a fit of enthusiasm usually fizzle out or fail in some other way. So *before* you launch a campaign, plan. Be thoroughly clear on:

- *Your objectives – both short- and long-term*   Never be vague about what you are trying to achieve. Write down your aims and objectives so that everyone has the same understanding of what you are working towards.
- *Your target*   Who is your campaign aimed at? Who must you influence? Who makes the decisions?
- *Your tactics*   What is most likely to influence your target? What are their weaknesses? How can you exploit these?
- *Your opponents*   Who are you up against?
- *Your weaknesses*   What are they? Can any weaknesses be turned into strengths?
- *Your support*   Who will support you? Are you likely to alienate any areas of potential support by your approach to your campaign?
- *The facts*   Research your case, know what you are talking about, and have all the relevant facts and figures to hand.
- *Your appeal*   What aspects of your case are most likely to appeal? (Different aspects will appeal to different groups of supporters.)
- *Your modus operandi*   What sort of campaign is most appropriate? A 'behind the scenes' campaign where you try to influence from within, or a public campaign? Don't launch a big media campaign if a problem or issue can be sorted out quietly behind the scenes. Always explore other ways of achieving what you want.

Bright idea

When presenting your case, try to put forward solutions to the problem. That way you are less likely to come across as grumbling, and more likely to be seen as constructive and forward-looking. A 'campaign for fair business rates' is better than a 'campaign against rate increases'.

- *Your technique*   Will you go for one big push and a blaze of publicity or a more drawn-out campaign? Which will work best for you? Can you sustain interest in a long-running campaign?
- *Your name*   Will your campaign have a name? What? What about a logo and letterhead?
- *Your budget*   How much will your whole campaign cost and where will you get the money from? How much money do you need right now? Can you do some fund-raising later?

The launch

Often a campaign is launched well before anyone has stopped to consider many of the above points. To really stand a chance of success you need to plan first, then launch. Not all campaigns have a clear beginning. They may start up slowly and gradually gain momentum. However, it is generally best to have a campaign start, or launch, even if it is a rather artificial beginning. That's because an official launch will present your very best opportunity for getting publicity, raising the issue you are campaigning on, and building support, so don't waste it. Have a high profile launch and get your campaign off to a flying start.

- What will happen at the launch? (A stunt-cum-photo opportunity? A press conference to explain the issues? A party for supporters?)
- Will you need to prepare any publicity materials for the launch? (Press packs, an exhibition, hand outs, photographs, factsheets, letterheads, news release paper, badges, balloons.)
- Who will organize the launch? Where will it happen? (If possible, ensure that your launch does not clash with another event which might detract attention.)
- Who will you invite? (Supporters? Other traders? The media?)

Don't let it flag

So much energy and attention is focused on the launch that the days and weeks that follow it can be rather anticlimactic. No one knows quite what to do next. Sustaining interest in the campaign, and keeping the momentum going, are major challenges. Any ongoing campaign faces the danger of petering out. To counteract this draw up a campaign programme, listing a series of events for the weeks and months ahead. These campaign highlights should be planned well before launch day, and scheduled into a campaign programme.

Bright idea

Morale is important in a long-running campaign. Whenever you achieve something, however small, let everyone know. It helps maintain interest and gives the impression that the campaign is going somewhere.

When drawing up your campaign programme, you will discover that there are limits to the number of ways in which you can keep presenting the same points. Finding enough different ways of saying the same thing requires real imagination.

Let's take a fictitious example. Your town council plans to ban parking outside the local parade of shops. You and neighbouring traders know that this will have an effect on your turnover. If people cannot park outside to nip into the shops, they may give up using your shops altogether. How can you keep up interest in a campaign like this?

- Arrange a photocall – do a mock boarding up of the shops to show what the future could hold if the yellow line plans go ahead. A fortnight later…
- Organise a stunt – carry a coffin with RIP LOCAL SHOPS written on it. Deliver it to the offices of the local council and ensure the local media are there to capture the event on film. A fortnight after that…
- Announce names of important local organisations that have pledged support to your campaign – the Chamber of Commerce, local community groups, etc.
- Get a petition going – announce the start of the petition, publicise how many signatories you have got to date, and have a photocall when you are ready to hand your petition over.

As you can see, a lively imagination and a strong sense of what is newsworthy can be used to maintain interest in a campaign that could otherwise disappear with little more than a whimper.

The campaign committee

Big or long-running campaigns require a committee to ensure smooth running. This may comprise:

- a chair (to chair meetings);
- a secretary (to call meetings and take minutes);
- a treasurer (to keep on top of the finances);
- a fund-raiser (this could be the treasurer, or you could have a separate person).

Bright idea

To help sustain interest, make sure that you don't release all your news in one go. If you have two really interesting bits of information, never announce them in one news release, but divide them between two sent out a week apart. That way you get two bites at the cherry.

You might also have:

- a coordinator;
- a membership officer;
- a press and publicity officer;
- a president or patron (a local celebrity or figurehead).

Assigning titles such as 'fund-raiser' to members gives them a clear role, with well-defined duties. That helps ensure that jobs get done. You might want to go one stage further and produce job descriptions so everyone knows exactly what is expected of them.

Your committee (and any subcommittees, such as a fund-raising subcommittee) will need to get together regularly at properly organised meetings. To ensure that business runs smoothly prepare agendas and stick to them, take minutes and circulate them, and keep on top of the inevitable correspondence and general paperwork that all of this generates. Even with informal campaign groups, record-taking is useful.

Bright idea

However passionately you feel about the campaign, don't lose your sense of perspective or become a campaign bore. If you appear reasonable, measured and objective, people will be more inclined to listen and to take notice. No one listens to fanatics.

Funding your campaign

Some successful campaigns have been run on thin air, but most need a budget of some sort. List what you'll need to spend money on, work out the grand total, and calculate when you will need it by. (Generally you will not need the full amount straight away.) Set up a fund-raising team and charge them with devising some money-making ideas.

Don't overlook the tried and tested ways of raising funds. They might not be glamorous, but they can still bring in the cash:

Bright idea

Find out what talent you have at your disposal and use the skills of those in your campaign group. Perhaps you have a photographer among your ranks, or someone with artistic flair. Ask supporters if they have access to useful equipment such as desk-top publishing computers. Also use the skills of the family and friends of your supporters.

- jumble sales;
- car boot sales;
- collections at meetings;
- donations/contributions from companies who are part of the campaign;
- fun sponsored events – bungee jumps, parachute jumps, runs and rides;
- social events – discos and dinners;
- fairs and fêtes;
- auctions.

The laws governing fund-raising are complex and it's best to seek advice before holding anything likely to require permission or compliance with regulations, such as a lottery, street collection or competition.

True story

During a Commonwealth heads of government meeting in Edinburgh, many road closures were planned for security reasons. Local traders were angry about the effect of these on their businesses and demanded compensation. One shop owner brought the campaign to the front page of the newspapers by displaying a huge home-made poster depicting colourful caricatures of the heads of government and explaining how he would lose £2,000 as a result of the summit. Often a simple idea can secure valuable publicity for a campaign.

An A-Z of campaign tools and techniques

A

Action   Tell your supporters what action they can take to help you win. Make it easy for them to act, and fun too.

B
Badges Another affordable way to promote the campaign message.

Balloons Printed balloons are a cheap and fun way to spread the word. Look under 'Promotional Goods' in the *Yellow Pages* for suppliers. (Don't forget to budget for helium canisters to inflate them.)

Banners Strategically placed banners can get the message across loud and clear.

Boycotts Boycotting campaigns can be effective, both in terms of attracting media/public attention, and in putting pressure on organisations to change their practices. Boycott campaigns have been organised by small businesses against certain high street banks who were accused of exploiting small businesses through their charging structure.

C
Car stickers Use them to get your campaign mobile.

Coalitions Form one with other interested businesses/groups then present a united front to show the strength of support for your cause.

D
Deputations Sending a deputation to talk to decision-makers can be a way of getting some media attention and encouraging the other side to listen to your case.

E
Engineering Sometimes you have to 'engineer' or set things up that would not otherwise happen, such as a photocall or stunt. If you base your campaign on events that happen naturally, you may get nowhere. Create your own news.

F
Forging links Establish as many links and alliances with others as you can. The more support you can get, the better.

G
Gimmicks Use gimmicks and stunts to attract attention from passers-by and from the media. (Consider your stunt carefully, as they can backfire. One insurance giant used homing pigeons in a media stunt, landing itself in trouble with the RSPCA and attracting widespread negative media coverage.)

H
Humour You can introduce humour into your campaign even with quite serious subjects.

I
Information Get as much information as you can and use it as a weapon, both to support your cause and to undermine the opposition.

J

Joining forces   Forming partnerships with other companies can make you a much stronger force, more likely to be taken seriously.

K

Kids   Children and animals have appeal so involve them in your campaign if you can. A photo of a child holding a placard with 'Help my mummy. Save our local shops' splashed across it holds more appeal to the general public (and newspaper editors) than shopkeepers on a march holding placards.

L

Lobbying   Lobby your MP to win their support. Big trade or industry campaigns employ professional parliamentary lobbyists, but you can do it yourself. Write to your MP, attend one of their surgeries, or phone them at the House of Commons (Tel: 020 7219 3000), where you will be able to talk to their secretary or researcher. Arrange to see them either in London or in their constituency and find out what they intend to do. You can also lobby your Euro MP (your MEP), your member of the Scottish Parliament, Welsh and Northern Ireland Assemblies, Greater London Assembly, and your local councillors.

M

Media coverage   See Chapter 8 on using the media to find out more.

N

Newsletters   Keep supporters informed of campaign achievements and other news, so they don't lose interest or lose touch. Use newsletters to inform potential supporters and encourage them to join the cause.

O

Orator   A good orator can put forward your case, give your campaign a face, and attract new supporters. If you have one, use them to act as media spokesperson, to address meetings and to rally support.

P

Petitions   They must include addresses and signatures if they are to be valid.

Posters   Keep copy to a minimum and remember that flyposting is illegal.

Public meetings   Book a room slightly smaller than you need and put out fewer chairs than you think you'll use. This will give your audience the impression that the meeting was more successful than you hoped. A large, half-empty room with 20 people signals failure. A small, packed room with 20 people is a success!

Q

Questionnaires and surveys   These are useful for backing up your claims, demonstrating support and attracting media coverage.

R

Rallies Rallies, marches and demonstrations pull together supporters, giving them a feeling of unity and togetherness. But beware; they can alienate potential supporters who resent the disruption. If you are planning a march, make sure you get permission from the police first.

Recruitment Ask each campaign member to recruit one new person to the campaign, thus doubling your number of supporters. Don't miss recruitment opportunities, such as at your public meetings or when you are asking people to sign your petition.

S

Sit-ins Sit-ins can attract attention, but they may lose you support if you are seen as being aggressive, and they may be illegal.

Slogans Try to come up with a catchy or clever slogan that summarises what your campaign is about.

Stalls Setting up an information stall in your town centre on a busy Saturday can attract both attention and support for your campaign.

T

Talks and presentations Spread the word and win support with a rallying-call talk. Use a confident and knowledgeable speaker with good visual aids (slides, videos or overheads) to help get your message across. Take your publicity material along to hand out, and a sheet of paper for potential supporters to leave their details on.

T-shirts Wear your message across your chest! Printed T-shirts are affordable, or you can buy cheap white T-shirts to decorate using fabric paints and stencils. For short runs, laser transfer printing is cheaper; screen printing is more cost-effective if you want a larger number produced.

U

Undercover Spy on the opposition. Go to their meetings, write to them for information, discover their plans.

V

Vigils Vigils are a more peaceful alternative to a sit-in.

W

Word of mouth It's the cheapest way of letting people know about your work.

Writing letters A letter to a newspaper is a great way of reaching thousands of people for the price of a stamp. For organised letter-writing campaigns (to, say, MPs or councillors), ensure supporters write personal letters, rather than simply sending a standard photocopied letter.

X

X-citement!   Make campaigning exciting and fun. Even serious campaigns should have a lighter side. Meet for a cup of coffee, hold a celebration for a minor victory, find ways to keep up morale.

Y

Yardstick   If your campaign seeks to influence opinion, carry out some initial research before you launch. This will enable you to measure your success and will provide you with a media opportunity to demonstrate it.

Z

Zany   Mad things, in their place, can attract attention. One businessman in dispute with his local council accused them of sticking their heads in the sand over the issue. Eventually, in frustration, he attended a council meeting dressed as an ostrich – to the embarrassment of councillors and the delight of press photographers. The element of humour in his stunt helped win him public support and showed the council up as stuffy, bureaucratic and humourless.

Bright idea

Come up with a name for your campaign – something appropriate and memorable. A good example is the campaign aimed at boycotting toys made in China using child labour – Toycott. Acronyms are useful if you can't think of a one- or two-word name. At university we had a campaign called CRAP (Campaign for Real Andrex Paper)! Aim for a pronounceable acronym.

Now over to you

Put on your thinking caps and have a go at being creative with these two very different campaigns (see Figures 13.1 and 13.2)

Figure 13.1   Campaign to save BT telephone box

Campaign one

Imagine you run a newsagents in a parade of shops in the small town of Redford. Outside your shop is an old-style red telephone box. This telephone box is loss-making and British Telecom plan to remove it. Initially they intended to replace it with a modern, vandal-proof kiosk. Now they will not replace it at all.

People using the telephone box often visit your shop, buying something to get change for their call. Not surprisingly, you want the telephone box to stay. You are about to mount a campaign, with 100 other residents, to get it saved. But hurry; BT plans to remove in it six weeks.

Your assignment

- Find a name for your campaign.
- Come up with a series of events, stunts, photocalls and anything else to attract attention and to put pressure on BT to give your telephone box a reprieve.
- You have no money in the campaign coffers, so you may need to fund-raise.

Figure 13.2   Campaign to reverse government's plans to introduce a 15 per cent tax on real ale

---

Campaign two

Your chain of 'real ale' pubs comprises 30 hostelries in the West Country and 20 in the north of England. The government plans to introduce a 15 per cent tax on real ale, on top of the existing excise duty and VAT. This will have a devastating effect on your business. As you serve only real ale, your pubs are going to be far more expensive than others and you fear that there will be a massive fall in trade. The big breweries and pub chains do not plan to campaign, as they produce or sell very little or no real ale.

Your assignment

- Find a name for your campaign.
- You want the government to reverse its decision. Come up with publicity-attracting events to help you get your message across and win public support.
- List who you will approach for support.

This exercise should have demonstrated the difficulties of campaign planning. Perhaps you surprised yourself with your creativity and ideas. You see, campaigning can be fun as well as serious. What did you come up with for Campaign One? (see Figure 13.1 and the following Figure 13.3) How about this:

Figure 13.3 Campaign One assignment – 'Keep Redford Red'

KEEP REDFORD RED

As a first step to getting some publicity and raising funds at the same time, organise a BT Boycott Day. Ask Redford businesses and residents to donate to campaign funds the money they would have spent on telephone calls that day. Get publicity for your stunt in the local paper. (See Chapter 8 for details of how to do this.)

- Register an application to get the telephone box listed. Use this to get some publicity in the local press.
- Have a sit-in at the telephone box, attracting attention and preventing it from being used. Organise a photocall for your sit-in, and get banners made to decorate the kiosk.
- Hold sit-ins at main telephones in the town centre for one hour, and hand out leaflets (printed on red paper) to people seeking to use the telephone you are occupying. Get them to sign your petition. Get your supporters to dress from top to tail in red, just like an old-fashioned phone box.
- Persuade your local paper to run a small feature on the history of the red telephone box.
- Get local radio along. Your story has great radio potential for telephone sound effects.
- Jam BT's switchboard with calls complaining about their intentions in Redford.
- See if another telecommunications company will take over the telephone box from BT.

That should be plenty to keep a campaign going for six weeks!

And what did you come up with for Campaign Two (see Figure 13.2 and the following Figure 13.4)?

Figure 13.4   Campaign Two assignment – 'Don't let Real Ale Ail'

DON'T LET REAL ALE AIL

Possible supporters include:

- your customers;
- brewers making real ale;
- other pubs selling it;
- CAMRA (the Campaign for Real Ale);
- famous real ale aficionados;
- beer-drinking MPs;
- your own MP;
- the breweries and pubs that do not sell or make real ale. (Warn them that unless they support your action, they may find that the tax is extended to other beers and lagers.)
- Launch the campaign in a famous pub – perhaps the set for Coronation Street's Rover's Return at Granada TV's studios in Manchester. Hold a news conference and photocall.
- Hold simultaneous photo opportunities at each of your 50 pubs in order to attract the local press.
- See if you can get real ale manufacturers to print a campaign message on beer bottle labels.
- Set up taste testings so drinkers can sample real ale. Explain how the intended tax will effectively wipe out many traditional beers. Give them a campaign leaflet detailing how they can support the campaign, for example by writing to their MP.
- Get coverage in trade papers and in the local, regional and national press. Also seek coverage on specialist programmes such as BBC Radio 4's *Food Programme* (which also looks at drink).
- Get a petition going and circulate it in pubs and clubs. Get a drayman's wagon to take the petition to 10 Downing Street (along with a crate of real ale) and organise a photocall.
- Have special pint-of-beer-shaped campaign beer-mats made, with the campaign slogan printed on one side and a postcard on the reverse (addressed to 10 Downing Street) so drinkers can add a stamp and send off the beer-mat to the Prime Minister.

---

14 Making a stand: getting the best from trade fairs and exhibitions

> Exhibitions (whether for the trade or for the public) offer a great opportunity for you to promote your product and win new business. This chapter will show you how to make an impact, how to get the punters to your stand, and how to follow up afterwards to clinch that deal.

The right stand at the right exhibition can transform the fortunes of your company. You could make a big enough profit in a couple of days to invest in some new machinery, or perhaps win a major new client. Some companies thrive by exhibiting. But that is not the experience of everyone. You might have had a poor time at a trade fair. If so, it is probably because you:

- chose the wrong exhibition to exhibit at; or
- did not know how to exploit the major selling opportunity that the right exhibition or trade fair offers a small business.

Sometimes you will be invited to take part in an exhibition. At other times the initiative to exhibit will come from you. Whatever the source, you need to decide whether or not a particular exhibition is the right one. To do this you must write down what you hope to achieve from exhibiting – your objectives. Now you can take a view on whether that exhibition is likely to help you achieve your aims, and you can evaluate success should you decide to go ahead.

Your objectives might be to:

- raise the profile of your company among key industry buyers;
- sell 300 copies of your new software package at the stand;
- attract new orders worth at least £8,000 for other software in your range.

If the exhibition is not likely to attract key industry buyers, or your stand will cost more than the money you hope to make, you might decide against exhibiting at this particular event. Having a clear idea of what you hope to achieve enables you to make an informed decision about whether or not to exhibit.

You need to decide:

- *Why* – why exhibit? Is there an easier or better way of achieving the same result?
- *What* – what will we be exhibiting?
- *Who* – who will we be exhibiting to? Who will come?
- *Benefits* – what will we get out of it?
- *Cost* – what is our budget? Can we do something to an acceptable standard for this budget? Is this the best way we can spend our publicity budget?

Five strong reasons for exhibiting

1. Staffed exhibition stands offer you a face-to-face opportunity to convert interested people into customers.
2. You can make new contacts which can be followed up later.
3. Exhibiting is a good opportunity for two-way communication. You can tell the punters about your product, and also pick up views, opinions and feedback from them.
4. You can use an exhibition to raise your profile.
5. Exhibitions can be a cost-effective promotional tool.

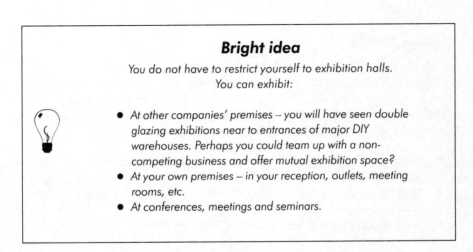

Bright idea

You do not have to restrict yourself to exhibition halls.
You can exhibit:

- At other companies' premises – you will have seen double glazing exhibitions near to entrances of major DIY warehouses. Perhaps you could team up with a non-competing business and offer mutual exhibition space?
- At your own premises – in your reception, outlets, meeting rooms, etc.
- At conferences, meetings and seminars.

Choose the right showcase

Exhibiting requires a big input of time and money, both of which you will want to spend wisely. You certainly don't want to waste cash or effort by taking a stand at the wrong exhibition. Make sure you select a showcase that will enable you to reach your target audience, and that will position you properly in terms of the image you are seeking.

Ask the exhibition organiser for an audience profile. This will provide you with a picture of who has attended the event in previous years and should also give you an idea of why they attended and what they hoped to get out of the event. Reputable organisers will produce an audience profile based on real research. If yours does not, perhaps you should consider finding a more professionally organised event.

Professional event organisers will produce a plan for promoting the event. Find out about it. Ask them questions about:

- Which media have been contacted about the event and whether features and coverage have been secured. (Get details of which publications will be running features and when.)
- Which journalists have been invited and which have attended in previous years.
- Whether they have copies of media coverage from recent years (ask to see it).
- Whether publicity flyers or mailings have been sent out and if so, how many, who to and when.
- When, where and how the event will be advertised.
- The opening – will there be a celebrity or other 'pull' to get people along?

Satisfy yourself that the organisers will work hard to draw in the target audience and to promote the exhibition.

Display materials

You don't want to make an exhibition of yourself when you set up your stall. Shabby, amateurish or unattractive exhibition displays will reflect a poor image of your company. Your stand is your showcase and you will be judged accordingly. Use a designer to produce your boards; home-made ones can look tacky and unimpressive. Brief your designer on:

- *Setting* Where will the exhibition be displayed? In a busy foyer or exhibition hall, or in a quiet corridor? Your display site will affect the design.
- *System* What exhibition display system will be used? A modular display system or display boards attached to a wall?
- *Audience* Who will it be aimed at? The trade? The public?

- *Key messages*   What do you want to get across? Keep it simple, preferably with just one clear message per board. (Your designer can commission a copywriter to come up with the wording, or you can provide your own text.)

Six ideas for exhibitions with impact

1. Exhibitions are about visual impact, so don't get too bogged down with text; few will read it if there's too much.
2. Go for lots of bullet points to make the text quick to read and easy to digest.
3. Try to represent as much as you can by using graphics, charts, tables and photographs, with only small chunks of copy.
4. Make your illustrations and text really large so they are easy to see and read.
5. Make good use of your corporate identity on your boards.
6. Don't forget lighting. Consider whether you will need additional lighting for your display. (If so, how will you provide this? Can the exhibition hall provide power? Will they charge you for it?)

Bright idea

'Mix and match' exhibition boards which can be chopped and changed are better than those that need to be shown in their entirety in order to make sense. If each panel can be a stand-alone, you have the basis for a much more flexible display. In a small space you can use just one or two of your boards.

Once you have gone to the effort of producing an exhibition for a particular event, find opportunities for displaying it again.

Staff your stand

Have staff standing at or near your display and available to answer questions and provide further information to interested people.

Top tips

- The seniority of staff should match the event. At a major forum attended by key buyers, those on your stand should be senior, confident in talking about your products, well-briefed and knowledgeable. If you are just handing out stickers and balloons to children, obviously there is no need for the top brass to be there.

- Brief staff on what is expected of them, how they should handle enquiries, and on what you hope to get from the exhibition.
- Staff should keep the stand (and themselves!) neat and tidy, with coffee cups well out of the way.
- Do not let staff (or furniture) block the entrance to your stand, or make it too narrow, thus making it difficult for visitors to get in. People don't want to have to negotiate an obstacle course to get to see your stand.
- Don't let staff huddle in groups laughing and chatting; always maintain a professional approach.
- Staffing a stand is tiring, so fix up a rota and ensure that no one does more that three hours without a break. For an all-day exhibition attracting 10,000 people, an average-sized stand requires three staff, two on duty and one available to relieve staff for their breaks, to free them to visit other stands, take lunch, etc.
- Be careful not to overstaff your stand. Visitors will feel outnumbered and reluctant to come over for fear of being pounced on and coerced into buying before they have had a chance to make up their own minds. Make sure your staff don't look as if they are hovering, ready to swoop on unsuspecting passers-by.

Bright idea

Staff should locate the loos, café, etc before the doors open, as they are bound to be asked where these facilities are, and will foster goodwill if they are able to help with directions.

Pulling the punters

However impressive your stand, it is worthless if it fails to attract customers. You must get people across to look at your display, to talk to your staff, to pick up your literature or to buy/order your product.

Do some footwork *before* the event. Ask the organisers if they have a list of people who have booked tickets for the exhibition. See if you can get a copy of it. Write to people on the list, tell them you will be exhibiting, enthuse them so they will want to see what you have to offer and will make the effort to seek you out. Consider giving them an incentive to visit your stand – perhaps a special discount voucher or a free gift.

Even if the event organiser cannot help you with a mailing list, there's nothing to stop you from creating your own. Use the exhibition as an excuse to write to customers telling them about it, and inviting them along to take a look. Send potential big customers free tickets. Issue a news release to your local and trade press (see Chapter 8 for details of how to write a release) to whip up a bit of advance interest. Publicise the exhibition in your customer newsletter and put flyers in your mailings.

Another piece of work you can undertake before the big day, to maximise your chances of visitors to your stand, is to make sure you get an optimum position in the exhibition hall. Visit the venue and ask someone to show you what the flow of people will be – where they will come in, which way they will head, where the seating and refreshment areas will be, where they will leave by, and so on. On the basis of this information, make a decision on the best site for your stand. Contrary to popular belief, the best position is not the stand nearest the entrance, but the second nearest one. People are still busy looking at their programme or putting their ticket away immediately they get through the door! If you don't take the trouble to visit the venue, you may end up in a backwater.

During the exhibition itself, there are various ways of attracting attention. Find a way of incorporating some activity or movement to your stand, perhaps with a video, talk or a product demonstration. Research shows that such stands attract more visitors. Avoid static stands.

Bright idea

Consider a prize draw at your stand in order to get people to it. Ask them to fill in their name and address, or to pop a business card into a box. Hey presto, you have an instant mailing list.

Consider who you want to attract when designing your stand. If you want to pull parents to your stand in a busy shopping centre, get your staff to dress up in Disney outfits to draw the children across, allowing you to talk to the parents. An exhibition displaying fashion clothes might do well with a small band performing at it, or pop music playing. Free cups of tea might be a magnet for older people.

When you use a gimmick to get people over to your stand, devise one that will attract the right people. There's no point in getting queues of punters if the

Bright idea

Most exhibition organisers produce an exhibition catalogue or programme. Take time to draft your entry for this. Write something that will encourage people to seek out your stand, then make sure that the stand lives up to the description so you don't leave visitors feeling short-changed.

majority of them are not interested in buying, just in getting a freebie or seeing a sideshow.

True story

A computer software company used a caricaturist to attract visitors to its stand in a busy exhibition stall. The tactic was extremely effective. Soon there was a long queue waiting for a free caricature, but they soon disappeared with their freebie. Few lingered long enough to look over the software.

Essentially there are three types of punter:

1. The *'want one'*, who will make a point of going to your stand. They are looking to buy and interested in what you have to offer. They have already decided to buy, your aim is to make them buy from you, preferably there and then (though be careful not to lay on the pressure or they will back off). If you cannot make a sale, give them information, product samples, price lists, brochures and so on to take away. Get their details and follow through later.
2. The *'don't want one'*, who has no interest in your product and will not be attracted to your stand. Don't waste your time here.
3. The *'might want one'*, who could be swayed. This person is perhaps considering your product, but has yet to decide to buy. They may need encouragement to come to your stand. When you get them, make sure they go away with information. Contact them in a few days, perhaps with a special offer.

Try to spot the different types. Be sensitive to whether or not someone wants to talk by watching their body language and looking out for other cues. Many people at exhibitions are paper collectors; they pick up every possible leaflet and digest it all later on back at the office or at home. Leave these people alone when they visit your stand, and select people who look as if they are interested in talking. Make visitors feel comfortable and at ease, not intimidated.

Bright idea

When you approach visitors at your stand, never say: 'Can I help you?' People frequently reply: 'No'. Think of an opening line that will start a dialogue.

Making your stand

Your exhibition stand is your company's own personal space. Don't feel that you have to limit it to a table and a few display boards. Decorate it. Use props. Put in seating if this is appropriate. Have flowers and plants. Play music. Do everything you can to make your stand attractive, welcoming, and eye-catching. Screen a video if it will attract punters, or set out an attractive and interactive product display. Plan your stand so that it is easy for passers-by to stop and take a look or pick up a leaflet. Exhibition-goers can recall fewer than a dozen stands; make yours one of the memorable ones.

Bright idea

Free coffee can attract people. The aroma brings them to your stand, and the hot coffee keeps them there. Use ceramic mugs not paper cups – people will wander away with a paper cup, but will not if you give them a proper mug!

The cost of making a show of yourself

Different venues have different pricing structures. You may:

- be charged per square metre of space you occupy;
- be given a space and told how big a display you can have on it;
- be charged extra for prime spots in the hall;
- be charged a flat fee (in such cases it is best to book early and reserve the best site).

Generally, when you are quoted a price for exhibiting, it will cover the space in the hall but anything else will be extra. Watch out for any hidden costs; there may be additional charges for a PA system, stand lighting, electricity, a video player or other equipment, for extra rooms (for seminars or a media launch, for example) and for extra seating or furniture. These can easily mount up, perhaps doubling the basic charge. Find out what you will be provided with, and check that it's OK for you to bring in your own seating or equipment if you wish.

Bright idea

Always have information, samples or publicity material for people to pick up and take away, or freebies such as badges and balloons. Keep a pen and paper handy to take details from visitors who want further information about you or leave enquiry forms for visitors to complete. Always respond to enquiries as soon as you get back to the office, while the enquirer's interest and enthusiasm are still fresh.

When you discuss prices with an event organiser, they will probably quote you a cost per square foot or metre. What you are quoted is not a price tag, so always negotiate downwards. The organisers will have a 'mean metreage yield' to aim for, so even if there is no scope for a reduction, there are other ways of getting a more favourable deal. Use trade-offs to get a better bargain; for example, agree to pay the full price but insist on free lighting, some free tickets and a more prominent entry in the catalogue. Be clear about what you can offer in exchange for a reduction and how you can work together to reach a deal. Remember that as a potential customer, you are in a strong position to drive a hard bargain.

When calculating the cost of your exhibition, include staff time in setting up the display and attending the exhibition, as well as accommodation and travel if the event is away from home.

Your budget may look something like this (see Figure 14.1).

Figure 14.1 Exhibition budget costings

EXPENDITURE	[£]
Photos for exhibition boards	£900
Design and production of boards	£1,500
Give-aways – pens and balloons	£200
Coffee and cups hire	£100
Staff time (two staff for seven hours)	£140
Stand fees	£500
TOTAL	£3,340
ESTIMATED INCOME	
Sale of new software: 20 packages @ £99	£1,980
	(ie £990 profit)
Orders for accounting software 20 @ £199	£3,980
	(ie £1,990 profit)
TOTAL	£2,980
PROFIT/LOSS	–£360

You might decide on the basis of the above figures that while you will make a 'paper' loss, you still wish to exhibit because:

● you will be reaching an important and influential audience and making useful contacts;
● the biggest item, the exhibition boards, will last you many years and will be used time and again;
● the photographs commissioned for the boards will be used in your next promotional brochure, thus spreading the cost;

- it will look bad if you do not exhibit, with competitors and customers wondering why you are not there.

Bright idea

When exhibiting, there's nothing to stop you from joining in too. Visit other stands, attend talks, network, form useful contacts, promote your business to other non-competing stallholders. Also take the opportunity to spy on the competition!

The practicalities

Some event organisers run a technical day for exhibitors, some time in advance of the event. It covers the practicalities, such as which loading bay to use, what you can stick on your exhibition shell and what adhesive you can use, how much time you have to set up and take down your stand, and when this is to be done. If yours does not offer this, make up a list of questions on practical points such as these.

Insurance

If you have anything valuable on your stand, or you are selling things, check the security arrangements, particularly if you have to leave the stand set up overnight. Also check insurance liability (your goods may not be insured once they are off your premises, so you need to check that they are covered by the organiser's insurance, or to make alternative arrangements if necessary).

Follow-up

It is obvious that following up leads after the event is essential – isn't it? It would appear not. According to research, up to 70 per cent of exhibitors fail to do this. Perhaps they have money to burn! Have a follow-up strategy in place *before* you exhibit so that you can follow up leads while they are still warm. Wait until they have cooled down and the opportunity is lost. Another reason to get in quickly with the follow-up is that you want your material to arrive before everyone else's; your prospect is bound to have left their details with other exhibitors. If yours arrives before the rest, it may get more time and attention from the recipient.

Bright idea

If you get a lead at an exhibition, fax a note off to the prospect that day. When they get back to their office and find your fax they will be impressed by your speed and enthusiasm. It will help you make an impact.

If visitors to your stand want follow-up, make a note of their needs. It's not enough merely to collect their business card; you need to know more, and to put it in writing at the time. What information do they want? Are they in the market for your product right now? In six months' time? Find out. That will allow you to make the right kind of follow-up afterwards, and to prioritise who gets followed up when. If possible, produce a tailor-made enquiry form. This will be a great help to you after the event. It might look something like this (see Figure 14.2).

Figure 14.2 Enquiry form

ENQUIRY FORM FOR PICKFORD PAPER PRODUCTS
Please complete the following so we can deal with your request promptly. Place your completed form in the red box.

Name: . . . .

Job title: . . . .

Company: . . . .

Address: . . . .

Telephone: . . . .

Please complete any of the following which are applicable:

Please call to arrange to see me about: . . . .

Please send me further information on: . . . .

Please add my details to your mailing list ☐

Please send me a written quotation for the following: . . . .
. . . .

You can, of course, arrange follow up visits there and then, by taking your diary along with you. Make that date while your prospect is full of enthusiasm, rather than leave it until they get back to the office and away from the buzz of the exhibition hall.

Finally, always hold a post-mortem. Check your achievements against your objectives to evaluate how successful the venture was. List anything that was particularly good, or that worked especially well. Do the same for the things that were not so good. Learn from your mistakes, and learn from others too. List ideas you picked up from other exhibitors and see if you can use any of them in the future.

15

Advertising and sponsorship

This chapter will show you how to get advertising working for you. Discover how to write your own advertising copy, how to use radio advertising, bus advertising, even the *Yellow Pages* to effect. Learn how to keep your adverts within the law. Collect tips on how to strike a mutually beneficial sponsorship deal.

Big companies wouldn't spend millions on advertising if it didn't work. But remember that big companies have big experts on big salaries to advise them. Many small businesses waste money on poor quality, badly targeted and ill-timed adverts, or throw money down the drain on ineffective sponsorship. Make sure you are not one of them.

Advertising can be expensive; a 30-second advert on network TV might cost you more than your annual turnover! But you don't have to hire the Saatchi brothers to make the required impact (though if you want to, Chapter 27 will advise on how to select an agency). A display advert penned in-house for your local paper might suffice and does for many businesses, helping them to:

- maintain awareness – to promote their name and remind customers that they are still there;
- advertise an event – a sale or special shopping evening;
- advertise special discounts or extended opening hours;
- advertise a service;
- sell a product;
- attract staff.

True story

Advertising need not cost a fortune and can help you make your fortune, as an unemployed sales manager discovered. Finding it impossible to get another job, he made a placard saying: 'I need a job – experienced in management – sales director', which he hung alongside a busy A-road. His local TV station featured his unusual advertising campaign and the next day he was offered a new job as international sales manager.

As this book is aimed at small businesses, and has a DIY slant, I will focus mainly on press advertising, which you can often do in-house; if you are planning TV or radio advertising, you will probably need to use an external agency (see Chapter 27).

Before embarking on an advertising campaign, consider:

- *Objectives*   Why do you want to advertise? What do you hope to achieve as a result?
- *Target audience*   Who do you want to reach? (Mothers? Book-lovers? Wealthy people? Pet owners? Anyone living in the Preston area?)
- *Key messages*   What do you want to say to them?
- *Medium*   How can you achieve this? What advertising channels will allow you to promote these messages to your target customers?
- *Frequency*   How often would you need to advertise to get your message across successfully and how big/long would your advert need to be?
- *Budget*   What is the cost of the various options? What do you need to spend to meet your objectives? (Remember to include hidden costs such as the cost of commissioning an advertising agency or designer, photographer, copywriter, scriptwriter, actors/voice-over artists, singers/musicians, etc.) Decide whether you could spend this money more effectively in another way.

Objectives

Set specific and measurable objectives before you advertise. It is no good saying: 'We want to advertise in order to attract new customers.' That's too general. All of the following objectives are measurable:

We want to advertise in order to:

- attract 100 new customers;
- attract sales worth £500,000;
- attract 100 enquiries, leading to 50 sales;
- increase by 50 per cent the number of visitors to our exhibition stand this year.

Also include some kind of time scale, for example:

- We wish to attract 100 new customers within one month of our advert appearing.
- We want to attract sales worth £500,000 within six months of our advertising campaign ending, all of them as a direct result of the campaign.
- We want to attract 100 enquiries, leading to 50 sales within two months and a further 20 within a year.

Which medium?

The next decision is *where*. The medium is as important as the message. A brilliant advert in the *Observer* is useless if 99 per cent of your customers read only *The Sunday Times*. Budget is often a primary factor when deciding where to advertise, but it shouldn't be. A company might say; 'We've got £1,000 in our advertising budget so we can only afford to advertise in the local press'. This is putting the cart before the horse. Work out what sales you hope to generate and from whom. Then decide how much you need to spend to achieve this. Consider what will reach your target and achieve your objectives most cost-effectively. A national newspaper advert for a sale in a local store might be madness (unless the store happened to be Harrods!).

There are various media advertising outlets.

Local paid-for newspapers

Pros:
- Great for geographical targeting. Some cover only a town or city. Others (the *Yorkshire Post*, *The Scotsman*) cover a whole region.
- Most will set your advert for free, although don't expect more than some basic layout of your text and logo.
- A representative from the newspaper will be happy to come and see you to discuss options and ideas.
- You can place an advert at very short notice because there is no long lead-in time.
- You can use coupon responses, essential if you want people to write in for information or place an order.
- It is quite cheap, especially classified adverts.
- Your advert can be read and reread.

Cons:
- Your advert has to compete for attention.
- People buy newspapers primarily for the news, not the adverts, so many just scan ads without reading them.

- Reproduction can be poor.
- Daily and even weekly newspapers have a short shelf-life, reducing the chances of your advert being seen.
- There is wastage; a paper's circulation might be 100,000 people, but not all of them will read your advert.
- Press adverts are static and two-dimensional.

Local freesheets

Pros:

- Cheap to advertise in and, because they are free and hand-delivered, they reach most households.
- Many people look forward to their local freebie, avidly reading both the news and the adverts.
- People use the freesheet as an information source for finding traders and other suppliers.
- Some free newspapers cover just a small neighbourhood, allowing very precise geographical targeting.
- Coupon responses can be used.
- It can be very cheap, especially classified adverts.
- Your advert can be reread.

Cons:

- Their only revenue is advertising, so freebies carry many more adverts than a paid-for newspaper. Your advert will have to compete for attention with many more adverts.
- Some people never read their freesheet. When someone takes the trouble to buy a paper, they will find the time to read it. Something delivered free to their door may not be valued in the same way.
- Many freesheets are so locally based that they do not reach a good cross-section of the population.
- Free papers are not always regarded as 'real' newspapers.
- Not all readers will read your advert.

National newspapers

Pros:

- Each paper has a clear readership profile, making targeting easy.
- There are fewer adverts to compete with than in local papers.
- You can place an advert at short notice.
- They are ideal for national companies to reach a wide, mass audience – perhaps millions of people.
- Because they reach many people, response rates can be high. Even if just 0.25 per cent of readers respond to an advert in a newspaper with a 4 million circulation, this will produce 10,000 replies.

- Coupon responses can be used.
- A quick response can be expected – coupons will be returned quickly.
- Although more expensive than local papers, national press advertising can be affordable if you use classified ads.
- Your advert can be read and reread.
- There is the prestige factor – a company advertising in a quality national will gain in terms of reputation.
- Sometimes you can get a cheap deal for 'distress' space – last-minute space the paper is desperate to sell.

Cons:
- Although some papers have a geographical bias (eg more readers in the north of England than in the south), geographical targeting is poorer than for local papers, so they are generally of less use to local or regional businesses. Some papers produce regional issues (eg the *Daily Mail*) or have a Scottish edition, so this does help targeting.
- Advertising is more expensive than in local papers.
- Because of cost, you may have very little space in which to get your message across.
- Reproduction can be poor.
- Daily newspapers have an even shorter shelf-life than weekly freesheets, though Sunday papers do lie around for longer.
- National papers often have a more stylish format and swankier adverts to match. So that your advert does not stand out for all the wrong reasons, you may have to have it professionally designed, thus adding to the cost. Many papers will want 'camera-ready artwork'; you will need a designer to prepare this for you.
- Not all readers will read your advert. Research shows that as few as 5 per cent of readers actually read any individual advert.
- Many readers will not be in the market for your product, so wastage will be very high.

Trade/consumer/specialist magazines

Pros:
- Targeting is much easier – architects read *Architects' Journal*. Only people interested in homes and gardens read *Homes and Gardens*. It is therefore easier to reach a particular profession or interest group.
- Reproduction is generally better.
- There are fewer adverts to compete with (except in the freebie trade publications and classified sections).
- There is high reader interest, so adverts are more likely to be read.
- The shelf-life is longer.

- Most trade publications are passed around the office and read by more than one person. Consumer titles are shared with friends and relatives, or find their way into the doctor's waiting-room.
- Professional and special interest publications are often filed for reference, making them even longer-lasting.
- Coupon responses can be used.

Cons:

- You may have to advertise in a number of journals to reach all of your audiences, whereas a newspaper advert in the right paper would allow you to reach them in one go.
- The longer lead-in times mean that you have to plan ahead.
- You may be asked to provide 'camera-ready artwork' and this will involve engaging a graphic designer.

Local commercial radio

Pros:

- Geographical targeting.
- It tends to attract social classes Cs, Ds and Es in particular, so if that is your market, it is ideal.
- It can be cheap, depending on the station. But the cheaper the station, probably the smaller the listenership.
- Most stations have staff to help and advise, and perhaps even an in-house production team to make your advert.
- Many local stations have a very loyal following and a strong local identity – perfect for small businesses.
- Most homes have more than one radio and 95 per cent of all cars have one, so there are many opportunities for people to tune in.
- Voices, music and sound effects can bring your advert to life.
- Listeners do not have to make any effort – the advert is brought into their home or car and read out to them.
- It is harder to ignore a radio advert. You can skim over a press advert, perhaps seeing little more than the headline, but a radio advert will be heard in its entirety.

Cons:

- Local radio is frequently on as background noise, with listeners doing other things while half-listening.
- It is more transient than a newspaper advert, which can sit around for days and weeks, and can be looked at again and again.
- You need to keep repeating your advert if you want to make an impact. That adds to the cost.

- It is more difficult to get a response to radio adverts: you cannot use coupons.
- Listeners may need a pen and paper to take down the details.
- You have just seconds to get your message across.
- You will need to budget for production as well as airtime. You will need a copywriter, a voice-over artist and perhaps music too. (Most stations will be able to help you with this.)
- Unlike both TV and press advertising, radio is not visual.
- Any 'small print' which is legally required (eg 'Your house is at risk if you default on the loan') must be read out on air. In a printed advert it can be, literally, small print.

National commercial radio

Pros:

- The growth in specialist channels in national commercial radio, such as Classic FM, Talk Radio and Viva, make targeting certain social groups easier. For example, Classic FM is popular with social classes A and B, and the middle-aged and elderly.
- It offers opportunities to reach a large number of people for less than a TV advert.

Cons:

- Apart from talk stations, some radio stations are not actively listened to.
- The drawbacks of local radio advertising also apply to national radio.

Commercial TV

Pros:

- It can be a powerful and persuasive medium. A clever advert can change people's buying habits.
- You can reach a mass audience.
- You can target geographically (by advertising on one or more of the local networks) or buy airtime on all of them to ensure national coverage.
- You can decide what time you want your advert to appear and during which programme, so as to reach the right audience.
- You can enter people's homes.
- Little effort is required by the viewer, as your advert is presented to them.

Cons:

- TV is expensive, in terms of both airtime and production, although some small businesses do use it locally.
- It's not a DIY medium; you would need an advertising agency.

- Many people video-record programmes and fast-forward during the adverts.
- Some viewers 'channel hop', using their remote control during commercial breaks.
- It is difficult to convey a complicated message in a few seconds.
- TV advertising is transient; it is over in a flash and cannot be retained in the way that a press advert can.

True story

During World War Two, Stork margarine was heavily advertised, even though it could not be bought on ration coupons. When the war ended and Stork became available again, the company ran an advert showing a stork in a prisoner's uniform being released from prison. Many products were forgotten about during the six-year war, but Stork had no difficulty in making its comeback.

DIY advertising

This section explains how to produce adverts for the print media. Writing scripts for radio and TV is very specialised, and probably best left to advertising agencies.

You might not have the ability of a professional copywriter, but you may still be able to produce effective press advertising in-house. Just take on board the following points:

- Know your audience. To communicate effectively you need to understand who you are writing for.
- Know the competition. Unless you know what they are offering, how can you offer something different or better?
- Know your UBP – your unique buying point. This is different from a USP (unique selling point) in that it focuses on what is of interest and importance to the buyer. USPs are product-centred. UBPs focus on what counts for the customer, at whom your advert is aimed.
- Keep your copy short and your message simple. Complex advertisements do not work because readers simply do not have the time, and often cannot spare the effort, to wade through your advert or to sort out what you are saying.

AIDA

Another way to produce effective adverts is to follow the AIDA formula. AIDA stands for attention, interest, desire and action.

> ### Bright idea
>
> A series of adverts needs to be seen to be from the same stable because adverts rely on the familiarity factor for recognition. You can make it clear that your different adverts are from the same company by using a standard layout, the same typefaces in each advert, and so on. If each advert looks totally different from the last you have to re-establish yourself every time. Build on the previous advert, don't start from scratch again.

Attention

We see up to 1,500 sales messages every day, but, remember only seven: the other 1,493 just pass us by! To be among the few that get noticed, your advert must be attention-grabbing. Try using strong photographs/illustrations, an arresting headline, bold colours (or striking use of black and white in a colour publication) and good design to make your advert stand out. Some sad advertisers resort to sex to attract attention. It doesn't work. Independent research carried out on behalf of the Advertising Standards Authority found that 64 per cent of respondents were offended by adverts that portrayed women as sex objects.

True story

This advert landed the advertiser in trouble with the Advertising Standards Authority. It showed a photograph of a young woman leaning against a piano wearing a short dress, which had ridden up to expose part of her bare buttocks. The caption read: 'GENTLEMEN NOW WE HAVE YOUR ATTENTION, WE WOULD LIKE TO ANNOUNCE THE ARRIVAL OF THE NEW SEASON COLLECTIONS...' Such pictures might attract attention, but do they develop an interest in the product? No.

Interest

Having attracted the reader's attention, you must now hold their interest and keep them reading. Make sure the body copy of your ad is a good read.

Desire

The reader has not only noticed your advert, but read it too. The next hurdle is to stimulate a desire to buy your products or use your service. Make them feel that they can't manage without you.

Action

Now you have to prompt them into action. Make clear what action is required. You may want readers to:

- complete a coupon requesting more information or a free publicity pack;
- send for a free sample;
- call you for details of a product or service;
- visit your store;
- take out a subscription/membership;
- ask you for a quotation for work;
- change their buying behaviour (eg by switching to your product);
- place an order.

Whatever action is required, ensure readers can take it with ease. There are various ways of doing this:

- Use a coupon device to make it really easy for readers to respond. Put your address on the coupon as well as in the body of the advertisement; that way, if a reader loses the advert having cut out the coupon, they will still know where to send it. Make your coupon big enough to be completed with ease – readers may give up if they have to squash in their details, or you may have trouble reading their writing.

Bright idea

Code coupons in the bottom corner so you can tell where they were cut from. That way you can monitor response to your advert, and assess which publication or which day/week produced the best response. You can do this for radio adverts too. Ask people to write to department X for one radio station and department Y for another. This is invaluable when it comes to discovering which adverts were most effective.

- Use a Freepost address if you can afford to (contact Royal Mail for details).
- Use a Freephone 0800 or 0500 number.
- Consider offering a credit card facility so readers have payment options and can order by telephone.
- Use a return address that is as short as possible and easy to spell.
- Include a list of outlets so they can take action by visiting your nearest store.

Bright idea

Never end your advert with 'We hope to hear from you soon'; it is too vague. Spell out what action they need to take: 'Return this coupon TODAY' or 'Contact us before 12 June to take advantage of this great offer'.

Slogans

Slogans can be useful in adverts. Try to come up with a slogan for your company that is both appropriate to what you do, and at the same time clever. Use puns, alliteration or other literary devices to introduce apt wit and humour. For example, The 3D Jigsaw Company might have as its slogan: 'Bringing a New Dimension to Puzzles'.

A good technique is to take a well-known company slogan and amend it in a comic way. I saw an advert for a small bicycle shop that applied this technique very successfully. It showed two topless men, one with a sagging beer-gut and the other with a washboard tummy. Over the flabby stomach was printed: 'This man bought a car'; 'This man bought a bike' appeared over the muscly midriff. Along the bottom, in large letters, it said, 'Reaches the parts other beers reach.' The advert worked because of its clever and humorous allusion to a famous advert.

True story

Perhaps this is no more than an urban myth, but I have heard that there is a firm of builders called Singh and Patel who use the slogan: 'You've tried the cowboys – now try the Indians!'

Five proven ways to boost the effectiveness of your adverts

1. *Colour*　Use it if you can afford to, as full colour advertisements in magazines attract twice the readership of black and white ones.
2. *Photos*　Research shows that good quality photographs have greater credibility than other illustrations and generate about 25 per cent more recall.
3. *Headline*　Use a powerful headline because only one person in five will read beyond it.
4. *Line spaces*　A line space between paragraphs increases readership by 12 per cent.
5. *A heavy dashed border*　Use one around a small advert to make it look like a coupon. It will increase impact and response.

True story

A new take-away placed expensive adverts in the local papers. It sounded so good that I decided to try it out, but the advert omitted the address and telephone number. I was left with a watering mouth; the restaurateur was left heavily out of pocket. His mistake was a surprisingly common one. The advert's copy was (presumably) supplied on headed notepaper, and no one thought to write out the contact details as part of the advert. Perhaps they assumed the newspaper would take care of it or maybe they simply didn't think. Don't make this mistake yourself.

Six steps along the eye path

Research carried out to discover how people 'read' adverts reveals that our eye follows a definite route when we see an advert for the first time:

1. *Picture*   We go here first, so make sure any pictures used in your adverts are large, dramatic and attention-grabbing.
2. *Headline*   Our eye then moves to the headline. Eighty per cent of readers stop there. If you want yours to read on, get them hooked on a hard-hitting headline.
3. *The bottom right-hand corner of the page*   This comes next. Most advertisers place their name and logo here.
4. *Caption*   For the few readers who get this far, the caption on the photo is the bit they read next. Captions attract twice the readership of the main text.
5. *Cross-headings, subheadings, other illustrations and graphs*   A scan of these follows.
6. *Body text*   Although this is the part of an advert that amateur copywriters give most attention to, it is actually the bit that is least likely to be read! Don't rely on your text to get people interested; most won't get this far.

True story

Topical adverts can be very powerful. During a national postal strike, Internet provider Pipex placed the following press advert: 'TODAY IT'S E-MAIL OR NO MAIL... We'd like to thank today's striking postal workers for the opportunity to bring the cause of e-mail to the notice of the British public. There's not much to say about e-mail except that it's faster, cheaper and more flexible than ordinary mail... Oh, and it never goes on strike.' Can you make your advertising as topical and direct as that?

A winning formula

You can see from the eye path research that an advert's picture and headline are its most important components. Combine a dramatic or eye-catching picture with a witty or intriguing headline to produce an effective advert. Here's a real-life example – an advert produced to demonstrate how economical the Honda Civic is when it comes to fuel consumption showed a car alongside a petrol pump, with the headline; 'Avoid painful fillings'. Simple but effective. Small businesses can use this formula too.

A picture and headline should work together, with each telling its half of the story. A picture that simply repeats the headline, or vice versa, will not work. Each needs the other to make sense, and together they should produce a strong enough message to stand-alone, without any body text. (Even if you have body text to give the detail, create a headline/picture partnership that can work well without it.)

Bright idea

In newspaper adverts, 'reversed out' copy (where text is not printed, but the surrounding paper is, making the text appear to be printed the same colour as the paper) is less likely to be read than ordinary text. Try to avoid it in adverts.

Hard-hitting headlines

You can make your headline more effective by:

- Using *why* in the headline. 'Why ten million Britons have bought a Pilkingford conservatory' is better than 'Ten million Britons have bought a...' The first makes people wonder, the second leaves them thinking 'so what?'
- Using *how*. For example, 'How to get a free MOT'.
- Using *do*. For example, 'Do you want to save money on your weekly shop?'
- Using a *signpost* to alert your intended audience. For example, 'PARENTS – hundreds of ways to keep your kids occupied this summer' or 'WINE BUFFS – connoisseurs of fine wine will love Bacchus, Newton's newest wine bar...'

Some headlines are so strong and self-explanatory that they can work without an illustration or body copy, making them ideal for businesses on a really tight budget that must produce all adverts in-house. For example:

- Cruickshank Insurance – 0800 100 100 – will save you money.
- MOTs only £10 at Mac Motors nationwide.
- Hike trainers – the best for less.

Such adverts work well on the side of a bus, for example, with just a logo, or as car stickers. Can you think of strong, clever headlines that could support your advertising?

Bright idea

Always put body text below your illustration. Our eye automatically lands on the illustration; don't ask your reader to defy gravity by having to read up to reach your copy.

The body text

A massive 80 per cent of people looking at your advert will not get as far as the body text, but don't let that dispirit you. Those who make it are likely to be interested in what you have to say. Use the body text to explain your headline (and photo/illustration, if you used one), to give more detail, to present any facts and information, and to persuade the reader.

Boost your body text

- *Don't* waffle. Get straight to the point.
- *Do* use short sentences and short paragraphs.
- *Don't* say too much; your reader will have trouble taking it all in.
- *Do* use the first person – lots of 'we', 'you', 'your', etc.
- *Don't* present too many ideas or propositions; it will confuse.
- *Do* use questions as subheads, to keep readers' interest. For example, 'Would you like to halve the time you spend on housework?' (But phrase your question so the reader answers in the affirmative.)
- *Don't* use too much unbroken text or small print; it will daunt would-be readers and may cause a headache for those who do tackle your text.

Bright idea

If you plan to run a series of different adverts, do not prepare and place the first one before starting work on others in the series. Have the whole series produced, or at least outlined, before the first advert is placed.

Advertorials

Advertorials (sometimes known as 'special features' or 'promotional articles') are laid out like editorial and comprise an article or feature rather than straight advertising copy. Why choose an advertorial when you can place a mainstream advert instead?

- Straight adverts must be short and punchy. As an advertorial is a feature-length article (or even a series of articles spanning several pages), it allows space for a more complex message or lengthier information. For example, it would be a good medium for promoting the benefits of creating a loft conversion; outlining things to look for when buying a new bed; showing recipes for lamb.
- There is space to go into detail and to illustrate, using photos, graphs, case histories and facts and figures.
- Unlike real editorial you can, within limits, say what you want to about your company or product (so long as it is true!).
- Sometimes it can be cheaper to buy half a page of advertorial space than the same amount of display advertising space.

Bright idea

If you decide to place an advert (not an advertorial) in a trade publication, ask them if you can have some editorial too. Although few publications will admit to their magazine being advertising-led, in practice you can sometimes secure editorial by placing an advert. It is always worth a try.

Speak to your target publication's advertising department to discuss an advertorial. They will explain to you how they go about it. Different publications have different approaches. Most will get one of their reporters (or a freelance) to interview you. A feature that satisfies your advertising objectives will then be written. Make sure you see this before publication to check for inaccuracies. The publication may provide a photographer (usually at a cost) or you can supply your own quality photographs. Occasionally you will be expected to supply the article yourself.

Are advertorials ethical?

There is some debate about the ethics of advertorials. Some feel that, in trying to pass themselves off as editorial, advertorials trick readers. (The Periodical Publishers' Association produces guidelines on the labelling of advertorials. The Committee of Advertising Practice says that advertisement promotions should be designed and presented so as to be easily distinguished from editorial.) However, many advertorials do look very much like ordinary features, and even use the same typeface and page layout.

Some regard advertorials as a waste of money because everyone knows that they are nothing more than advertising imitating editorial, so readers don't bother to read them.

Quite a few journalists feel that because advertorials are not independent articles, they erode a publication's credibility and bring their profession into disrepute.

Advertorials have a place for companies that would otherwise find it difficult to attract editorial coverage. They can be very useful if they are well written and genuinely informative. For example, a special promotion by a paint company that demonstrated how to achieve various special effects with paint would be regarded as a real plus by readers. By contrast, corporate claptrap explaining how fantastic the paint company was would not get a second look.

Bright idea

Some publications make extra money by charging advertisers an additional fee for 'colour separation'. This is a necessary technical process involving separating your colour photos into the four printing colours. If you are asked to supply photographs, enquire if there is an extra charge for colour separation, and if there is, you might find it a great deal cheaper to opt for black and white photographs instead, or to get your pictures colour separated elsewhere.

On the buses

Now for a look at bus advertising, a high profile advertising medium that is affordable for even very small businesses. You can advertise inside or outside the bus in a variety of configurations. You can specify the type of bus (double-decker, a single decker, etc); you can say which depot(s) you want your bus to run from; and you can specify towns and cities for your campaign (but you cannot select particular routes).

If you are considering bus advertising, arrange for a sales representative to visit you and explain what bus advertising can do for you. Remember that they are trying to sell to you, so evaluate carefully what they say; it may not be objective! Ask to see examples of adverts and to speak to local businesses who have used the medium successfully.

Should you decide to go ahead, the company will advise on your copy (or they can write it for you), they will get artwork produced and will arrange for your adverts to be printed. You can arrange your own printing, but it is as cheap – and less hassle – to buy a whole package.

The benefits

Those who sell bus advertising say it is wonderful because:

- you cannot throw it away;
- you cannot switch it off;
- you cannot turn it over;
- it lasts longer (radio and TV adverts last seconds, press adverts last hours, but bus adverts last months);
- a bus campaign can reach up to 90 per cent of the urban community;
- bus routes follow the movements of the population;
- you can run a very local campaign (eg in just one town, or one part of a city) or you can go national (or any combination in between), making bus advertising very flexible;
- bus advertising is as good for big business as for small companies;
- over 80 per cent of bus routes pass through town/city centres;
- the average bus crosses a town or city 15 times a day;
- the average bus will pass over 200,000 people a week.

The cost

One advert inside one bus can be as little as £10 per month. However, you need to add to this the cost of commissioning artwork and producing your vinyl panels. A rear of bus advert (size 20" × 48") would cost around £65 per panel per month. Remember to multiply these figures by the number of buses you need to advertise on in order to achieve the right level of awareness for your advertising.

The rep will give you a rate card setting out the cost per panel per month for the various permutations. You will almost certainly be able to get the quoted price reduced. If they won't budge on the overall price of your campaign, there's still scope for negotiation. See if you can have two months for the price of one, or ten extra buses free.

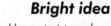

Bright idea

Rear panels are read by motorists and pedestrians on the move, so keep it short – just who you are, where you are and what you do. Make type sizes really big; small text cannot be made out.

When selecting where on a bus to slap your advert, budget plays a part but there are two other factors you should consider.

1. *Target audience*   Those reading your advert *on* a bus may be very different to the sort of people who drive along *behind* buses. Are you advertising to bus travellers or car drivers?

2. *Length of message* External advertising has to be short and sweet because you are displaying on a moving vehicle to people who are themselves on the move. Internal advertising can be more expansive; it will be read by people with time to kill – people sitting on buses.

Just the ticket

Bus ticket advertising is also an option. Obviously only bus passengers get to see your advertising (unlike adverts on the back of a bus), but if this is your target market, why not consider it? Those who sell bus ticket advertising say the benefits are that:

- Tickets must be retained for the duration of a bus journey, so passengers have ample time to look at your advert.
- It is as effective for small businesses as for the big brand names like McDonald's, Butlins and American Express who use it.
- Tickets are full colour for maximum impact.
- You can advertise in just one bus depot, just one town, or a much wider area.
- The promoters can help you plan a campaign. They will make the booking with the various bus companies, do your artwork, printing, delivery and campaign monitoring.
- For around £2 per 1,000 adverts (including campaign and creative planning, artwork, printing and distribution) it can be really cost-effective (although there is usually a minimum spend of around £450).
- A full-scale nationwide campaign can deliver up to 60 million adverts in just one week.

Bright idea

If you want to measure the success of bus ticket advertising, offer shoppers a small discount if they present their promotional ticket when buying from you.

Who travels by bus?

Image Promotions, the company responsible for over 95 per cent of all bus ticket promotions in the UK (see Appendix 2), provides the following figures for what it terms 'typical bus users':

Socio-economic group (per cent)

A	3
B	17
C1	26
C2	25
D	18
E	11

Age group (per cent)

15–19	9
20–34	22
35–44	16
45–54	14
55–64	12
65 and over	20

Reasons for bus use (per cent)

Shops	56
Work	18
Social	12
School	14

Local radio advertising

Many small businesses use local radio. Just tune into your local commercial station and have a listen. Are your competitors advertising? Could you sell your product or service on local radio? Should you? (Will you be reaching the right audience?) If you think that local radio might be for you, call your local station and ask for the sales department. Chat with a rep about:

- The benefits of radio.
- The process involved in producing an advert.
- The likely costs.
- How much help is available from the station and the cost of that help.
- What sort of person listens to the station. (The rep should be able to tell you their ages, interests and other lifestyle information. They will also tell you how their listener profile varies according to time of day or night, programme, and so on. This will help you plan when your commercials are broadcast, to ensure that you reach your intended audience.)

True story

EMAP Radio Yorkshire owns five radio stations in Yorkshire. It claims that it would take you 104 years to speak to each of its listeners for 30 seconds (if you never eat and sleep, and everyone is in when you knock). Alternatively, you could achieve it in just 30 seconds using the radio!

Be heard, not seen!

Writing for radio is difficult. The first lesson in radio is: write to be heard, not seen. Because radio is aural, that rules out anything visual. The biggest drawback of this is that you cannot show your product. However, you do have music and sound effects at your disposal, powerful tools that are not available for print promotion. When using music, you have to budget for the right to play the music, and the airplay royalties. This can really eat into your budget.

The second lesson is: remember that you have very little time to make an impact. The average commercial is 30 seconds, allowing you around 70 words. It's not a lot. A 70-word poster would be fine, as you could get a photo or illustration to provide much of the message.

Research shows that the most memorable type of radio advertising is what is termed 'mood/fantasy'. It involves the listener and paints a picture in their mind. Ensure your advert talks directly to your listener, and in the same way that they would speak.

Provide a good brief to whoever is making your advert. This should include information about your product, its benefits, USPs, and details about competing products.

Most people listening to your commercial will not be in the market for your product, but you still want them to listen to your advert. If it makes the necessary impact, they will think about you next time they want to buy one of your products. To achieve this your adverts should be interesting, entertaining or funny – or all three.

Bright idea

When broadcasting telephone numbers, get your number read out in a way that will make it more memorable. Take the number 383 940, for example. This would be easier to recall when read as 'thirty-eight, thirty-nine, forty' than 'three eight three, nine four zero'.

Creativity is what will win the day. That does not necessarily mean producing an 'off-the-wall' or totally wacky advert. It just means using the medium in a clever way. Why produce a 30-second commercial when you could produce one lasting 20 or even 10 seconds? Or three different versions? Break the boundaries so long as it works.

Like other advertising, radio adverts must clearly signal to the listener what action they should take. Tell them one or more of the following:

- Where they can buy your product.
- Which number to ring for further information (preferably a Freephone number, and something easy to recall).
- Where to write for details – addresses must be short and easy. (The Royal Mail runs a service called 'Freepost Name', which was devised to make responding to radio and TV adverts easier. Freepost Name allows customers to respond to an advert by writing to Freepost, followed by the name licensed by a particular company. There is no need to write a full address or postcode, or to use a stamp.)

Radio fact file

- 72 per cent of listeners listen in the kitchen.
- 27 per cent listen in the bathroom (43 per cent of 15- to 24-year-olds).
- Under-24s spend more time listening to commercial radio than any other group.
- 17 per cent of commercial radio listeners who listen in the car between 9 am and 12 noon are either female part-timers or housewives.
- 25 per cent of female shoppers are likely to be listening to the radio when planning their food shopping.
- 61 per cent of the adult population listen to commercial radio.
- The UK's first radio advert was for fish fingers – back in 1973.

Bright idea

When you listen to your completed commercial, it will be in a studio with professional equipment. The quality will sound great. Ask to hear it on a basic radio set, as this is how most of your listeners will hear it.

Yellow Pages

The *Yellow Pages* is perhaps the one place that all businesses advertise. Given that it is one massive advertising tome, you need to be on the ball to get your advert noticed among the thousands of others. There was a time when some businesses deliberately chose names like Aardvark Plumbing or AAAAA1 Glaziers to ensure their place at the front of their section in *Yellow Pages'* alphabetical listings. I am told that this is no longer allowed. In any case, the best way to get your advert noticed is to pay for a display advert and to use the space you have bought creatively.

Bright idea

You can get 'Find us in the Yellow Pages' stickers. If it is appropriate for your business, use these stickers in company vehicles as a mobile advert.

You will find yourself alongside competing businesses, so promote your USP – hard. Readers look in your section of *Yellow Pages* because they need someone to provide your service or product, but why should they choose you? Your advert needs to tell them why.

Top tips for *Yellow Pages* adverts

- The paper is really poor quality, so don't use photos – they will reproduce badly.
- There is a mass of information on each page, so make your advert different by making maximum use of 'white space' (or, in this case, yellow space!) – it will help your advert stand out.
- Place your advert in a box so it is set apart from the other adverts.
- Be big and bold in your design and text. The rows of small text on the other pages will make people squint. Your advert should provide optical relief.

Bright idea

Often little thought and consideration goes into job adverts, and great opportunities are therefore missed. Regard a job advert as dual purpose; it should attract applicants for a particular job and it should promote your company to those who are idly scanning the jobs' pages. Instead of simply passing on information about the position you are advertising, use it to say something about your company or products. Don't write; 'Anytown Carpet Warehouse needs an HGV-qualified driver. 39 hours per week. Salary £...' Write, 'By offering the best choice of carpets in town, our business has expanded. Now we need an HGV-qualified driver to join our growing team...' Anyone reading that would have a much more positive impression of your company, whether they want to apply for your job or not. They might even pay you a visit next time they need a carpet, simply on the strength of that job advert.

Be ready to respond

You advertise in the hope that people will take action and get in touch. Be ready for them when they do.

- Make sure you have sufficient supplies of advertised goods. There's nothing more likely to lose you goodwill than unfulfilled or delayed orders. You may want to offer enquirers an information pack. Ensure that you have prepared packs before your adverts appear, so you can respond swiftly and efficiently. You might wish to include in the packs:
  - a personalised covering letter thanking the enquirer for getting in touch;
  - any sales or publicity material;
  - a sample (if appropriate);
  - an order form or other response device;
  - a list of local outlets where your product is available.

Bright idea

If you advertise in trade publications, be prepared for enquiries to continue to arrive in dribs and drabs for some months, as these publications tend to have a longer shelf-life than newspapers.

- Take on temporary staff if you anticipate the need, or ensure that you are not short-handed because of holidays.
- You may get enquiries or orders by phone, mail and e-mail, by fax and in person. Make sure that your receptionist/sales staff know what to do when someone calls. They must know what to say and what details to take down. All enquiries and orders must be handled professionally.
- Have a distribution/response system in place *before* you place your adverts.

Bright idea

Prepare a pro forma so that enquirers' details can be fully recorded. Make sure you include all the relevant information and that there is a clear system for processing the pro formas, sending out information/orders, and adding enquirers' addresses, etc, to your database.

The media plan

Too many companies place an advert as a knee-jerk response. They see their sales falling or competition increasing, and regard a hastily placed advert as the solution. If this is your attitude, advertising will fail you. Advertising is one part of your marketing armoury. It should be built into your marketing strategy, alongside your other marketing activity. But if advertising is a major component of your promotional work, a separate media plan is a must. It should include:

- what adverts you will be running;
- when;
- where (in which publications/radio stations);
- at what cost;
- for what effect.

There's no need to prepare a media plan if all you intend is a very occasional advert to publicise a sale or special offer, for example.

Staying within the law

The Advertising Standards Authority (ASA) is responsible for ensuring that advertising meets the standard and is in the public interest. It has the power to investigate complaints about advertisements; many of these are about small businesses. It's not just the big boys who fall foul!

True story

When a company claimed a 'major advance in stairlift design' and described itself as 'world leaders in stairlift technology', another stairlift company reported it to the ASA and their complaint was upheld. Nothing will delight your competitors more than catching you out. If they are monitoring your advertising, any breaches they spot will be reported to the ASA with great speed. Many of the complaints made to the ASA come from other businesses.

You don't have to deliberately try to mislead the public in order to have a complaint against you upheld. You can be in breach unintentionally, so make sure that any claims you make in your adverts can be substantiated.

The Committee of Advertising Practice (CAP) is the self-regulatory body that devises and enforces the British Codes of Advertising and Sales Promotion. They produce a really useful guide to the codes, which can be downloaded free of charge from www.asa.org.uk. More useful advice is available at cap.org.uk. CAP also offer a free and confidential advice service to advertisers, to help ensure that they stay within the Codes. (Telephone 020 7580 4100 and ask for the copy advice team or e-mail copyadvice@cap.org.uk.)

The Codes apply to adverts in newspapers, magazines, catalogues, mailings, brochures and posters, but not to broadcast commercials on TV and radio. These are policed by the Independent Television Commission and the Radio Authority, respectively. A full copy of the Codes is available; get hold of one if you are planning any advertising. The main points are:

- all adverts should be legal, decent, honest and truthful;
- all adverts should be prepared with a sense of responsibility to consumers and society;
- advertisers must hold documentary evidence to prove all claims that are capable of objective substantiation;
- if there is a significant division of informed opinion about any claims made, they should not be portrayed as universally agreed;
- no advert should cause fear or distress without good reason; advertisers should not use shocking claims or images merely to attract attention.

The cost of a campaign

There are two sources of information about the cost of advertising. Advertising departments produce 'rate cards' setting out the cost according to size, position, and so on. Another source is a monthly publication, *British Rate and Data* (*BRAD*), which lists all the UK's advertising media, their rates and their readership. You can subscribe to this, or consult a copy at central reference libraries.

Bright idea
Often the rate printed on a rate card is negotiable, so always try to get the official rate reduced.

For press advertising, factors affecting price include:

- *Time of year*   There are slack periods when you can get a better deal.
- *Demand*   The less the demand, the less you pay.
- *Size*   The bigger your advert, the costlier it will be. A half page will cost more than a quarter page, though not necessarily twice as much.
- *Circulation*   The bigger the circulation, the more you can expect to pay for your space. However, your advert will reach more people.

- *Situation* Front page adverts cost more than those on the back.
- *Colour* Black and white is cheaper than colour, and 'spot colour' (adding a splash of red to your black and white advert, for example) is cheaper than full colour.

For broadcast adverts, the price depends on:

- *Station/network* Some are more costly than others, depending on the area they cover, the listening/viewing figures.
- *Time* When the advert will be seen/heard. Obviously peak times are more expensive.
- *Programme* During/after which programme the advert is aired.

Bright idea
If you are planning to place a series of adverts in the same place, you can generally negotiate a discount.

Monitoring and evaluation

Evaluation should be an integral part of your advertising. When you place an advertisement, keep a log of enquiries so that you can see where's best to advertise. This will be invaluable should you decide to rerun a campaign; you will be able to see at a glance whether publication A or radio station B came up with the goods. See Figure 15.1, an advertising response log that can be adapted to suit your purposes.

Figure 15.1 Advertising response log

Name/ address	Saw advert in (publication)	Requested catalogue (tick if applicable)	Made purchase from advert (amount of sale)	Made purchase from catalogue
Jeremy Allison Finch Street Preston PR98 1PZ	Preston Gazette	✓	£25 (credit card) 31/12/01	£100 (credit card) 27/1/02
Yasmin Shah 27 Cambridge Court Lancaster LN11 4SS	Lancashire Evening News	✓	✗	Not as yet
Michael Pascale 311 Maryvale Street Blackpool	Lancashire Evening News	✓	✗	£50 cheque 15/3/02

Prepare an analysis of your logs. Refer to Figure 15.2 of a log analysis to see what facts you could draw out.

Once your campaign has ended, sit down with your log and your objectives. Have you achieved your objectives? Look also at income and expenditure. If you spent more on your adverts than you received in orders, perhaps you failed. On the other hand, if one of your objectives was to build up a database of potential customers, and your campaign has achieved this, you might be able to claim success – if the database goes on to prove its worth.

Figure 15.2 Advertising response log analysis

FASHION FLAIR SHIRTS
Analysis Of Advertising Campaign

The facts

The main findings of the analysis of the log sheets are:

- we received 600 orders, 50 per cent from the *Preston Gazette* advert, 14 per cent from Central Lancashire Radio and 36 per cent from the *Lancashire Evening News;*
- in total we received £25,000 in orders;
- although *Lancashire Evening News* readers represented only 36 per cent of respondents, they bought in total £12,500 (ie 50 per cent of total orders);
- the average order was £42;
- as a direct result of the catalogues sent out, 327 further sales have been made so far, totalling £10,175.

The conclusions

1. Our experiment with radio did not work well, producing relatively few sales and enquiries. We failed to cover our costs and I recommend that we concentrate future efforts on local press advertising.
2. While on the face of it the *Lancashire Evening News* appears to have produced most money upfront, it brought in fewer requests for catalogues and less in follow-on sales. Nevertheless, the average order total per customer was well above average and it could be useful in the future for one-off campaigns. It was, however, more expensive to advertise in.
3. The *Preston Gazette* was best for attracting requests for catalogues. We have a better chance of developing a relationship with regular catalogue buyers than we have with one-off purchasers. Also, the cost of advertising in the *Gazette* was less than the *Evening News,* so all in all it appears to have been the best option.

Now over to you

Read through the following advertisement (see Figure 15.3(a)), which has been written for the national press, and itemise what is wrong with it.

Figure 15.3(a)   Advertisement for national press (version one)

LONGMAN SHIRTS

You may not have heard of Longman Shirts, yet they have been making bespoke shirts since 1902 from their purpose-built factory in the Wirral. Now the company has decided to branch out, with a new line of off-the-peg shirts. You could soon be the lucky wearer of one of these prestigious shirts. Just write to:

Catalogue Offer
Sales Department
Longman Shirts
Longman House
Unit 17
The Walrus Business Park
Anytown
The Wirral
WR12 2ZA

Within 14 days you will receive a catalogue featuring an extensive range of shirts. You will then be able to order from the comfort of your armchair. So send for a copy of the catalogue today.

Discussion

So many mistakes have been made in the way this advert has been written and presented that it is likely to be quite ineffective.

- The advert would be more powerful if written in the first person.
- Responding is too complicated. You have to write in; there is no simple coupon, and the long return address makes it even more off-putting.
- Its headline is not designed to attract attention and encourage you to read on.
- It contains too much irrelevant background information and facts.
- The copy is dull.
- It is better not to mention the factory; it detracts from the exclusive nature of the shirts. The copy should try to conjure up images of talented tailors, not dirty old factories.

A better version is contained in Figure 15.3(b).

Figure 15.3(b)   Advertisement for national press (version two)

WANT A BESPOKE SHIRT FOR AN OFF-THE-PEG PRICE?

A tailor-made shirt is so much nicer to wear. The sleeves are a perfect fit, the tails don't come untucked, and collar sizing is just right. Now you can have all the benefits of a bespoke shirt at an off-the-peg price. How? By ordering a shirt from our new mail order catalogue. For nearly a century Longman have been making bespoke shirts. Now we have introduced ready-made shirts in a wide range of fabrics and designs, with a choice of sleeve lengths, body lengths and collar sizes, and the option of a button cuff or a double cuff for links. To get your copy of our exclusive selection of shirts, just complete the coupon below.

. . . . ✂ . . . .

Please rush me a copy of your new catalogue of exclusive, quality shirts at affordable prices.

Name: . . . .

Address: . . . .

Postcode: . . . .

Return to: Longman Shirts, Walrus Business Park WE12 2ZA

DM12/01

Discussion

This is much better because:

- the headline attracts attention and interest;
- it is written in the first person, making it more direct;
- it has a coupon response to make replying easier;
- it cuts out unnecessary background material and detail;
- the return address is much shorter, making it easy to reply;
- the coupon is coded, so the advertiser can evaluate the success of the adverts placed, enabling him to work out which newspapers and which days were most effective.

True story

A London PR company seeking a new account manager made a huge job advert out of a sheet and hung it from the office window. As there were many local PR consultancies, their staff inevitably saw the advert and many applied for the job. The advert was so eye-catching that a photo and story found its way into *PR Week*, the magazine read by the kind of professionals at whom the advert was aimed. Great exposure for the cost of an old sheet!

Sponsorship

Sponsorship is a form of advertising which can be used to position and promote your company/products. If you run the local sports shop or leisure centre, you could perhaps sponsor a local football team and get them to wear strips featuring your logo. Depending on what business you are in, you might consider sponsoring a conference or research report. By being associated with something significant, high profile or prestigious, you can enjoy both reflected glory and positive media coverage.

True story

When HSBC reviewed its £1 million charitable budget, it realised that it was seeing very little return on its charitable giving. Big businesses these days expect to see a return on their investment, even when it comes to charitable donations. The bank decided to make a bigger impact by supporting a smaller number of charities in key fields. A short-list of charities was invited to tender. They were told what the bank was looking for and had five weeks to come up with ideas for specific projects to meet the bank's requirements. They then had to pitch for the business. Do you approach sponsorship in a businesslike way like this?

Sponsorship checklist

Too much business sponsorship is reactive. Companies are approached by charities and asked to support them. The business reaches sponsorship decisions based on their budget and the merits of the good cause. Be proactive. Find a project that helps you meet your marketing aims and produces demonstrable results. There's probably no point in sponsoring a children's painting competition at a village school if you are a nationwide business manufacturing garden ornaments. A national gardening competition would be a much better choice, because however worth while the cause, there needs to be something in it for you. Be clear from the outset what you are getting out of it. Are you going to gain by association? Will it help you position your company? Find out before you commit yourself. Ask yourself:

- Who do we want to reach?
- What message do we want to get across?
- What is our budget?
- How do we want to 'position' ourselves?

Now start thinking about what you could support. Sponsorship is about promotion, so manage it in the same professional and objective way that you handle other promotional decisions.

16

Through the letterbox: taking the junk out of direct mail

Direct mail is the third largest advertising medium in Britain and growing. Just look at the mountain of so-called 'junk mail' on your doormat if you want proof! This chapter will show you how to put together a powerful and effective direct mail package that hits its target.

Direct mail is advertising by post. Letters have long been used as a way of attracting business, but direct mail is a bit more sophisticated than the humble business letter. It can be used to:

- find new customers;
- sell to existing customers;
- provide information, for example to let people know you are holding a sale;
- distribute product samples;
- send out postal questionnaires to obtain marketing information;
- build up awareness of your company or product;
- reinforce your other marketing activity.

The pros and cons of direct mail are summarised below:

The pros

- Direct mail is an efficient way of targeting potential customers, so cutting down on wasted effort.
- A campaign can be very affordable; you can often undertake the whole process in-house.
- It can be cheaper than other forms of advertising.
- It can be used by very small businesses, unlike TV and national press advertising.
- It is harder for other businesses to monitor your activities; unlike press advertising, your message is not slapped across the page for all to see.
- Small mailings can be organised at fairly short notice.
- It can be used for 'test mailings'. (By sending one mailing to half your list and a different one to the other half, you can see which approach is more effective.)
- You can convey a lot more information than in, say, a press advert.
- You can include enclosures.
- You can be more imaginative and creative.
- Response is easy to measure.
- Mailings can be personalised.
- Messages can be tailored.
- The message can be timed to arrive on a particular day or time of year, so it is ideal for seasonal promotions, such as Christmas catalogues, January sales or summer offers.
- Relevant and interesting direct mail is welcomed by consumers.

Bright idea

Look at the direct mailings you receive from other companies. Put them to one side in a large box until you have collected at least a dozen different packages. Look at each one in turn and write down what you like and what you dislike about each. What works well? What turns you off? Turn your list into a checklist of dos and don'ts for your own mailings.

The cons

- It has a poor image.
- The hidden costs can be high – design, envelopes, updating or hiring a mailing list, stuffing envelopes, etc.
- You can waste money mailing to people who have moved away.
- Unless your mailing list is made up of the right profile, your cost per enquiry might be too high.

- Not all recipients welcome unsolicited letters. Some bin 'junk mail' unopened.

Bright idea

Look through newspapers and magazines for coupon responses – you'll see plenty. Send off a few and see what is sent back to you. Now look out for follow-up. Do the advertisers phone you, write again or better their first offer? See what you can learn from the way others do their mailings.

Objectives

A direct mail campaign should not be undertaken on the spur of the moment. It should be a part of your overall marketing strategy. To be sure that it is the right method, first establish what you hope to get out of it. Answer the following questions:

- What do you hope to achieve? Be specific. It is not sufficient to say, 'To attract more customers'. You need to quantify, for example, 'To attract 100 new customers and £100,000 in sales from them' or 'To attract 300 enquiries and to turn half of the enquirers into customers within six months'.
- Who is your target? Who do you need to write to? Again, be specific. It is no good saying, 'People likely to want new carpets'. You need to say, 'People in the south east of England who have just moved house and may therefore be considering buying new carpets'. You might target previous enquirers, existing or lapsed customers.
- How will your mailing fit into your company's marketing strategy? Will it just be a one-off mailing or one of a series? A mailing that is backed up by PR or press advertising? A mailing to back up other activity? View your mailing in context.

Test mailings

One big advantage of direct mail is that you can undertake 'test mailings', systematically changing elements of your mailing and monitoring the response. This approach could, for example, help you discover what sort of covering letter or enclosure produces the best results. Do you get a better response when you offer free postage? A test mailing could help you find out. Does a speed incentive or free gift make a difference to the quantity and quality of responses? Does price affect response? Again, use a test mailing to help you discover.

Bright idea

When doing a test mailing, do not introduce more than one variable in each test. Otherwise you will not know which factor led to increased or decreased response. (You can run several test mailings simultaneously – see below.)

Test matrices

You can split your mailing to try out different things at the same time. For example:

- you want to try a new mailing list (List X) and to test its performance against the mailing list you usually use (List Y)
- you want to see whether offering a free pelmet will increase the response to your designer curtains mailing
- you want to know whether reducing the cost of the curtains is more effective than offering an incentive.

Your test matrix would look like this (see Figure 16.1).

Figure 16.1 Test matrix

	List Y (usual list)	List X (new list)
Usual pack (control)	A	B
Free pelmet incentive	A1	
Lower price curtains	A2	

To find out whether your new list was better, you would compare the results of A with B. This is done using a control, namely, your standard mailing pack. You also want to find out whether other factors affect response. Comparing the results of A1 and A2 will tell you whether the free pelmet was more of an incentive than lower prices.

You can carry on testing until you find the most successful combination of factors. To measure which mailings are more successful, code the response device by writing or printing a code (eg M1, M2 or M3) on the coupon/form that the respondent returns to you.

True story

Greenpeace did a split mailing to test envelopes. A manila envelope was used alongside a white one. The manila outperformed the white by 94 per cent.

Don't be listless

Direct mail experts say that a mailing is only as good as the name and address printed on it! Do you really want to waste money sending lavish catalogues containing expensive goods to people who hardly have enough money to pay their rent? Or mailing catalogues for cement and bricks to plumbers or glaziers? No, you don't. But without a good list, you might just be doing that.

The strength of direct mail is its targetability; good targeting maximises your return. Effective targeting that hits people with a proclivity to buy your kind of product requires the right mailing list. Essentially you have three choices when seeking a mailing list:

1. You can rent a ready-made list.
2. You can have a list created for you.
3. You can compile your own list.

Off-the-peg lists

Like a suit, an off-the-peg list will cost you less than its tailor-made equivalent, but the fit might not be so good. Ready-made lists can be hired cheaply via list brokers. (You can get a list of approved list brokers from the Direct Marketing Association – see addresses in Appendix 2.) A list broker will advise you on the sort of list that is most suitable for your needs, or which selections from within lists. Their advice is normally free; their earnings come from commissions paid by list owners.

Lists are generally *hired* not *bought*. You will agree how many times you will use the list, with the hire price dependent on this. The price is usually per 1,000 names. Don't give way to the temptation to use the list more times than you have paid for; you will get caught out. Each list contains people paid to report back to the list owner/broker!

Those on your list are known as 'cold prospects'. If they respond to your mailing they become 'warm prospects' and can legitimately be added to your own mailing list and mailed to again as often as you wish.

Bright idea

Two non-competing, complementary businesses can benefit from sharing a mailing. For example, a video repair shop could team up with a video hire store. By sharing costs and contacts, both sides gain.

When you hire a mailing list, it will be compiled so that everyone on it shares certain characteristics; they may all have a similar income or lifestyle, attitudes and beliefs, live in similar housing, or a combination of these factors. For example, people who live in a:

- particular area (eg Leeds or West Yorkshire);
- particular *type* of area (eg a high status retirement area with many single people);
- particular type of housing (eg owner-occupied housing on new estates).

You can be quite precise about the type of person you wish to mail to, although inevitably there will be some wastage in even the best mailing lists. Describe the sort of person who buys from you and hire a list matching this as closely as possible.

Bright idea

It is preferable to address a mailing to a named person, but if you do not know the name of the person your mailing is for, try using their job function. Write across the envelope for example 'For the attention of the training manager'.

When speaking to a list broker:

- *Compilation*   How was the list compiled? Where did the names come from?
- *Performance*   How has the list performed? What have response rates been for other users of this list?
- *Updates*   How up to date is the list? How often is it updated and when was the last update? (Around 10 per cent of people move house each year, and around 40 per cent change company or get promoted, so both consumer and business lists get out of date very quickly.)
- *Cost*   What do you get for your money? How often can you use the list and over what period? Are there any additional costs?
- *Data protection*   Is the list registered under the Data Protection Act?
- *Mailing preference*   Has the list been cleared against the Mailing Preference Service's list? (See below.) If so, when?
- *Format*   Is the list available in the form that suits you best (eg sticky labels, computer disk)?
- *Post codes*   Is the list post-coded so you can sort it and qualify for Mailsort postage discounts? (See below.)

> ### Bright idea
>
> *Don't waste money or spoil your reputation by writing to people who do not want unsolicited mail. Consumers who do not want 'junk' mail can register their details with the Mailing Preference Service (see address list in Appendix 2), who produce regularly updated lists of everyone who has contacted them. The list can be bought for £100 plus VAT and used to 'clean' consumer lists. Hopefully this makes everyone happy; consumers do not get unwanted mail and companies do not waste money writing to people who are not interested.*

Tailor-made lists

A tailor-made list will more closely fit what you are looking for. It will not be compiled from scratch. It will use parts of a list, perhaps merged with another mailing list, giving you the sort of coverage you require.

> ### Bright idea
>
> *If using more than one list, 'de-dupe' to ensure that if names appear on two or more lists, they do not receive two or more mailings. Clearly this would be both irritating and wasteful. Specialist companies will de-duplicate for you. If names appear on more than one list, they might be particularly good prospects, worth singling them out for a very special offer.*

Home-made lists

Many companies believe that a home-made list is cheaper because they have not had to pay a broker for it. But when you take staff costs into account, your own list could work out very expensive if you are constructing it from scratch. However, research has shown that the names and addresses of your existing customers are, on average, three times as likely to respond to your mailings as cold prospects.

> ### Bright idea
>
> *A good way to expand your mailing list is to include a card inside your products. Suppose you sell computer software through various outlets. A card inside the packaging could ask people to return it with their details if they want to know about offers and new products from your range. I recently found such a card in something I had bought. It added, 'This is not an offer of junk mail… we dislike it too!' I thought this was a nice touch, so I duly completed and returned the card. Why not try it yourself?*

The best home-made lists are those you already have, and there are few excuses for not compiling lists as part of your everyday work. (You can buy software to help you construct mailing lists and databases on your computer.) You might need to refine a list, and you must spend time keeping lists up to date, but hopefully you will already have the makings of one. This might be made up of:

- people who have bought from you in the past (refer to invoices and other sales records to get their details);
- current customers;
- people who have telephoned or written in for further information, both recently and in the past;
- people who have entered any competitions you have run (this can be a good way of building up a list in-house);
- people whose business cards you have collected at exhibitions, conferences, etc;
- people's details left in visitors' books.

You can also source lists using the local telephone directory, *Yellow Pages* and *Thomson* directories (for business addresses). Don't forget the listings in trade directories too.

Bright idea

The Royal Mail's 'Mailsort' is a discount (of between 13 per cent and 32 per cent) for 4,000-plus letters of the same size and weight which you sort by postcode and bundle yourself. They also provide free collection for 1,000 letters or more and a range of other services from which companies using direct mail could benefit. Contact the Royal Mail for further details.

Databases

Mailing lists and databases are not the same thing. A mailing list is simply a list of names and addresses. A database includes other details too, such as:

- when and how often people have bought from you;
- what they have bought;
- average size of their order;
- average buying frequency;
- how they have paid;
- sex, age and other personal characteristics.

A database gives you a clearer picture, and enables you easily to extract particular groups. A good database might, for example, enable you to pull out all

female customers aged 40–60 who have spent £100 or more on garden ornaments in the last six months.

Use your database for better targeted mailings. Segment it so that you can
target particular products to particular customer types. For example, a loyal
customer is likely to know a lot about your company and your products. By
contrast, someone who has bought from you just once in the last two years is
perhaps less familiar with what you have to offer. It might be better to do
different mailings for these two groups.

An effective database will help you avoid wasted mailings and unhappy
customers. There is no point in sending your lawnmower catalogue to people
who have just bought a lawnmower from you. However, target these customers
with a mailing referring to their new mower, and telling them about your exciting
lawn-enhancing products, and your mailing will be appreciated and more likely
to lead to further sales.

If you plan to do a lot of direct mail, make sure you have a proper database. It
is the only way to organise all your data efficiently and meaningfully. You can
have one created for you by an information technology (IT) consultant, or you
can buy some ready-made database software which is easy to use and available in
applications such as Windows.

Bright idea

*Don't put every scrap of information you have on your database. This will
slow your computer and make information retrieval tedious and frustrating.
Record only the information that you will use and keep it all up to date.*

The Data Protection Act

If you use data, you are required by law to register with the Data Protection
Registrar. This is not complicated and a quick telephone call to the DPR on
01625 545745 will provide you with all the information you need. (See
Appendix 2 for address.)

True story

I have found my way on to two different mailing lists, in one case as Ms A and in
the second case as Mr Moy. One particular mailing made heavy use of the
personalisation, which, of course, it had got wrong. This just compounded my irritation and showed up the 'personal' touch for what it was. Any mail arriving for me
so addressed goes unopened into the bin. It is really important to get people's
names right. If you are hiring a mailing list, find out from the list broker or owner
what steps they take to check their lists for accuracy.

The mailing package

Having got your list sorted, time to turn your attention to the contents of your mailing. This will include:

- the envelope you send the mailing in;
- the covering letter;
- any other enclosures.

If your mailing list is good, your mailing will reach people who are likely to regard your business or product favourably. But that's only half the battle. The contents of your mailing need to persuade them to buy. Successfully targeted mailings can be let down by a poorly produced package.

The envelope: more than a carrier

Think of your envelope not just as a container for the mailing, but as a vital part of the package. It is the first thing your recipient will see. If they don't like it, your entire package could end up in the bin however wonderful the brochure inside and however terrific the product or offer. You can use off-the-shelf stationers' envelopes, or you can have envelopes specially printed for you with a design or message on the outside.

True story

A 'split test' mailing was carried out by a firm of direct mail consultants to assess whether the appearance of direct mail has any effect on the response rates. Five types of envelope were sent out. The one that looked most like a proper letter, with typed address and postage stamp, was found to be twice as effective as the one that looked most like 'junk' mail, even though the enclosures were identical.

Many companies have envelopes designed and printed specially for them, with messages urging the recipient to open the mailing. You know the sort of thing – 'Open now to save £500' or 'We've a great offer inside, but hurry – stocks are limited'. Companies using this approach do so because they believe that the cost of design and print are more than recouped. However, as the true story above shows, at least one company has found that mailings that look like 'normal' letters elicit the best response for them. Perhaps recipients feel that a plain envelope has to be opened, if only to check what's inside. It is easier to bin mail if you know at a glance that it is unsolicited. To work out what's best for you, carefully weigh up the costs and benefits and ideally do a split test mailing.

Bright idea

If you have specially printed envelopes, you will get a message across even if the envelope is never opened. I recently received a mailing from Oxfam, and printed on the envelope was the message, 'Over 90p in every £1 goes to fund our vital work on behalf of the poorest people of the world'. This important message could influence the recipient at some later date, even if they fail to respond to this particular mailing. Is there a slogan you can print on your envelopes?

If you are having envelopes printed, link the message on the envelope with the covering letter. For example, if your envelope says, 'Want to save £100 a year on your phone bill?' then the headline of your covering letter should say, 'Here's how we can help you make massive savings on your quarterly bill'. Another technique is to start a sentence on the envelope and complete it in the first sentence of your enclosure. Use the envelope to get the reader reading your letter. (This can be a risky ruse for business mailings, where a secretary might open mail and discard envelopes before passing the contents on to the addressee. For business mail, produce a package that will still make sense without the envelope.)

True story

I once received a letter in a plain white envelope. Across the envelope's opening, at the back, stamped in red ink, were the words, 'Opened for inspection'. The envelope had indeed been opened, and resealed with Sellotape. I was furious at this intrusion. On opening the letter, I discovered that it was an elaborate gimmick to attract my attention. The enclosure was a mailshot from the *Observer* newspaper which began, 'Imagine the outrage you'd feel if you discovered your mail had been tampered with.' It was promoting a series of articles on censorship. It was gimmicky but highly effective.

Bright idea

Use standard-sized small envelopes (eg approximately 9" × 4") as these tend to get opened first because they most resemble 'normal' mail. Larger envelopes delivered to people's homes tend to get opened last, or not at all.

Size matters

Whether using ready-made envelopes, or specially printed ones, decide on the size. This will be dependent on the size of the enclosures.

The Royal Mail find it easier to process some envelopes than others, now that their sorting is automated. They recommend that envelopes are:

- between 140 mm and 240 mm long;
- between 165 mm and 90 mm wide;
- oblong in shape;
- proportioned so that the longer side is at least 1.4 times the length of the shorter.

The common envelope sizes DL (designed to take one third A4) and C5 (for half A4) fall into the Royal Mail's preferred range. They cannot handle envelopes smaller than 100 mm × 70 mm, or larger than 610 mm × 460 mm.

Bright idea

Do not use commas and full stops in addresses. The Royal Mail's automated sorting machines find addresses without punctuation easier to read.

The covering letter

The covering letter is the heart of your mailing, holding the whole package together. If the letter is the only enclosure, getting it right becomes all the more important; it's your only chance to make a sale. There's no fancy brochure to do the work for you.

Many amateur copywriters write terrible covering letters. The main mistake they make is to follow a logical order. They begin with the background, gradually building up to the climax; the offer/proposition. They wrongly assume that the reader will read from the beginning, working through it in an orderly and methodical fashion. This is not how most people tackle direct mail; we tend to give a quick scan. If anything jumps out and grabs our attention, we may read on. If not, it's straight to the waste-paper basket. Take account of how people read when you write your copy. The trick is to use:

- headlines;
- subheads;
- underlining;
- bullet points;
- emboldened text;
- call-outs/pull quotes
- highlighting of key text in a different colour.

These are all great attention-grabbers.

Bright idea

Research shows that the 'Courier' typeface generally produces a better response. No one is sure why, but if it works, why not use it! If you don't want to use Courier, use another 'serif' typeface; 'sans-serif' fonts are apparently harder to read. A serif face has 'tails' on letters, whereas a sans-serif face does not.

Every letter should have a beginning (the hook), a middle (the facts, detail, background), and an end (the call to action). Too often the hook is found at the end of the letter, the part few readers will have reached. Hook them first or they will get away.

Bright idea

Try to keep your letter to one side of paper. If you go on to two sides, end page one with a split sentence to encourage the reader to turn the page.

Opening lines

Your opening line is crucial. It must grab attention. One great opening technique is the problem-solver. Here are two examples:

1. 'We can eliminate the problem of employee theft.'
2. 'Banish unwanted hair – for ever.'

Both address head on the reader's problem and suggest that you can help solve it. Such openers are so much better than a ponderous one like, 'I am writing to introduce the DZ47 Depilator, a unique product from Hirsute Developments Limited. It is designed to provide a unique unwanted hair remover facility…'

Bright idea

Many companies print a PS (postscript) on the letter in a hand-written style, so that this stands out from the rest of the text. It often says something like, 'Hurry – offer only available until…' or 'Remember, we cannot repeat this offer at these spectacular prices, so order today…' The PS should leap out and be enticing enough to make a reader read the letter they might otherwise have ignored. It should have a tone of urgency, or should aim to encourage action.

Other enclosures

Your covering letter should be navigational, guiding the reader through the mailing and signposting them to the enclosure(s). Enclosures might include:

- A mail order catalogue.
- An order form.
- A membership/subscription leaflet.
- A questionnaire.
- A promotional or information leaflet.
- A newsletter.
- A product sample; take care that the packaging you use is suitable. There is nothing more likely to put customers off than a damaged and thus useless sample.
- A money-off voucher.
- A prepaid envelope.
- A promotional video; some companies mail videos in place of leaflets and brochures. How better to show the luxury of your hotel than in moving pictures? Video can help bring to life a product in a way that a brochure never could. (You can get special lightweight video cassettes to reduce duplication and mailing costs.)

Bright idea

Aim for your covering letter and contents to emerge from the envelope the right way up. Preferably the letter and enclosures should be folded in the same direction, to make opening the mailing that bit easier.

Avoid too many enclosures; jumbo-sized mailings will burden the recipient and swell your postage bill. Decide on the maximum weight of your mailing before it is produced, and make sure you do not exceed it to the extent that you are pushed into the next mailing cost band.

True story

Eurostar wanted to publicise a special incentive for first class ticket purchasers. To symbolise the incentive they decided to include a carrot with the promotional package. Fifty thousand fresh carrots were mailed to Eurostar's database and the mailing did indeed attract attention, in many cases for the wrong reason. Some carrots were mouldy or shrivelled by the time they arrived, creating quite the wrong impression of the offer and of the company. The stunt also generated some negative press coverage, adding to the damage.

Get a good response

Remember 'AIDA'? (See Chapter 15 on advertising.) Your mailing should attract attention, stimulate interest and desire, and prompt action. Your success lies in the ease with which you enable people to act. Use a combination from the list below to ensure that action is easy:

- *Response device*   People are much less likely to write you a letter than to complete a simple tear-off slip or coupon. Remember this when designing your mailing. Include an order form or another device to allow easy response.
- *Business Reply*   This is one of the Royal Mail's response services, which have been designed to encourage customers to respond by enabling you to pay their postage. Research by the Direct Mail Information Service showed that paying the postage for your customer's reply increases response. Envelopes or cards prepaid and preprinted with your address make it really easy for recipients to respond. If you think this is likely to increase take-up for you, and that the long-term benefits will outweigh the cost involved, try it out.
- *Freepost*   Your enquirers can write to you post-free, although you will have to pick up the tab. It will cost you the postage charge, plus an annual licence fee, plus a small handling charge per item. Talk to your local Royal Mail Sales Centre (Tel. 08457 950 950). All calls are charged at local rates.
- *Freephone*   Freephone (0500 and 0800) numbers work in a similar way to Freepost. Call your telephone company for details. Don't forget to include the cost of staffing telephone lines to handle responses when drawing up your budget. Research has shown that people generally prefer to respond by post than by telephone.
- *Credit card payment*   If customers can pay by credit card, orders can be taken by telephone. A Freephone credit card hotline makes it easier still. Remember to include the 'merchant fee' charged by the credit card company in your calculations.

Bright idea

You can encourage response to your mailing by including a 'speed incentive'. For example, your mailing could say, 'Reply before 1 July and get a free summer hamper'.

Coping with success

You undertake direct mail campaigns with the expectation that they will be successful. You want a good response, and the bigger the better. But are you prepared to cope with the response? Do you have enough staff available to process orders, send out catalogues, or answer the phone? It is vital that you do, for two very important reasons:

1. If you do not fulfil enquiries/orders swiftly, you will create a poor impression of your company in the eyes of your prospect. They might not want to buy from you again.
2. If you are slow, your prospect may place their order elsewhere. It is possible that they will have asked various companies for information: the one responding first is likeliest to get the order.

Don't leave planning to the last minute. Have response plans in place before your mailing begins.

Bright idea

Your direct mail letter and other enclosures should reinforce your corporate identity. Make good use of your logo, print in your house colours, etc, so recipients can see at a glance who their mailing is from.

Unlike press advertising, where you are unable to control response, you do have a little more control with direct mail. If you target 10,000 people all in one go, you might have difficulty in coping with the flood of enquiries. But you can break your mailing list into more manageable chunks, perhaps mailing 1,000 each week or month. Don't make your chunks too small or you will lose your Mailsort discount.

Bright idea

In business-to-business mail, it can be difficult to get your mail past secretaries and on to the boss's desk. If it is the boss you are trying to reach, consider dressing up your mailing as a package and couriering it. By making the package look important, you can often get it past the gatekeeper. (As this method is expensive, it is not suitable for every mailing.)

Perfect timing

I am often asked when the best time is to do a direct mail campaign. The best time is the time that is right for the recipient. If someone is looking to buy a major piece of equipment, and you happen to sell that equipment, ideally your mailing should coincide with the recipient's intent to purchase. A mailing reaching them the day after they have bought the equipment is useless to you and useless to them. Unfortunately no one has yet invented the magic crystal ball that enables us to know what our prospects are thinking or doing at any particular time (or what next week's Lottery numbers are!). So we have to use educated guesswork. A mailshot for bulbs and plants needs to be done before the growing season starts. Mail order catalogues full of small gift ideas should go out before everyone's finished their Christmas shopping.

January, supposedly, is the best month for doing a non-time-sensitive mailing, February the second best and June the worst. Others say, perhaps not entirely tongue in cheek, that there's no good month – they're all bad! It has been claimed that Tuesday is the best day, though I'm not sure why. If you are writing to other businesses, it's better to aim for delivery earlier in the week than later. Decide when the right time is for you. This depends on a range of factors, including when you have the time to do a mailing, when you are able to fulfil the orders/enquiries that result from it, and what you are selling. For your own sanity try to avoid big mailings coinciding with a really busy period in your company because responding to resultant enquiries is hard work.

Bumping up your budget

Postal charges are not the only costs involved in direct mail. The hidden costs can really bump up the bill. Here are some others you will need to budget for:

- *The mailing list*   Whether hiring one or building your own.
- *Envelopes*   Whether buying them from the wholesalers or having your own designed and printed.
- *Design*   The cost of having envelopes, covering letters and enclosures (such as leaflets) designed.
- *Printing*   The cost of having the above items printed, including the cost of paper.
- *Copywriting*   If you want your enclosures professionally written, you will need to budget for this.
- *Photography*   You may need to commission photography for a brochure or other enclosures, perhaps even for the envelope.
- *Response device*   Add to your overall budget the cost of a Freepost address or other response device to encourage recipients to reply.
- *Stuffing envelopes*   There are companies who will stuff envelopes for you – mailing houses – or you can do it in-house, possibly using students. However, do not underestimate the time and effort (and boredom!) involved in stuffing, sealing and sorting envelopes – I speak from experience!
- *Project management*   Whether you coordinate all of the above in-house, or use a specialist direct marketing agency to oversee it for you, it will cost.
- *Follow-up/fulfilment*   Processing responses to direct mail takes time and costs money (though it hopefully generates money too!).

Combining direct mail with other advertising

Sometimes direct mail is used as a stand-alone activity. It need not be. Direct mail can be combined with press advertising, and the two can work very well together. Press advertising enables you to reach a wide audience (even if you advertise in a specialist publication), while direct mail lets you narrow that down even further and target it even more sharply.

Let's say you sell stencil equipment mail order. You have a good customer base, but your business needs to expand. It might be impossible to get a mailing list of stencillers and would-be stencillers. By including advertising as part of your campaign, you now have a method of getting that all-important list. Place an advert in a craft magazine promoting your extensive range of stencils and stencilling equipment and offering a free brochure to all enquirers. Existing stencillers will be eager to get your brochure, as will those contemplating stencilling. When they write in, you create the mailing list. Now track your customers to see if enquirers became customers. A proforma like the one shown in Figure 16.2 will help you.

Figure 16.2   Customer tracking form

Name	Address	Saw advert in	Placed order after first mailing (value)	Placed order after second mailing (value)
Mrs J Smith	12 High Street Gilgate G10 2MP	Crafts R Us	£90	£15
Sima Singh	The Hayloft Stenning Village Kempster	Craft and Home	No	£100
D Jones	103 Jamieson Street Totteridge TR1 2CP	Craft and Home	No	No

If you take the time to complete such a log, and to analyse it, you will have valuable marketing information. In the example above, a simple analysis would reveal:

- which publication produced most enquiries;
- which produced the highest value orders;
- whether enquirers placed an order after the first mailing, and if so, how much they spent;
- whether a second mailing was valuable in getting new customers to buy some more;

- whether a second mailing was effective in getting those not responding to the first mailing to place an order.

Direct mail in cyberspace

Many small businesses use the Internet as an effective vehicle for sales and promotion on a global scale. (You can read more about the Internet in Chapter 17.) People who visit your Web site can be direct-mailed using e-mail. The benefit is that mailshots can be sent from one end of the country to the other, or even across the globe, for the price of a local phone call. At the time of writing, legislation is under consideration to outlaw 'spamming' – the mass transmission of junk e-mail. It is likely that Europe-wide legislation will be introduced to compel customers to positively 'opt-in' to receiving sales e-mails, rather than the current voluntary opting-out system.

Measuring success

Measure the cost and effectiveness of direct mail campaigns in the same way as you would measure the success of a press advertising campaign. The two standard measures used are:

1. *Cost per response*   Add all the costs associated with your direct mail campaign, then divide by the number of responses received.
2. *Cost per conversion*   Divide the cost of the mailing by the number of sales. The cost per response will inevitably be lower than the cost per conversion.

Work out in advance how much you can afford to spend on each sale. There's no simple formula for this; it all depends on how much a customer is worth. If you have to spend £25 to get one customer, but each customer will spend around £7,000 with you in their lifetime, and one in ten customers will recommend you to seven others, £25 is a small price to pay.

Set targets at the outset, based on your allowable cost per conversion. Review these targets as part of your evaluation. Suppose your allowable cost per conversion is £50 and your mailing list is 1,000 people; you will need to make 20 sales (assuming each mailing costs £1) to break even. Anything above that number is a return on your direct mail investment.

Your evaluation should include a post-mortem to see what lessons you can learn to improve future mailings. The post-mortem checklist shown in Figure 16.3 shows some of the factors that you may wish to consider when reviewing the success of a campaign.

Bright idea

Get hold of the Royal Mail's excellent Direct Mail Guide, full of tips and advice on direct mail. It is available free from the Royal Mail Customer Sales Centres (see address list in Appendix 2).

Figure 16.3   Direct mail post-mortem pro forma

Campaign name: ....

Mailing date: ....

Quantity mailed: ....

Number of 'gone aways' returned: ....

Number of orders received following initial mail-out: ....

Number of enquiries for more information: ....

Percentage of enquirers who went on to make a purchase: ....%

Total cost of mailings (incl. inserts and staff time): £ ....

Cost of sending out additional information: £ ....

Cost of mailing per sale: £ ....

Average order size: £ ....

How could the mailing package be improved?
- Letter design –
- Letter content –
- Enclosed leaflet design –
- Leaflet content –
- Envelope design –
- Other –

How did the various suppliers perform? Any comments?
- Designer –
- Copywriter –
- Printer –
- Stationer –
- List broker –
- Royal Mail –
- Others –

Where could savings be made?

Were there any additional costs we had not anticipated?

How did we handle responses in-house? Could we have done better? How?

Overall how could the campaign's success be rated? Did it meet its objectives?

What are the recommendations for future mailings?

Direct advertising

Don't confuse direct mail and direct advertising. Direct mail is *mail* which goes direct to a household. Direct advertising is *advertising* dropped through people's letterboxes (not mailed), often though not necessarily in a free newspaper, and is usually in the form of a leaflet without an envelope.

Direct advertising has many advantages for small businesses because:

- it is cheap;
- it can be used by very small businesses;
- it is especially effective for local businesses;
- it can be targeted at particular types of neighbourhood.

The Royal Mail offers 'Door-to-Door', a service which enables you to deliver promotional material nationwide (or just in one or two areas, depending on your needs), reaching recipients at the same time as their regular post. The cost depends on the volume and weight of the items you are sending, but works out very reasonable.

Now over to you

You run a company making mattresses. You have just launched a range of hypoallergenic cot mattresses made using natural fabrics. You have been lucky enough to get hold of a mailing list of pregnant women, whom you want to persuade to buy your cot mattress. The following covering letter is sent out with an order form and brochure (see Figure 16.4(a)).

Figure 16.4(a)   Direct advertising covering letter (version one)

The Natural Bedding Company
Great mattresses for a good night's sleep
Sleep Easy House, 11 Somnambulist Street, Snooseland SL3 3P
Tel. 014452 332267 Fax. 014452 332268

Dear Mrs Smith,
We have been making mattresses for over five years and are delighted to inform
you that our latest mattress was launched last month. Using the very finest
materials, the best craftsmanship and the latest technology we have produced
the ultimate mattress. We are also making a mini-range for junior, so your baby
can sleep on the same type of top quality mattress that you yourself enjoy.

Many mattresses lack proper support, and this is no more true than in cot
mattresses. Another problem with the average cot mattress is that it is made of
synthetic materials. Our range is all natural, with a choice of cotton or feather
filling wrapped in cotton or linen. Add to this the range of colours and designs
our mattresses come in and you'll be spoilt for choice. Just look through the
enclosed brochure and you'll see what we mean.

Yours sincerely

Johnny Dormer

Johnny Dormer
Marketing Manager

Discussion

If that letter landed on my door-mat, along with the rest of my mail, I'm afraid it
would rapidly become a resident of the waste-paper basket. What was wrong
with it?

- The letter begins by talking about mattresses in general rather than going
  straight in with the relevant bit for a pregnant woman; cot mattresses.
- It proudly announces that they have been making mattresses for over five
  years; that's not very long in my book.
- It is from the Marketing Manager, so it seems too much like a sales letter.

The version contained in Figure 16.4(b) is far better.

Figure 16.4(b)   Direct advertising covering letter (version two)

The Natural Bedding Company
Great mattresses for a good night's sleep
Sleep Easy House, 11 Somnambulist Street, Snooseland SL3 3P
Tel. 014452 332267 Fax. 014452 332268

Dear Mrs Smith,

BOUGHT YOUR BABY'S MATTRESS YET?

If you haven't yet bought the mattress for your baby's cot – great! Mothers who want the very best for their babies buy them the best. Our new cot mattress *guarantees* excellent support for your baby's growing body. It also offers protection against the allergies and irritations many babies experience from lesser mattresses. So all in all, **you can't buy a better night's sleep for your baby** – and yourself! And what's more, your purchase can help raise money for the Cot Death Trust, which is carrying out pioneering work into the causes of sudden infant death syndrome.

Allergy-free
Because our mattresses are made using only natural fabrics, they will not irritate your baby's delicate skin. Nor will they make baby itch, scratch or sneeze. They are the closest baby will come to being wrapped in cotton wool.

Easy-clean
To ensure complete hygiene, our mattresses are fully washable. Just soak in soapy powder for an hour, rinse and dry. It's as easy as that.

So if you are lucky enough not to have bought a cot mattress already, order one from us today. If your order reaches us within ten days, we will make a £1 donation to the Cot Death Trust as part of a £10,000 fundraising initiative we are supporting.

Yours sincerely

Julie Nocturne

Julie Nocturne
Baby and Child Division

PS
Remember to order within ten days if you want to help the Cot Death Trust.

Discussion

What makes this second letter so much better?

- The opener asks a question designed to attract mothers who have not yet bought a cot mattress (ie potential customers).
- It makes the reader feel that they would be selling their baby short by buying any mattress other than yours. It hints that other mattresses may not support your baby as well, might cause an allergic reaction and might be less hygienic: it makes mothers question what might happen if they do not buy your mattress.
- It uses some powerful arguments for buying from you, and highlights them in the form of subheads. Other key text is emboldened to make it stand out.
- It has joined forces with a relevant charity, to show how much it cares about babies.
- The time-limited offer (of a donation to charity) acts as a prompt for action.
- The postscript reminds the reader of the need to act quickly.
- Emotive copy such as: supporting 'your baby's growing body'; 'wrapping your baby in cotton wool'; and 'a better night's sleep for your baby' go straight to the heart.
- It is from someone in the 'Baby and Child Division' so it carries an air of authority. Even if in reality you don't have such a division, you can add credibility by naming parts of your company so they sound more official, impressive or relevant than they are.

17 Promoting your company: the Internet, other promotional tools and how to select the right one

In addition to the obvious promotional vehicles, such as advertising and direct mail, there are masses of others for you to choose from. This chapter presents you with a selection of the many promotional methods available and will help you work out which one is right for you.

You don't have the megabuck budget of a large corporation, so your promotional budget must work that much harder for you. Fortunately there are many promotional tools that are just perfect for small businesses.

Promotion in cyberspace

Initially the Internet was for anoraks. Now nearly everyone uses it – to find information, to communicate, to buy and to sell. Cyberspace is a very democratic place in that access is available to businesses large and small. While a one-person operation could not advertise alongside big businesses in the press and on TV, you can on the Internet. The Internet is a great leveller, giving even local businesses a chance to go national or international. If you don't already have a Web site, perhaps it's time you got one. Whether you intend to trade online or simply use it as a publicity tool, a Web site is a must. It can generate interest that you can translate into sales offline. It offers an opportunity to build up a list of potential customers who can opt-in to receive further news and information by e-mail or snail mail. You can publish an online catalogue or newsletter and make it available to a vast audience without any printing and mailing costs (and update it virtually cost-free). You can elicit feedback on your products and services, even carry out research. And, of course, you can use it to sell. Although there is still consumer caution about online sales, more people are trying it and feeling reassured.

Getting online

Getting a Web site has never been easier. What's more, you don't need to be a 'techie' because there's now plenty of affordable help to get you online. Specialist consultancies and skilled freelances are available to help you with all the steps involved, from creating an attractive and enticing site using suitable text and images to securing a domain name and registering the site. They will take care of the technical side for you. They can help you to ensure that your site is picked up by search engines, they can configure it so that you can keep tabs on the number of hits, and they can explain how to update the site yourself so that it remains fresh and interesting to visitors.

You can create your Web site in-house and there are plenty of books and software to assist you. However, people are more Web-savvy these days and they expect to see business sites that look professional. Don't jeopardise your good image with an amateurish Web site. Do it well, or get in the professionals. And if you plan to create a virtual shop, you'll definitely need professional help to ensure that the so-called backroom functions are effective and that online ordering is secure.

Attracting hits

OK, so you've got a site. What now? First you need to ensure that everyone knows about it. Check that the address is on all stationery, all publicity material and all ads. Use direct mail to let customers know about your cyberspace presence. Attract them to your site with a competition. Put your Web address on press releases so that journalists get used to using it for background material. File recent press releases there, price lists, product photos and information, company history, useful tips, facts and information. Make it into an interesting resource that is well worth a visit.

True story

Ann Summers sells erotic lingerie and sex toys. Aware that the embarrassment factor prevented many potential customers from entering their shops, the company set up online trading. Through their 'virtual' shop they can sell to people who would never otherwise buy from them.

Webvertising

Whether or not you have a Web site, there's nothing to stop you from advertising on someone else's. You can sponsor relevant sites or place ads on other sites likely to attract the kind of customer that you wish to reach. Specialists in Webvertising can help you identify suitable advertising opportunities to achieve your objectives.

Audio cassettes

Many people drive to work and 90 per cent of motorists have cassette players in their car. Audio tapes are a novel way of reaching potential customers. Because we are bombarded with written material demanding our attention, it makes a nice change to have information read out to us, helping us profitably to use the otherwise 'dead' time we spend stuck in traffic. Because they have a higher perceived value than a newsletter or leaflet, tapes are perhaps less likely to be binned. Your tape will have to be interesting and informative if you want it to be listened to. Some types of material are particularly well suited to an audio tape. Here are some examples of promotional material that would go down well on tape:

- Twenty things to ask when choosing a management consultant.
- How to get planning permission for a house extension.
- The benefits of fee-paying schools.

Tapes can be made to sound like documentary radio, with interviews, experts, music and sound effects. Bring your material to life in this way, for a relatively low cost.

Bright idea
Keep a supply of leaflets in your bag and car, so there is always one to hand when you need it and you are away from your office/premises.

Promotion from A to Z

Don't overlook the more mundane (but often equally effective) promotional methods available to small businesses. Many of them are featured in the following A-Z of promotional opportunities. You will find that quite a few can be done in-house at little or no cost and minimum effort. Inevitably some require significant expenditure or major planning. Take your pick from:

A

Advertising trailers   These are mobile billboard displayers. Special trailer vehicles drive around town displaying your advert. They are great for raising awareness, especially if you are new to a town.

B

Bags   If you run stores, promotional bags are a must. But other businesses can also make use of the humble plastic carrier bag with their logo and message. They can be really useful at exhibitions, allowing visitors to your stand to carry away all your bumph with ease.

Business cards   Regard your business card as a wallet-sized advert. Use it to list your services as well as to pass on your contact details.

C

Cinema   Cinema advertising is cheaper than TV advertising and a good way to reach the 15–24 age group. You have a captive audience and the screen size offers maximum impact for your commercial. On the downside, it is expensive to make a decent commercial, you have to pay for the 'air time', and you would need external expertise.

Commemorative covers   You can have commemorative covers produced by the Royal Mail (so long as you are willing to pay). Telephone them for full details.

Bright idea

Use your office answering machine message as an advertising opportunity. Record details of how callers can place an order or get hold of a sales catalogue. That way you can make sales while you're out of the office.

D

Directories   Adverts and listings in relevant directories and handbooks can be effective if the readers form part of your target audience. If you are a business-to-business company, consider an inclusion in the trade directories of your key customer groups.

E

Envelopes   Why not consider getting a promotional message printed on your envelopes? It is a cheap way of publicising yourself every time you send a letter.

F

Flags   Flags are surprisingly good value for money and offer a novel way of promoting your message. Various companies specialise in flag-making. (See the *Yellow Pages* for a company near you.)

Fridge magnets   A cheap but clever way of getting your name in front of your customer every time they open the fridge. Great for dairies, frozen food companies and others in the food and drink industry.

G
Give-aways   Free promotional items such as balloons or biros can carry your advertising message, but bear in mind that cheap and tacky gifts might give you a cheap and tacky, throw-away image. (See below for more information on promotional gifts.)

True story
Food can be used as a promotional vehicle. British Telecom was the first British company to use 'eggvertising', where messages are blown with high-pressure jets on to the outside of fresh eggs. It was also the first to use apples. When it cut the price of calls to America, the price-cut message was printed on small fruit labels stuck to apples, which were handed out to transatlantic travellers arriving at Heathrow. (New York is known as the 'Big Apple'.) Baskets of apples were also delivered to leading US companies with offices in London, with a photocall staged to secure media coverage too. It was a cost-effective and imaginative way of attracting attention.

H
Hoardings   Hoardings form part of a type of advertising known as 'outdoor'. Research shows that two weeks is the optimum time for a hoarding advert to be displayed; awareness peaks on the tenth day and then declines. Each poster site has an OSCAR (Outdoor Site Classification and Audience Research) which is an individual score based on traffic flow past the site, position of the board, and so on. An OSCAR of 89 (about average) means that the poster is passed by around 89,000 people each week. Motorists seeing your poster have around seven seconds to take it in, so it must be big, bold and very simple.

I
Inserts   Leaflets inserted into magazines and journals are a cheaper method of distribution than direct mail.

J
Junk mail   This is the derisory term for direct mail (see Chapter 16).

K
Key-rings   Many companies produce key-rings with their logo or promotional message. They are cheap to make and have a long 'shelf-life'. But if you want people to use your key-ring, make it attractive or useful (eg by incorporating a torch, whistle or pen into it).

L
LED displays   Some public places such as swimming pools and sports centres offer an advertising service via large LED displays which display your message. This is a cheap and easy way to advertise.

M
Mouse mats   These can be produced to your own design and offered as gifts to your customers, ensuring your name, message and logo are under their nose every day.

N
Notepads   Some businesses have notepads (and other desk accessories such as blotters, rulers, etc) printed with their logo, contact details and list of services. This sits on customers' desks where it reinforces your name and ensures that your telephone number is to hand when they need it.
Noticeboards   Use other people's boards to display your publicity.

O
Outlets   See if you can use other companies' outlets (shops, offices, etc) as opportunities to promote yourself, via exhibitions/displays, or by leaving posters and leaflets. For example, if you run a sandwich delivery service, leave leaflets in nearby offices.

P
Pay and display car parking tickets   In most towns and cities you can advertise on the back of these.
Phone cards   You can have special promotional phone cards produced for you.
Playing cards   You can get cards made up with your own design printed on the reverse. These can be an attractive and unusual give-away.
Postcards   Most trendy cafés and restaurants in our major towns now have postcard dispensers. Customers can pick up attractive and free postcards, while advertisers can benefit from a new advertising option that is also cost-effective.
Post Office franks   If you don't have your own franking machine, you can still get your message across by getting the Post Office to frank other people's letters with your logo.

Q
Questionnaires   You should not conduct a questionnaire survey merely as a way of promoting your company, though surveys can serve the dual purpose of collecting useful information *and* helping you promote your name and products.

R
Roundabouts   Some local authorities allow small businesses to sponsor its traffic roundabouts. In most cities you can sponsor bins and other bits of local authority furniture.

S

Screen savers   Have a computer screen saver designed to incorporate your logo and promotional message. Give them to clients on disk as freebies or put it on your Web site for downloading.

Stationery   Your own letterhead, compliments slips and other stationery offer a good opportunity to promote what you do. If your company does not have a strapline (a short and snappy statement of purpose, eg quality paper at low prices) why not devise one and use it on your stationery to explain your work or promote a product?

Stickers   Once stuck down, stickers have great staying power and so your message remains on view for a long time, thus increasing the number of opportunities for it to be seen and read.

T

Taxis   Taxi cabs can display adverts inside and outside the cabs and some are also fitted with leaflet dispensers.

Town criers   This is an unusual and arresting way of announcing that you have arrived in town!

Transport advertising   This covers everything from bus adverts to posters on the London Underground, in lifts, escalators and trains. Transport advertising can be an effective method in that you are reaching an audience which is bored, often stationary, and in need of something to occupy them.

U

Umbrellas   Golfing umbrellas were once synonymous with serious corporate entertainment, but many small businesses now produce promotional items of this sort. A wide range of promotional products is available from many different companies at quite reasonable prices. They can be personalised with your logo and message.

V

Vehicles   Use your company cars, vans and lorries as mobile adverts.

W

Windows   You don't have to run a shop to make good use of a window display. If your office is a shopfront, learn a trick from the big department stores and arrange attractive promotional displays. (You will need more than a collection of yellowed press cuttings, dusty products and decomposing bluebottles to achieve this!)

X

X-tra time   Your own staff can be your best advertisements. What they say about your company 'after hours' will have a significant bearing on your reputation.

Y
Year planners Planners remain in use and on display for a whole year, making them very effective.

Z
Zany gimmicks Use your imagination to devise gimmicks that help you promote your company. In a bid to get news editors to notice their release, an upmarket cashmere boutique delivered its releases to the fashion press by goat! It certainly attracted attention, but was it directed at the release or at the less fragrant deposit left by the animal? Can you do anything mad to gain the right sort of attention?

Bright idea

Never overlook the obvious when it comes to promotion. A sign outside your office is a cheap and effective way of promoting yourself, particularly if you are on a busy street. Remember to check out planning permission.

Promotional gifts

Gifts, give-aways and other items bearing your promotional message, logo and contact details can be a good way of winning new business or a big waste of money. If you want your promotional items to work really hard for you, here's how:

- Decide what you want to achieve by giving a gift. It might be:
  - to show appreciation of a valued customer or;
  - to put your name in front of existing and potential customers.
- Select a gift that is appropriate, for example a jewellery pouch if you sell expensive jewellery; a letter opener if you sell stationery.
- Make sure your gift is fun, useful, desirable or attractive.

True story

When Lyons launched 'Signature', a new instant coffee, they asked key journalists to sign and return a postcard, which was then analysed by a graphologist (and the results sent back to the journalist). An amazing 98 per cent of journalists responded! It was a far better way of grabbing their attention and engraving the product name on their minds than merely giving them a free jar of instant coffee.

Which tool for the job?

You need to use the right tool for the job. To help you select the right one, think about:

- what you are hoping to achieve;
- what your budget is;
- who you are trying to reach;
- how long you need to run a promotion for.

Bright idea

Use your fax header sheet as a promotional tool. Think whether you could add a short and simple promotional message. Or perhaps an advert for a sale, event or product. After all, it won't cost you anything to do, but could gain you some new business.

You will probably use a mix of methods to produce the desired effect. For example, let's say you are opening a new hire shop for DIY equipment. To promote it you might choose to:

- Produce a leaflet and door-drop to homes in your catchment area.
- Run a competition in conjunction with the local evening paper, offering free hire to the winners. See if you can get the paper to tie this in with a feature on DIY and home improvements.
- Use press advertising.
- Use an advertising trailer.
- Persuade a skip hire business to give out one of your leaflets when they deliver a skip (where, presumably, householders are undertaking improvement work and might therefore need to hire equipment).

Select methods that are appropriate, cost-effective and will reach the target audience. Incorporate your choices into your marketing strategy and use them to reach out, win new business and expand your enterprise.

True story

Research among classic concert-goers revealed that half of them do not listen to BBC Radio 3. To increase awareness and promote Radio 3 to them, cough sweets wrapped in special, non-rustling wrappers branded with the Radio 3 logo and wavelength details, have been placed in special dispensers (also with Radio 3's branding, and the strapline 'Music Sweet Music') in concert halls. Concert-goers can help themselves to the sweets. What a great idea! It is cheap, effective, appropriate and it even improves the quality standard of Radio 3's live broadcasts by reducing coughing! What's more, the launch of the 'silent sweet' attracted massive local and national media coverage, thereby gaining yet more valuable exposure.

18 Getting the facts: marketing research

Marketing research is a vital tool for small businesses. Research provides you with the information on which you can base your marketing decision-making, enabling you to make informed decisions rather than stabs in the dark. It can even provide you with information that will help you avoid costly advertising and promotional mistakes. This chapter will show you how to use research to the full.

You will be familiar with the term 'market research', research into your market. 'Marketing research' goes much wider. It involves market research, as well as other types of research designed to help you get all the information you need to make the right marketing decisions. It can be used at the 'ideas stage' to gauge responses to your proposed new product or service, and again post-launch to establish the level of customer satisfaction. You can use it to help you develop new products and services and to improve existing ones. Use it to uncover information:

- *About your service* What do customers think about it? Can they suggest any improvements? Would they like to see any changes?
- *About your products* Why do people buy them? What do they think of them? Are there any gaps in your 'product line'?
- *About new products* What is the potential market? How big is it? Who would buy?
- *About your company* What do people think about your name, logo and image? About your staff? About your premises?
- *About your competitors* Who are they? What are they doing that you're not? What do their customers think of them and their products?
- *About your customers* Who are they? What types of people? Where do they live? How much do they earn and spend? How can you get them to buy more? What do they think of you?

- *About customer satisfaction* Are you caring for customers? What do they think? Have they been treated badly by you? How have you handled complaints?

Marketing research can take many forms – questionnaires, interviews or reviewing existing material, for example.

True story

Market research is a fantastic tool, but you sometimes need to be wary of its findings. The *Daily Mirror* newspaper used masses of market research to find out what its readers wanted. Then along came the Sun, offering a diet of sexy pictures, sexy stories and sexy offers. Before long it had overtaken the *Mirror's* circulation and pinched many of its readers. People asked by market researchers what they wanted to see in the *Mirror* were unlikely to ask for sex. However, when a newspaper came along offering it, they were happy to switch. The moral? Ask the right questions and be aware that there are certain issues that people are unhappy to discuss with complete strangers who stop them in the street.

Consult a book on marketing research and the list of contents will probably terrify you – Z scores, finite population correction, bi-variate analysis... But don't let the jargon put you off. This is the most technical area of marketing, and a mathematical bent will be helpful, but you don't need a PhD in statistics to do a bit of basic research.

You will probably have undertaken research before you set up in business. Most banks expect to see some kind of research (usually as part of a business plan) before they agree to lend. The problem is that after an enterprise is up and running, you may find yourself so busy that there is little time to stand back and take a look at research. If you are in this position, do try to create the time. The benefits are clear.

The raw material for marketing research is information. There are two types: secondary data (published sources of information) and primary data (newly gathered information).

Secondary data

This is cheaper and generally more readily available. Secondary data include:

- trade and specialist journals;
- government publications and statistics (eg the *Census of Population*, the *Family Expenditure Survey*, reports from the Registrar General, *Monthly Digest of Statistics, Social Trends*);

- published research carried out by others;
- information available on the Internet;
- surveys published by market research companies.

Bright idea

Many professional bodies have comprehensive specialist libraries. They may allow you access if they regard your research as worth while. You may also be able to get access to university libraries. Ring up, explain your need and see what they say.

The drawback with secondary data is that they are non-specific and more likely to be out of date. Nevertheless, they have their uses. Large reference libraries are an obvious starting point for tracking down secondary data. The Chartered Institute of Marketing run a library and information service, Infomark, for general marketing information. Some of the services it offers are open to non-members for a small fee. (Telephone Infomark on 01628 427333.)

The Internet is also a great source of information. Use 'search engines' to find relevant research from all over the world, from the comfort of your desk, all for the cost of a local telephone call. Some of the sources of data on the Internet attract a fee for downloading, such as Dun and Bradstreet's company service, but most are free or inexpensive.

Bright idea

MORI produce reports (based on opinion gathering) covering a wide range of issues. It is a great deal cheaper to buy one of their reports than to commission your own survey, though obviously they will be less specific to your business than something you commission yourself.

Primary data

You have to gather primary data yourself, or commission someone else to do it for you. That's why they are more expensive and take longer to gather. On the plus side they are more specific to your needs. You can get primary data by:

- *Consulting experts* Academics, specialists, gurus.
- *Observation* Watching reactions and behaviour, for example showing customers your proposed new adverts and seeing how they react, watching people's buying behaviours in supermarkets.

- *Survey* Postal questionnaires, telephone surveys, personal interviews, focus groups, online surveys (see below) etc.

Bright idea

MORI, Gallup, Harris, NOP and the other big market research companies run regular 'omnibus' surveys which track consumer attitudes. They ask a number of very wide-ranging questions and you can pay the research company to have your own question included in one of these. It will set you back around £600. This may sound a lot, but it is a very cost-effective way of getting a national survey carried out by a leading market research organisation.

Your hypothesis

What is your hypothesis? What are you trying to find out? What do you need to prove or disprove? What do you want to learn? Once you are very clear on what you are trying to achieve, you can select the best way of getting the information you need.

Methodology

This is jargon for how you intend to get the information you need. For example, you may decide to use a postal questionnaire plus depth interviews with a sample of customers.

Asking questions

Aside from reviewing secondary data (also known as desk research), there are numerous ways of gathering marketing information. The best way is to ask questions. You can do this:

- in a formal way (eg a questionnaire);
- informally (eg sitting down with a target group for informal discussions);
- face to face (by reading them out and completing a questionnaire for the interviewee);
- by sending out a postal questionnaire;
- by being direct (eg 'How much do you spend on food each week?');

- by being indirect (eg 'Why do you think people prefer packaged meat to fresh cuts?');
- by asking closed questions (yes/no questions, or multiple choice);
- by asking open-ended questions (eg 'How do you think second-hand car salespeople could improve their image?').

Direct, closed questions produce very structured questionnaires which are easy to administer and analyse, but the responses can be less helpful than you might wish. Take the following example:

'Have you ever eaten at Gustave's Restaurant?   Yes   No'

Replies to this question will not tell you why people have not eaten there, how often they eat there, and whether or not they like it. Multiple choice questions can be useful. For example:

'I have never eaten at Gustave's because:

(a) I have never heard of it
(b) It is too far away
(c) It's too expensive
(d) I'm a vegetarian
(e) Other.'

Multiple choice can be too prescriptive. Perhaps someone will not eat at Gustave's because the proprietor once threatened him with a machete! There may be scores of possible answers, but no questionnaire could list all of them. Open-ended questions (eg Why have you never eaten at Gustave's?) can get you this sort of information, but they produce answers which are difficult to record. With closed questions, your interviewer or interviewee can tick boxes on the questionnaire, and an 'other' option does to some extent get round the problem. With anything open-ended you have to do one of the following:

- Tape-record it (which respondents might object to. Also, the tapes will then have to be analysed).
- Get the interviewee to write responses (which is time-consuming and off-putting. It also excludes people who are illiterate or whose first language is not English).
- Get the interviewer to write responses during the interview (they will need shorthand to keep up, their attention will not be as good if they are having simultaneously to write and listen, and you will be relying on their interpretation and summarising of responses, which might be unreliable).
- Get the interviewer to write it up afterwards (which means relying on their memory of events and interpretation).

In spite of all the drawbacks of open-ended questions, to which we must add time and cost, they do provide better insights. Judge which is best for you, depending on what you want to find out, how much time and money you have, who you need to interview and where they are. Questionnaires can contain a mix of open and closed questions.

When you ask people questions in order to obtain marketing information, you are conducting a survey. You can conduct your survey in a variety of ways.

Personal interviews

These take place face to face and are generally regarded as the best type of survey.

Pros

- They tend to elicit the highest level of responses.
- The interviewer can prompt respondents, or help them understand questions with which they are having difficulty.
- They can be very structured (a questionnaire with closed questions) or only slightly structured (a focus group interview).
- They can take the form of a dialogue, being very much two-way and allowing respondents to ask questions as well as answer them.
- Interviewees can see, feel and taste products.
- They can allow perfect targeting for certain types of survey. For example, if you want to know what customers think about a competitor's store, you can stand outside it and question people. It would be very difficult to get this information from a telephone or mail survey.

Cons

- Face-to-face interviews, particularly one-to-ones, are generally more costly.
- Interviewer bias can creep in.
- Respondents might be reluctant to talk about certain things face to face – contraception, death, personal habits.

There are three types of personal interviews:

1. face-to-face questionnaires;
2. one-to-one depth interviews;
3. focus group interviews.

Face-to-face questionnaires

This is when you read out questions from a questionnaire and record the responses given. Often these take place in the street, with passers-by being stopped and invited to help, although they can be carried out elsewhere – on your premises, in your customers' homes or workplaces, for example. With street interviews, try to pick a sheltered spot such as a shopping centre, or a place where people have time to kill, such as a bus stop. (Select somewhere that will enable you to talk to a representative group.) Remember that you are relying on respondents' goodwill. Start with a brief introduction, explaining why you are doing the survey and asking if they are willing to take part. Carry something official, such as an ID card, to reassure respondents that you are bona fide. Your opening question should be interesting and easy to answer, to give the respondent confidence. Some interviewers like to start with an open question that gets people talking. Rapport is important in face-to-face interviews. Pay attention to how interviewers dress, and what assumptions respondents might make about them on the basis of how they look.

Bright idea

Interviewing is tiring. Give staff breaks so they are fresh and alert. Also ensure they are properly equipped for outdoor surveys, with appropriate footwear and clothing, plenty of spare pens, a clipboard and bag or briefcase.

One-to-one depth interviews

A depth interview aims to uncover feelings, attitudes and motivations. It is structured (insofar as the interviewer has a framework and a clear idea of topics/areas to be covered) but it is far less rigid than a questionnaire-based interview. Such interviews offer opportunities to delve deeper and to get qualitative insights. They can be carried out in-house using your own staff, although training will need to be provided first. Ideally interviewers should be encouraging but not leading. They should be friendly and easy to talk to.

Focus group interviews

These are rather like group depth interviews, involving anything up to a dozen or so people. An experienced facilitator introduces an issue and encourages the group to discuss it and offer views, opinions and insight. The interview could, for example, focus on looking at some proposed new adverts for your business, or it could examine one of your products by bringing together a small group of people who currently use it.

- Carefully select members of the group so they are representative of your target audience.
- Use only a trained or experienced facilitator.
- Structure the session so that all the necessary issues are covered.

- If necessary, reassure participants about confidentiality.
- Ensure participants receive a copy of your findings, if appropriate, or at the very least a thank-you letter and update.

Mail questionnaires

The pros and cons of mailed questionnaires include:

Pros

- Questions that people would probably not answer truthfully face to face might be answered honestly in an anonymous postal questionnaire, for example 'Do you have bad breath?' or 'Are you worried about baldness?' Personal interviews tend to have an urban bias; postal questionnaires can be sent to more remote places. This is particularly useful for a national company doing its research in-house. You couldn't possibly question people in Land's End from your HQ in John O' Groats, except by telephone (see below) or by mail.
- Respondents can work through the questionnaire at their own pace.
- Interviewees can complete the questionnaire when it is convenient. A problem with telephone and face-to-face surveys is that people are often approached when they are in a hurry or busy doing something else.
- They can be cheaper than face-to-face interviews, though don't forget to take into account the cost of envelopes, printing and staff time to do the mailing, as well as the cost of the stamps. Questionnaire return rates are increased if a stamped addressed envelope is enclosed, though this does add considerably to the cost of the exercise. (To avoid expenditure on wasted stamps, talk to the Royal Mail about a Freepost address, so that you will pay the cost of postage only on those returned.)
- You can reach many more people for the same cost as face-to-face interviews.
- If appropriate, questionnaires can be left in your reception, where you have a captive audience with nothing better to do. (Remember to have a postbox available for the questionnaire, and plenty of pens.)
- They can include illustrations, unlike telephone interviews.

Bright idea

If you send a tactful and encouraging reminder to those who have not completed their postal questionnaire, enclose a spare; the original may have been mislaid.

Cons

- Response is usually low, casting doubt on the validity of the sample. Professional market researchers are pleased to get a response rate of 30 per cent for postal questionnaires, though don't be surprised if you get as few as 10 per cent back. You need to be confident that the non-responders are not significantly different in their attitudes and opinions from those who have responded. This is not easy. Effectively you have a self-selecting sample.
- They have to be questionnaire-based and therefore are less flexible.
- They often comprise closed questions because respondents are usually unwilling to complete anything that will take too much time or effort.
- You need to pay more attention to design and layout, so that the questionnaire looks attractive and easy to complete. This could mean the extra expense of having to pay a designer. Remember that attractively presented questionnaires are more likely to be completed and returned.
- You may need to go to the trouble and expense of enclosing stamped, self-addressed envelopes to encourage returns, or setting up a Freepost address.
- You may have the effort and cost of doing a follow-up mailing to encourage response.
- Unless you have an appropriate mailing list, you will need to construct or hire one (see section on mailing lists in Chapter 16).
- They are not an ideal tool when surveying people with low literacy levels, or whose first language is not English.
- Because these questionnaires can be read through fully before answering, bias can creep into the answers. 'Funnelled' questions (see below) are therefore less effective.
- Sometimes the answers you get back come from more than one person. Perhaps someone in the household starts answering the questionnaire, gets bored and finds it completed by another member.
- The observations which interviewers can make when working face to face with respondents are impossible with a postal questionnaire.
- They take longer; you need to wait for questionnaires to reach people, allow them a week or more to complete them, and then wait for them to be returned to you. It can take several weeks in total.

It is usual to include a covering letter explaining who you are and what you do (if necessary), what you hope to achieve through your research, and why you hope people will participate – what's in it for them.

True story

An experiment was carried out in which identical questionnaires were issued, each with a covering letter. Half the covering letters were polite and tactful, half short and authoritarian. Surprisingly, the questionnaires sent with the curt covering letter elicited a better response!

Leave a space at the end of a questionnaire for additional comments. Sometimes this can reveal some interesting and relevant insights about issues not covered in your questions, issues that may not have occurred to you.

Bright idea

Research has shown that sponsored surveys can elicit a better response than identical unsponsored surveys. For example, a trade survey on heating and ventilation might be more successful if backing could be obtained by one or more of the professional bodies or publications representing plumbers and heating contractors. A covering letter accompanying the survey could come from the chief executive of the professional organisation, on their own headed notepaper, thus making the mailing immediately more relevant to the recipient.

Fact file

- There is no significant difference in response rates between questionnaires sent in a hand-addressed envelope and those with a computer-generated label.
- Self-addressed envelopes with proper postage stamps on them, when enclosed in postal questionnaires, produce a higher response than preprinted business reply envelopes.
- If respondents are really interested in the subject matter of your survey, they will be willing to complete quite lengthy and detailed questionnaires.
- The more interested respondents are in the subject matter of your questionnaire, the sooner they are likely to complete and return it.
- The status of the person signing the covering letter has an effect on response rates: the higher it is, the higher the return figures.
- Design of postal questionnaires is important. Research has shown that response rates can be affected by typeface and type size, type of paper used and even the choice of colours.
- Single-sided sheets produce more responses than double-sided ones.
- Setting a deadline for returns increases the return rate (see Figure 18.1).

Figure 18.1 Mailed questionnaire

GOURMET CAT FOOD EXPRESS

Thank you for your custom over the last year. We want to make it easier for you to care for your pets, and we would welcome your input into how we can achieve this. So please spare a few minutes to complete this questionnaire.

Please circle any applicable replies. There is space for additional comments at the end of the questionnaire.

1. Currently we deliver fortnightly. Would you prefer weekly deliveries?
   Yes   No   Makes no difference

2. Do you own one or more dogs? (if no, go to Q4)
   Yes   No

3. If yes, would you switch to us for your dog food if we offered free home deliveries? (Assuming we stocked your favourite brands and we were price competitive.)
   Yes   No   Would consider it

4. If we stocked other pet supplies such as cat litter, flea spray and vitamins, would you consider buying these from us? (Assuming we stocked your favourite brands and we were price competitive.)
   Yes   No

5. Currently we ask for payment in cash on delivery. Would you prefer any of the following payment methods? (Please tick any which you would prefer.)

   Cheque on delivery   ❑
   Cheque payment by post   ❑
   Direct debit   ❑
   Credit card   ❑
   Other (please state)......................................

6. Any other comments?

Thank you for completing the questionnaire. Your comments will help us to provide you with a better service. We will write to all customers in September with the findings of this questionnaire and news of what action we propose to take as a result of what you have said.

Please return this questionnaire to:
**Ailoria Felix, Gourmet Cat Food Express, Catford Street,
Brippington BR1 1PR
by 1 July**

If you want to achieve 1,000 responses from a mailed questionnaire, and you expect a return rate of around 20 per cent, you will need to send out 5,000 questionnaires.

Bright idea

To encourage more people to respond to your mailed questionnaire, offer an incentive. For example, give respondents a 10 per cent discount voucher or enter them for a prize draw.

Telephone surveys

Telephone surveys have benefits, although they also have a great many draw-backs, as you can see:

Pros

- You can reach out nationwide.
- You can ask open-ended questions.
- Research has shown that the quality of data obtained by telephone interviews is as good as that from personal interviews.
- It can be much faster.
- You can do away with the need for a paper record, which then needs to be keyed into a computer. Technology means that you can now use computer-assisted telephone interviewing (see below).

Cons

- You might ring at an inconvenient time (eg meal times, children's bath time or during *Coronation Street*!) and irritate the respondent.
- If you are calling someone's home, they might regard this as intrusive or wonder how you got their name and number.
- There can be difficulties in building up a list of people to ring and in ensuring representative samples, although you can buy lists.
- It can run up huge telephone bills, especially if you are calling long-distance or during peak rate office hours.
- People might find it difficult to answer questions honestly when speaking to a real person.
- You cannot do an anonymous survey this way.
- Depending on what time you call, you might find that you fail to get a representative sample, for example calling a home number between 9 am and 5 pm on a weekday is not a good way of reaching working people.
- Communication is limited to oral responses; surveyors cannot pick up on visual detail as they could if interviewing someone face to face. Visual cues which indicate that a respondent has perhaps not understood the question are lacking on the telephone.
- Visual aids cannot be used. For example, you could not use telephone techniques to test the reactions of the public to three press advertisements you were considering running.
- Products cannot be sampled over the telephone.
- The growth in the number of people owning answering machines and call-screening devices can pose a problem.
- Some telesales people have given telephone research a bad name; they claim to be doing research when really they are making a sales call. As a result, many people will not take part in telephone surveys.
- People can be wary of strangers calling their home.

Computer-assisted telephone interviewing (CATI)

In such surveys, respondents are telephoned and questioned in the usual way, but instead of the interviewer writing down their responses, they are keyed into a computer terminal, saving the need to have to do this later and making it faster and cheaper. You need to develop a computer program to deal with it, the cost of which should be added to your research budget. There are a number of companies specialising in this field that will carry out a survey for you. Computers can also be used for personal interviews (CAPI), thanks to portable laptop computers. And they can be used for self-administered testing. In this case, the questionnaire is set up on a computer screen (perhaps in your reception, at an exhibition or in a shopping centre) and people can complete a questionnaire directly on to the computer. It's a good technique for sensitive questions which respondents might find hard to answer face to face with a real person. This is not widely used, but it has great potential. If you are a computer whizz-kid, why not consider producing your own?

Research in cyberspace

Marketing research can be undertaken on the information superhighway as well as the high street. There are thousands of interest and discussion groups. Here you can ask questions or seek views on particular issues. You can also conduct online questionnaires. Condom manufacturer Durex have online questionnaires and offer a free screen-saver as a reward to those taking the time to complete their questionnaire. Car manufacturer Toyota uses its Web site to encourage owners of one of its range of cars to talk to each other. Their conversations are analysed by professional researchers, providing the company with valuable information.

Bright idea

Before launching a questionnaire for real, test-drive it. Check for ambiguity and clarity of questions and correct any errors. Try it out on friends and colleagues, or better still on a sample of potential respondents.

Which method?

The survey method you opt for will depend on what you want to find out, from whom, how quickly you want the findings, and what your budget is. Some surveys automatically rule out certain methods. For example, if you want to do a taste test, clearly this cannot be done on the telephone. If you need to ask very personal questions, it's best done by a self-completion questionnaire.

Ten musts for effective questionnaire design

1. *Make analysis easy*   Choose questions and a format that will make it easier for you to collate the results in numerical or percentage terms. You want to be able to present your findings in a meaningful way. For example, 80 per cent of respondents shopped at Pinky's Postal Presents just once in the last year, and nearly half of these people said that they would buy more often if they could pay by credit card.
2. *Keep to the right*   Research shows that the best place for answer spaces is at the right-hand side of the page, as this is where the eye rests after reading your question. Remember this when designing the layout of your questionnaire.
3. *Don't lead the way*   Never ask leading or biased questions. Phrase all your questions carefully so that you do not inadvertently suggest that certain answers are more acceptable than others. For example, if you ask, 'These days few people wear nylon underwear; cotton is regarded as more fashionable and healthy. Do you wear nylon underwear?' then you will probably not find out what is worn on British bums. Certainly you must never ask, 'You don't think... do you?' Be careful, too, of intonation when you are reading questions aloud. This can lead the listener to a particular answer. For example, 'Do you agree that fresh vegetables are more nutritious than frozen?' By stressing the word 'agree', you might influence interviewees. Always try to come across as neutral.
4. *Use a funnel*   Many questionnaires use the 'funnel technique' to avoid bias in responses. First you ask general or unrestricted questions and gradually you start to home into more specific questions. In this way the respondent creates the frame of reference for his or her responses to the general questions. It should be a smooth process in going from the general to the specific and helps to warm up the respondent, making them ready for more detailed questioning.
5. *Filter them*   'Filter questions' are a useful technique. For example, 'Do you eat out more than once a month?' If a respondent answers yes, you ask them a series of questions about where they go, what they eat, how much they spend, etc. If they answer no, you move to a block of questions on whether they would like to eat out more often, what prevents them, etc.
6. *Getting personal*   Questions about the respondent, such as age, name, income, education, marital status and so on, should be left until the end. If you start with these questions, before a rapport has been established, you will not get far. Even at the end of the interview respondents may wonder why you need to know, so it helps to preface the questions by explaining the reason and stressing confidentiality. This applies to self-completion questionnaires as well as those conducted face to face and on the telephone.

The only exception to this rule is when using a 'quota sample'. This is when you decide that in order to be representative, your sample must include, for example, 20 per cent of respondents in the 18–24 age group, 25 per cent in the 25–44 age range, and so on. Here you might need to know how old respondents are at the outset, so you can meet your quota.

7. *Dealing with attitude*   Sometimes you may need to ask questions that are 'difficult', threatening or on taboo subjects – for example, questions about attitudes to sex, religion or fears about personal health. If so, save them until the middle or near the end of the interview, so that you can build up confidence and reassurance in advance. Unless a rapport has been established, respondents will not be willing to answer these types of question. Many may refuse to answer them full stop. That's their right. If they terminate the interview, at least you will have gained some information from them during the first part.

8. *What's your job?*   Sometimes you need to find out someone's occupation as part of your survey data. It appears straightforward enough, but the fact is that many people when questioned in the street will inflate their status and importance. One man claimed to be 'transport manager' when in reality he was in charge of trolleys at a local supermarket. Probe gently to find out what people actually do. Even when people are not trying to hype their job, they may give an answer that is too vague, such as 'I work for the Health Service' or 'I'm a manager'.

9. *Order, order*   The order in which questions are asked can have an influence on the answers received. Experiments have been carried out in which half the group is asked questions in one order, and half in a different order. The responses of each group to the questions were very different. The order of the answer choices can also make a difference. For example, if you are doing a multiple choice questionnaire and offer 'strongly agree', 'agree', 'strongly disagree' and 'disagree' as answer options, always listed in that order, 'habituation' can take place. People may start ticking the same boxes without properly considering the answers. Choices nearer the start of the list are often selected. The way to avoid this is to aim for a mix of question types, or to change the question phrasing. For example, instead of stating, 'Kapital Kash and Karry offer a range of products that cannot be bettered', say, 'The range of products at Kapital Kash and Karry could be bettered'. By switching the way you phrase questions, you are gently forcing respondents to give a more considered answer.

10. *Complete cover*   Ensure that any question you ask covers the possible answers to it. For example, if you ask, 'Do you eat mainly fresh or frozen vegetables?' you have reduced the possible answers to two. What about those who eat equal amounts of both? Or those who eat tinned, dehydrated or ready-cooked vegetables? Or those, like my brother, who refuse to eat any vegetables!

True story

When the film *Gone With the Wind* came out, a survey was carried out to investigate readership of the book. When asked, 'Have you read this book?', an overwhelming number of respondents said yes, as this was the hip answer. When rephrased to, 'Do you intend to read *Gone With the Wind*?', a more accurate response to the original question was elicited. Many people who perhaps did not intend to read it said that they would, but those who really had read the book made this very clear.

Measuring attitudes

It is easy to measure facts using questionnaires. Questions such as, 'How often do you get your hair cut?' can be answered easily in a simple questionnaire and the responses quickly collated and analysed. But what if your questions involve delving into views, such as what people think of dyed or permed hair? That's where it gets harder, especially if you are using a simple, self-complete questionnaire. There are two methods that are widely used in marketing research, known as the 'Likert method of rating' and the 'semantic differential technique'. Don't let the jargon put you off! They sound horrendously complicated, but they are actually quite easy – you have probably seen and possibly drawn up questionnaires using these methods.

Bright idea

Avoid too many hypothetical questions, as the information they reveal cannot always be relied upon. For example, a question like, 'If the government reduced income tax by 5 per cent, would you consider spending more on your next new car?' is not likely to yield information that will be useful to you in your planning. Questions relating to people's actual experience usually elicit more accurate information.

The Likert method of rating

Using this method, respondents are asked to state their degree of agreement or disagreement with a number of statements. For example:

'The Churchill' is a traditional, established and solid-sounding name for a hotel that emphasises old-fashioned values:

1. strongly agree;
2. agree;
3. tend to agree;
4. tend to disagree;
5. disagree;
6. strongly disagree.

Semantic differential technique

Here respondents are given statements from the top and bottom of a scale and they are asked to indicate their feelings in one of seven positions offered for each set of paired statements. It sounds complicated when described like this, but the examples below show how easy it is:

7 6 5 4 3 2 1

The staff at our Leisure Centre are:
friendly and courteous   – – – – – – –   unfriendly and unhelpful

The food at our hotel is:
excellent value for money   – – – – – – –   poor value for money

innovative and exciting   – – – – – – –   dull, ordinary and boring

Survey errors

When you conduct a survey, you cannot always take the results at face value. Errors can creep in. Below are the three main ways in which this can occur.

1. Errors in interpreting

A respondent might misinterpret what is meant by the question, thus giving the wrong answer. For example:

Q: How much do you spend on groceries?
A: (scaled response from 'a lot' to 'none')

The first problem is that no time period is specified. Does the researcher mean over a year, a month or a week? What do they mean by 'groceries'? Does this include petrol, newspapers, flowers, nappies? It is not clear and respondents are left to interpret the question, inevitably leading people to different interpretations. Also, 'a lot' to one person might be 'a little' to another.

Q: How many shops do you visit in a week?

Again interpretation is required. What is meant by 'visit'? Do the researchers want to know how many shops you actually spend money in, or how many you step inside? What if you visit the same shop five times in a week? Does that count as one or five? Respondents are likely to interpret this question differently, leading to inconsistent answers.

It is also possible for the interviewer to misinterpret. If the respondent is ambiguous, the interviewer might misunderstand.

2. Errors in reactions

Some respondents feel that in being asked to take part in a survey they are in some way regarded as special, for they have been singled out. They may wish to present a good impression, and perhaps be tempted to give what they regard as the 'right' or socially acceptable answers. If asked how much they spend on their children's Christmas presents, people might be tempted to lie or exaggerate, so as not to appear mean. When asking about attitudes to controversial issues, you might find yourself getting the answers people think you expect, not what they really think and believe.

3. Interviewer-induced errors

A face-to-face interview is a social interaction. In some survey interviews, the interviewee simply plays back to the interviewer the views and attitudes that they believe he/she will share. They pick up what they think are the interviewer's values and reflect these, not their own.

Know where errors can occur. It will enable you to avoid or take account of them.

Bright idea

If you are doing blind taste testings, do not call one product 'A' and one 'B'. People tend to think that A is superior to B. Opt for X and Y instead, as these are more neutral.

Twelve tips for questionnaires

1. Put questions into a logical order.
2. Avoid ambiguous wording and make your questions clear and easy to understand. One survey asked, 'How did you find your last job?' expecting the

reply to be 'Through the local paper' or 'At the Job Centre'. Instead many people responded, 'It was really interesting' or 'I hated it'.

3. Keep the questionnaire as short as possible; people are put off by anything too long.
4. For mailed questionnaires, make sure your address is on the questionnaire, so people know where to return it.
5. Give respondents the opportunity of returning the questionnaire anonymously if you want really truthful feedback.
6. Ensure your questions are not biased or slanted. If respondents feel you have already made up your mind about the sort of answers you want, they may not bother to complete the questionnaire.
7. Ensure that the layout of your questionnaire is clear and simple; if it looks a mess, it will put people off filling it in.
8. Make it as easy as possible to complete, by giving boxes to tick or multiple choice options to circle.
9. Limit the number of open-ended questions; they are difficult to process and off-putting to respondents.
10. Have a deadline for the return of completed questionnaires.
11. Don't ask two questions in one, for example, 'Have you ever eaten at Gustave's and, if so, did you think it offered value for money?'
12. Avoid jargon and acronyms.

True story

Use plain and simple language and short, easy-to-understand questions in surveys. What's clear to you might be gobbledegook to your respondent. Research has shown that words in common use, such as 'incentive', 'proximity', 'discrepancy', and 'paradox', are not widely understood. It is reported that in one survey, 10 per cent of respondents thought that 'devolution' was Jeremiah's brother! In another, one respondent, when asked for the definition of 'nostalgia', said it was Welsh for 'goodnight'.

Samples

Decide what you want to find out (your hypothesis) and how you plan to find it out (your methodology). Next you must decide on who will be surveyed. With the exception of the government's ten-yearly census, no survey can cover the whole of the population. Researchers use instead a 'sample', which is a smaller group that is representative of the 'population' they wish to survey.

If you run a small mail order business and you want to find out what your customers think about your customer care, it should be possible to survey your entire customer base. You will know exactly who your customers are and how to reach them. But let's say you are thinking of setting up a chain of Indian fast food outlets, rather like burger bars but offering quick Indian meals instead. It would be impossible to ask every fast food eater in the country whether they would use such an outlet, when and how often. That's when you would need to select a sample. By surveying a representative sample, rather than the entire relevant population, your survey is made more manageable and affordable.

To select a sample, first define your population. That can take some thought. Let's look at the example above. You would need to ask:

- Do we want the sample in our survey to represent:
  - all fast food eaters?
  - everyone who likes Indian food?
  - just those who like Indian food, but not burger-style fast food?
  - a mixture of fast food lovers and Indian foodies?
- Do we want to survey only those in the catchment area of our proposed outlets?
- How many people will we need to interview? (The larger the sample, the more precisely it reflects your population (if it is carefully selected). But bear in mind that increasing a sample from 250 to 1,000 requires four times as many people, but it only doubles the precision.)

Be very clear on what your population is and ensure that your sample is representative of it. Then locate your sample. Will you ask people coming out of Indian restaurants? Burger bars?

There are a number of ways of selecting a sample from your population.

Random sampling

With random sampling, every member of your survey population has an equal chance of being selected. First you start with your 'sampling frame' – this lists everyone in the population you wish to survey, which might be:

- everyone who has ever bought from you;
- all adults living in Anytown;
- anyone who uses anti-dandruff shampoo.

Next you need to select a random sample from the list. You can do this in two ways:

1. *Simple random sample* Give every name on the list a number and then get a computer to generate numbers randomly.
2. *Systematic sample* Give every name on the list a number, select your first name randomly, then select every, say, fifth or tenth name.

Judgement samples

Here you use your judgement as to who to interview. This method of sampling is useful only where you are dealing, say, with an issue requiring expert judgement. You may decide that you need only speak to a handful of key people – a dozen at a nearby housebuilders, nine people working in local architectural practices, and three local contractors – to get the information you need on the likely interest for your proposed new construction management scheme.

Quota samples

You select people in order to be sure that you have a list that represents the population. For example, you may decide that it is necessary to interview a certain percentage of men and women, a certain number of people in particular age groups or social classes. If you want to ask about people's views on fizzy drinks, you might need to ensure that drinkers of the top brands are represented in your sample (perhaps in proportions according to each drink's market share.)

Avoiding biased samples

Biased samples produce unreliable results. Asking regular customers about your customer care might produce glowing (but unreliable) results. They presumably (though not necessarily) shop with you regularly because you are doing something right. Including former customers in your sample would help balance the findings.

Getting data from observation

Questionnaires are not the only way of getting marketing data. There is another way which has been used to great effect by others and is relatively easy to do – observation. Here are two real-life examples of observation being used to collect important marketing information:

- *Honda* watched how people go about loading their car boots and used the information to redesign the Honda Civic hatchback.
- *Philips*, the shaver maker, watched men shaving (with their consent) through a two-way mirror. Information gathered was used to modify its products.

You may be able to think of examples in your own work where simple observation will provide you with some valuable marketing information. For example:

- using observation to see if customers look at your publicity leaflets in reception; if they do, it could be an effective way of communicating with them;

- using observation to see how many people visit the premises of your main competitor.

There are ethical issues when it comes to covert observation.

Undertaking a survey

1. *The research brief* This involves developing survey objectives. What is your hypothesis? What are you trying to prove or to find out? Who are you trying to find it out from? The brief is a broad exploration of these issues. (If you are using external consultants, you will need to give them a brief and talk through it with them – see Chapter 26. If you are doing research in-house, you still need to produce a brief. This gives colleagues who are involved an opportunity to have an input into the research.)
2. *The research proposal* This is where the broad discussions held previously are now firmed up. The problem is set out, the 'population' defined, a way of selecting a sample recommended, the methodology, and estimates of time and costs worked out. If you are using consultants, they will prepare a research proposal for you to approve. If the work is being done in-house, a research proposal can be used to seek approval for the project from your co-directors. It can also be used to ensure that everyone understands what the research is about, why it is necessary and how it is being undertaken.
3. *Data collection* This is the bit we most readily think of as marketing research. Here you put into practice the methodology recommended in your research proposal.
4. *Data analysis and evaluation* Having got your raw data you need to process it into a form that is meaningful. Your findings need to be analysed and related back to your original objectives.
5. *Preparing the findings report* This is where you write up all the work you did in the preceding stage. You will also need to draw conclusions and make recommendations. Then you must ensure that your report does more than just sit on a shelf collecting dust. You need to ensure that you take action.

Desk data

Many companies have existing data, in a raw form, that could be extremely useful to them if they were to analyse them. For example, if you are a national business, you might find it useful to go through your records to build up a picture of where most of your customers live. You could classify people according to town or city; county; England, Scotland, Wales and Northern Ireland; north or south, east or west. There's no point in undertaking such an exercise, though, unless you have some thoughts on how you plan to use the information. You may wish to focus your publicity drive on the parts of the country where sales are low, or to concentrate efforts on those areas where you appear to be already successful.

Desk research of this sort can help you uncover all sorts of useful information, for example:

- your most profitable geographic areas;
- the preferred payment option (eg credit card, cheque, debit card, etc);
- whether you have more male than female customers;
- the peak times of the year for orders.

Think about what information you already have which, if properly analysed, could be helpful to you in your marketing work.

The effective marketing research checklist

- Ensure your survey staff are properly trained and know what they are doing.
- Check that your questions are not slanted.
- With each question ask, 'What will we do with the information?' If you can't answer, leave the question out.
- Ensure you have not added a few extra questions 'because you are doing the survey anyway'. Split questions into 'must know', 'useful to know' and 'like to know' categories, to help you decide what to leave out.
- Ensure the sample is a valid one and large enough to be both relevant and credible.
- Be aware of how errors can creep in.
- Opt for the right survey method.

Column inches from surveys

Many companies commission research with the sole intention of using it to gain a few column inches. A survey on surveys revealed that 3,000 stories a year in the national press are based on surveys! Perhaps your survey findings can be used to get some publicity for your business. For example, if your research reveals that most people eat your oven chips when they are in bed (sounds rather unlikely!) you could try to get some light-hearted tabloid coverage along the lines of chips being a love food. Announce it on 13 February and you've created a quirky Valentine's Day story for the following day's papers.

The media will not accept survey stories that amount to nothing more than blatant advertising. There needs to be an interesting angle to your story; journalists are looking for relevance, hard information, surprise, topicality and novelty (according to a survey among journalists). Barclays Bank, for example, do an annual survey on student debt. This gets them massive media coverage because their findings are real news, while at the same time it helps position the company as a good bank for students (the high earners of the future). The media will be more likely to carry stories based on professionally conducted research than on in-house research (which they might regard as more biased). They will expect you to say who conducted the survey, what the sample size was and what methodology was used.

To get your story in the media you will need to issue a news release. Information on how to do this can be found in Chapter 8.

Now over to you

Think about what you have read on questionnaires and then take a critical look at the questionnaire in Figure 18.2. It has been prepared by a fictitious book club in order to discover how the company can improve the service it offers to members. What mistakes does it make?

Figure 18.2 Research questionnaire

BOOKWORMS

1. Do you like the monthly newsletter?

   Yes   No

2. Would you mind if we scrapped the newsletter or reduced it to a quarterly publication?

3. Would you take part in a 'member get member' drive? (This would involve you in persuading friends and relatives to join us. In return you would get a free gift from us for each member introduced.)

   Yes   No   Would consider it

4. Would you be willing to pay an extra £5 in exchange for enhanced membership benefits?

   Yes   No

5. Would you be more likely to renew your annual subscription if we were to give away a free book?

   Yes   It would make no difference   It might make a difference

6. Do you have any other comments?

Return this questionnaire as soon as you can to Bookworms.

Discussion

There are some plus points about the questionnaire. It is brief and therefore quick to complete, it does make some very important mistakes, which include:

- There is no introductory paragraph – it launches straight in with the questions. This is a more serious omission if such a questionnaire is sent out without a covering letter.
- Q1 is not a simple black and white issue, but it is presented as though it were. People are unlikely simply to like or dislike the newsletter. Some will like all of it, others will like parts only, some will like none of it, some will like some editions but not others. How can you answer with a clear-cut yes or no?
- Q2 asks two questions in one, which is confusing. Scrapping the newsletter altogether is a very different option to reducing it to a quarterly.
- Q2 also raises too many 'ifs'. Some members might be happy for the newsletter to be scrapped, for example if the membership fee were halved.
- Q3 is not an easy one to answer. Surely it depends to a large extent on what gifts are offered? Not enough detail is given to allow respondents to answer this question.
- Q4 is unclear. Do they mean £5 a year? £5 per order? What would the enhanced benefits be? You need to know before you can judge whether or not they merit an extra £5.
- Q5 is also unclear. What book? Pulp fiction? A Mills & Boon? A worthy tome? Would there be a choice of books? Would the book be hardback? People might be influenced if the book were a best seller or an expensive edition, but not if it were a cheap paperback on a subject that held no interest for them.
- There is no closing date for returns, which means that respondents may delay completing it and then lose it or decide not to bother. Alternatively, questionnaires may be returned in dribs and drabs, with returns coming in well after you have begun to analyse the results.
- The return address is not included. If people have to hunt around for the address, they may not get around to sending it back.

If you want to use professional market research consultants, read Chapter 26 for advice on how to select a market research agency and how to write a brief.

19 Putting customers first: how to establish a customer care culture

Customers are vital to your success as a business. Treat them badly and they won't come back. If you recognise the positive impact that good customer care can have on your balance sheet, read on to find out how to put in place an effective customer care plan. This chapter will also show you how to deal positively with customer complaints.

You must have experienced this. You are in a restaurant having given up on one of the worst meals of your life. The waitress removes the plates of half-eaten food, asking mechanically if you have enjoyed your meal. The temptation to answer truthfully is resisted. After all, you know she's only asking because she's been told to. She's not interested in you or your meal. So you say nothing, but vow never to return. You tell everyone how awful the restaurant is. They avoid it like the plague. That's what poor customer care is for customers: a bad experience. But it is bad for businesses too, because dissatisfied customers won't come back.

Before you sit back smugly and say that your business is not like that, stop and think. Do you really treat customers well? Really well? Do you exceed their expectations? Can you say hand on heart that 100 per cent of your customers are 100 per cent happy with your business, your products and your services 100 per cent of the time? If you can, then you fall into a very tiny minority, because the fact is that most businesses are not good at customer care. Some get it right sometimes, but most get it wrong too often.

Few people cannot tell stories of poor customer service from their own recent experience. We all come across it every week – in restaurants, shops, in railway stations and on buses, face to face, over the telephone and in writing. Poor customer service is so common that it is likely that your company is as guilty of it as any other. Common sense tells you that poor customer care will lose you customers. But what do you gain by applying good customer care? A heck of a lot! Here are some reasons why you should tackle customer care:

Five reasons why you should care

1. It is cheaper to keep a customer than to attract a new one – experts say it can cost between 3 and 30 times as much to win a new customer as to keep an old one.
2. Happy customers make repeat sales.
3. Happy customers win you new business by recommending you to their friends.
4. Good customer care can help you differentiate yourself from competitors offering otherwise similar goods.
5. Good customer care is good for your reputation; bad customer care will damage reputation and dent profits.

True story

The Korean car company Daewoo branded itself customer-friendly right from the outset. Despite getting cold reviews from the auto press about the style of its cars, it captured 1 per cent of the UK car market in just 12 months. Not bad for a complete newcomer, especially given the prejudices against Korean cars. It was the company's emphasis on customer care that made it both distinctive and appealing to consumers.

A formula for success

So as you can see, good customer care makes good business sense. It affects your bottom line, but by how much? There is a formula you can use to calculate roughly what each customer is worth to you (see Figure 19.1).

Figure 19.1 A formula for success

1. Start by working out your average sale (annual sales in £s ÷ number of transactions). Write the answer in the column alongside:	A =

2. Now make a guess at the number of sales you get each year from each regular customer. Write the answer in the column alongside:	B =
3. Multiply this figure (B) by the number of years a customer buys from you on average. Write the answer in the column alongside:	C =
4. Now think about the number of referrals/ recommendations your existing customers make (i.e. how much new business do they put your way?) Write the answer in the column alongside:	D =

Use these figures to work out the sums below:

A............ × B .... = F.............. (sales per customer per year)
F............ × C .... = G............. (sales per customer over a lifetime)
G............ × D .... = I .... (gross sales from referrals)
G............ + I............. = £.............. Grand total

This grand total is the total value of a satisfied customer.

It looks a little complicated set out like this, but it is really a very simple formula. Here's an example. Suppose you run a beauty parlour.

Your average sale is £17.50 (A)
Each regular customer visits you six times a year (B)
Your customers stick with you for around 7 years (C)
Each recommends two of their friends to you (D)
Here's how you work out the value of one customer:

Sales per customer per year = A × B (ie £17.50 × 6) = £105 (F)
Sales per customer over a lifetime = F × C (ie £105 × 7) = £735 (G)
Gross sales from referrals = G × D (ie £735 × 2) = £1,470 (I)
Total value of a satisfied customer = G + I (ie £735 + £1,470) = £2,205

So next time you feel irritated with a customer, don't think, 'Oh well, it's only £17.50.' Remember that the real cost to you of a lost customer is much higher. So grit your teeth and keep that customer happy.

True story

I was writing a book on marketing (not this one) and telephoned a bus adverting company to ask them to send me details of their work, their costs, etc. I explained what I was doing, why I needed the information, and how they might find it a useful plug. Nothing arrived from them. As a result they were not mentioned in that book, they are not mentioned in this one, and I did not use them for a major bus advertising campaign for one of my clients. Good customer care would have paid dividends for the company concerned. How much goodwill and custom do you miss out on without ever knowing it?

So far we have concentrated largely on why you should take customer care seriously. Now for a look at what happens when you do not. If you visit a shop and the assistant ignores your obvious need for help because she is too busy telling her fellow assistant about a recent night out, you form a bad impression not only of that shop assistant, but of the store as a whole, and all the other stores in the chain. You judge it all by your one experience of one member of staff. That's how you are judged too. If just one of your staff is rude or unhelpful on just one occasion, that reflects on the rest of your business and on you personally. Companies do not exist as entities in their own right. They are made up of staff and judged on the basis of the skills and attitude of those staff.

Starting with staff

So it's down to your staff to deliver excellent customer care. Don't expect them to do this by instinct. Show them how. Apparently, new staff working in shops get far more training in handling money than in handling people. This is a short-sighted approach, because unless they handle people properly they won't be handling much money! Staff who need to use a computer are given computer training, those who interview and appoint staff are given recruitment and selection training, yet staff who handle people are not expected to have any special skills – because this activity is regarded as common sense, something we can all do with ease and competence. Yet clearly it's not that easy. Staff need to be trained in the importance of customer care and in customer care skills.

Each member of staff should be trained, for everyone will come into contact with customers. Many hospitals train nursing staff, receptionists and telephonists in customer care, but they forget about the cleaners, who probably have a great deal of contact with the public. Lost visitors ask them directions all day long, yet without customer care training, cleaners will be unclear about what is expected of them. They will continue to regard visitors' questions as unwelcome interruptions that get in the way of their real task: cleaning the corridors and wards. If customer care is part of everyone's job description (and their appraisal), and everyone learns how to do it, you will begin to see real customer care in action. Remember that once you've got your customer care right, you should include customer care training as part of the induction process for all new staff. That way you can keep up the standard.

So-called 'front-line' staff – receptionists, telephonists and sales assistants – are especially important. They are the ones who create the first impressions of the business and, as you know, first impressions count. How friendly are they? Do they smile and welcome visitors or shoppers? Do they answer the telephone quickly and deal with calls courteously and efficiently? Is there a clear system for offering visitors a cup of coffee, or is it left to chance? Try to see your front-line staff as strangers would. What impression do they create? What improvements could be made?

Even if you have just one or two staff, do look at customer care. Discuss it together and agree an approach.

Avoid over-programming

How often have you rung a number, only to hear, 'Good morning. Thank you for calling Hewbert, Harbert and Hare Solicitors Limited. This is Karen speaking. How may I help you?' Over-programmed staff are little better than under-trained ones. So if you are guilty of asking your staff to recite a turgid script when they answer the phone, stop it. Apart from being very boring for the receptionist, it sounds insincere to the caller and strips staff of their individuality. Don't be afraid to let your staff's personality come out when they answer the telephone, as long as they respond promptly and in a friendly way.

Teamwork

Don't forget that you may have internal customers too – your partners, directors or staff. And they, too, will have internal customers. The receptionist, for example, is providing a service to others in the company by answering the phone for them, welcoming visitors, perhaps doing some typing. So while you all do different jobs, you work for the same company and ultimately you are doing your job to further the aims of the business. No one should be allowed to see their job in isolation; it needs to be seen as a vital cog in the machine, just as important as all the other cogs, yet useless on its own.

Three steps closer to customer care

1. *From the inside* When you are a customer, what things annoy or irritate you? List all of them. Now think of situations where you have received poor customer care. What went wrong? Add these to the list. How can you make sure that your company is not guilty of these things? Draw up some ideas for ensuring that the things on your list are never experienced by your customers.

2. *From the outside* Get a friend to ring your company with a difficult or awkward question and see how they are treated. Ask them to write in with a request and see how promptly and efficiently it is handled. Try out your company using friendly outsiders and get some critical feedback. Now draw up an action plan for tackling any shortcomings.
3. *From another company* Try the same thing with other companies and see how they compare. If you come across any good ideas from them, see if they can be adapted for your own use.

Getting your premises right

Having dealt with staff, take a look at your premises – they are the first thing your customers see. What image does your reception convey about your company? Or your retail outlets? Arrange your premises to make everything as good as it can be for your customers. What are customers' needs when they visit you? Cater for them.

Go by recommendation

Earlier in the chapter I explained how to calculate the lifetime value of your customers. A crucial element of the calculation was the recommendations made by happy customers. Of course, only happy customers will recommend you; unhappy ones may be hell-bent on putting as many people off using you as possible. For some companies, recommendation is the most effective way of gaining new custom. My own bank, First Direct Bank, carries out independent research to establish their customers' satisfaction rating and the percentage of customers recommending them to friends. Due to the Bank's emphasis on customer care, First Direct customers have both the highest satisfaction rating and make more recommendations than the customers of other main banks. First Direct even send customers business cards and leaflets to hand out to friends. One leaflet begins, 'We have found from research that 89 per cent of our customers recommend us to their friends or colleagues. We have also learnt from our customers that they would appreciate some assistance when recommending us; hence this leaflet. If you know someone who… give them this leaflet'. Only a company confident that its customers were truly satisfied would dare use such an approach. First Direct also train staff answering their phones to recognise whether the caller is chatty and wants to talk, or businesslike and wants to get on. This way they can tailor their responses to the needs of their customers.

> ### Bright idea
>
> Make sure that at least one person in your company (yourself or someone senior) is charged with the task of overseeing customer care, even if you are a very small business. Make sure that person sees every customer complaint and is informed of the outcome.

Everyone with whom you have dealings is a customer of sorts. So remember that customer care is not just about the way you treat your obvious 'customers', it is about how you treat anyone you deal with through your work. It is fundamental to your relationships with your customers and potential customers. I try to be helpful and pleasant with all my suppliers, and there have been times when this has paid off. Designers I use have recommended my PR and marketing services to their clients, for example.

> ### Bright idea
>
> Regard everyone as a potential customer. If you have a meeting with a supplier and you are running late, call to say so. Not only is it the polite thing to do, it shows your company to be thoughtful and efficient. If you stroll (or indeed rush) in late with no forewarning and no apology, it will give quite a different picture. Does that really matter? Yes. Although you are your supplier's customer, you never know when your supplier might be in a position to recommend your services to someone else.

Set the standard

Good customer care can be measured (eg by counting the number of customer complaints and the number of complimentary letters you receive). Specify the standard you expect from staff, and ensure that it is met. Now you can be sure that you have consistent quality throughout your company. Standards need to be genuine, demanding, yet achievable. Review them if they prove too easy or too ambitious. When setting standards, always try to quantify, so they can be measured and monitored in an objective way, for example:

- all calls to be answered in three rings and put through to the right person first time;
- all telephone calls to be returned within 24 hours;
- all mail to be acknowledged within two working days;
- fresh flowers to be put in reception every Monday and Thursday;
- old magazines to be cleared out of reception at the end of each month;

- every customer to be greeted on arrival and offered coffee;
- all customers to be served within two minutes;
- 90 per cent of orders to be processed and despatched within 24 hours of receipt.

Publicise the standards you are aiming for, measure your performance regularly and publish this too. Failure to meet your standards needs to be explained – to staff and to your customers. (This may involve nothing more than displaying performance and standards on a noticeboard in your reception.)

Here are some examples of good and bad customer care:

Bad: 'She's not here. You'll have to ring back later.'
Good: 'I'm sorry, but Janet's out of the office just now. I can take your details and get her to ring you back within the next hour, or perhaps I can help you myself?'

Bad: 'It's nothing to do with me. It's not my department.'
Good: 'I'm sorry to hear that our training department appear to have made a mistake. I'll have a word with the training manager and ask her to ring you back this afternoon with an explanation and apology.'

Bad: 'You're not the only one who has had to wait three weeks for your delivery. We're snowed under at the moment.'
Good: 'I will personally ensure your order is despatched today. Please accept our apologies for the delay.'

Bad: 'Frankly I don't think you've got a leg to stand on.'
Good: 'We take all complaints very seriously. Thank you for telling us about it. We will look into it and get back to you within a week.'

Corporate responsibility

The key to handling situations like this is to get your staff to accept corporate responsibility. The customer does not care that you are short-staffed or that you work in another section. They regard you as a representative of the company, and therefore they hold *you* responsible. Accept that responsibility, with the customer at least. Bawl out one of your colleagues later if you must, but make sure that the customer's problem is sorted out first. Never pass a customer from pillar to post – it will only add to their bad feeling and give them another cause for complaint.

If you want staff to accept corporate responsibility, you need to involve them in the process of improving customer care. Ask them for their ideas on what can be improved (if you're large enough, you could even introduce a staff suggestion scheme), have brainstorming sessions and tackle problems together. Consider a small 'quality circle' (a customer care working group) to examine customer care, to come up with ideas for achieving it and to set and monitor standards.

True story

An NHS chiropody clinic wanted to provide better customer care. Staff were asked for ideas, and one suggested that the clinic should sell chiropody products to patients at less than the price they could be bought at the chemist. They introduced the idea, which was warmly welcomed by patients. The small profit from the sales was invested in plants and pictures to make the waiting-room more comfortable.

As well as including staff in coming up with ideas for improved customer care, bring in the real experts – your customers! Ask them what they think, and encourage suggestions (perhaps via a suggestions/ comments box) and feedback.

Customer or client charters

Consumers are now familiar with customers' charters – we have a Citizen's Charter and a whole series of other charters, such as the Patient's Charter – which set out clearly what we can expect as consumers of public services. What can your customers expect? Better still, have you asked them what they expect? This is what marketing is about. Charters will be eyed with scepticism unless they are seen to work. Why not commit yourself to a standard and show your customers their rights set out clearly and displayed prominently? Show customers that they matter to you.

True story

Recognising that lack of good child care can be a barrier to parents seeking an evening out, an Edinburgh theatre became the first in Britain to offer a free baby-sitting service to theatre-goers. Real customer care (indeed, real marketing) is about meeting your customers' needs.

Customer care mission statements

Many companies have mission statements setting out what they are about. The problem is that all too often they are simply wish-lists drawn up in a moment of enthusiasm at a directors' away day. They need not be like this. If you take it seriously, a statement can help you focus your mind on your mission. Why not produce a customer care mission statement for your business? My own mission statement for my company is to provide a top quality public relations service that is flexible and responsive to clients' needs and results in complete client satisfaction. When a client requires me to attend an evening or weekend meeting, it can be a real pain. That's when I have to remind myself that I am committed to being responsive and flexible! What is your customer care mission statement?

True story

I took my raincoat to my local dry cleaner. The assistant said that they might not be the best company for the job, as their chemicals might damage the waterproof coating. She recommended a place where they would be able to tackle it. Far from losing a customer, the assistant gained a loyal one. Her friendly, helpful and impartial advice gave me confidence in the shop. With the exception of my raincoat, I now take all my dry cleaning there.

Be a copy cat

If you come across a customer care idea that works, copy it, adapting it as necessary to fit your company. A manager running an NHS chiropody clinic spotted a good idea at her local hairdresser, which showed people pre- and post-coiffure. She adapted this at her clinic to show feet before and after treatment, so that patients would have a clear idea of how their feet would look. This was found to take away much of the fear and anxiety about treatment and to give patients something positive to focus on. Have you encountered any good ideas that would translate to your own business?

Giving them what they want

Real customer care is marketing's best friend. Like marketing, it involves asking customers what they want/need and delivering on that – not giving them what you think they want and hoping for the best.

Find out what customers want by asking them. Consider:

- a questionnaire or survey (see Chapter 18 for details of how to compile one);

- a seminar or focus group for customers to say what they want and for you to listen, take note and take action;
- visiting a cross-section of your customers to ask for their views;
- introducing a comments' and suggestions' book, box or card;
- setting up a customers'/users' panel (many large stores do this to good effect);
- talking to ex-customers to find out why they stopped buying;
- trying to find out about customer satisfaction levels with your competitors, so you have a comparison to measure yourself against.

True story

A hospital equipped a separate waiting-room in casualty specially for children, since it felt that it would be less traumatic for children and their parents to be separated from the adult accident and emergency patients. It decided to fill the room with toys and games to keep the children occupied, but someone suggested that perhaps it would be a good idea to take guidance from parents as to what they would like to see in the room. 'A doctor,' replied one mother, 'for what's the use of toys if my child is too sick to play?' The parents clearly had a different view of need to the hospital authorities. Then they asked the children, who unanimously wanted to see a TV and sweets in the waiting room. This was at odds with the view of the parents. The moral? Seek the views of all groups of customers, don't rely on your own guesswork.

Suggestions/comments schemes

At last the benefits of comments and suggestions schemes have caught on and many businesses are using them to gain useful customer feedback, ideas on how to improve their offerings and vital marketing information. Alas, many companies produce comments cards simply because others do; they are failing to ask the right questions and to use the information they gather.

The primary purpose of a comments/suggestions card is straightforward: to seek comments (bad as well as good) and to get ideas and customer feedback. You can also use them to get general information, for example by asking one or two questions such as, 'How often do you visit this cinema?' or, 'How did you hear about us?', followed by options boxes to tick.

Once you have gathered all this information, for heaven's sake use it! If your business is criticised, don't be defensive or make excuses. Take a serious look at the criticism and see if there's anything in it. If so, put it right. If good ideas are suggested, put them in place and, if you know who suggested the idea, thank them, give them a meal on the house or in some other way acknowledge their contribution.

True story

My local café has a comments card. Each quarter it produces an in-house newsletter, which it leaves on tables, detailing what comments have been received and what action has been taken. I get the feeling that they are genuinely interested in what their customers think, and I like their interactive style. I'm sure that many comments cards I have completed elsewhere have ended up in a black hole.

Get a 'can do' attitude

Perhaps one of the best ways of keeping customers happy is to ensure your company has a 'can do' attitude. Too many companies have complex and unnecessary rules and regulations that get in the way of good customer care. Staff in these companies are drilled with 100 reasons why customers' reasonable requests cannot be accommodated. Here's a real-life example. I visited a pizza restaurant with my three-year-old son. We were told we had to stand at the door while a table was cleaned for us. I explained that as we were tired, we would rather sit at the table while it was prepared. I was told that was not possible; it contravened company policy! When I asked to see the manager, she asked us to leave, saying that she did not want customers like us. Needless to say, I have not been back. Nor have the 30 other people I have told about it. I cannot believe that our request was such a big problem. After all, other restaurants allow this. Their 'can't do' attitude created enormous ill will and lost them custom.

Here's another example, again involving my young son, which shows how counter-productive it is to have a 'can't do' mind-set. In a museum café my son asked if he could have chips and beans for his lunch. Although chips and beans were clearly on display, I was told that I could not have them together as they were not a 'recognised meal'. I could buy chips on their own, or beans with something else, but not chips and beans together. Apparently the problem was to do with a computerised till. The situation appeared ludicrous to me so I persisted with my request. Eventually the counter staff agreed. Why could they not have done so at the outset? A can do attitude would have averted a problem and left everyone feeling positive. As it was, the staff upset a little boy and made his mother very angry.

Hallmarks of a can do company

Can do companies:

- see problems as challenges to be overcome;

- pull out all the stops to meet a customer's requests;
- do not have rules and regulations designed to make life easier for staff, at the expense of customers;
- empower staff to be flexible, bending the rules when appropriate in order to keep customers happy;
- are not afraid of unusual or difficult requests.

Keep customers by building brand loyalty

As it costs a great deal more to attract a new customer than to keep an existing one, first-rate customer care makes sense; it is the best way you have of keeping your customers and, via their word of mouth, attracting new ones. Your customers will remain loyal to you only if you treat them well (by getting your customer care right) and offer the right products (which is what marketing is all about). On top of all this there are things you can do to enhance a customer's loyalty:

- Thank them for being customers and show their custom is appreciated, perhaps by sending them money-off coupons.
- Keep them up to date with news, special offers, new products.
- Consider giving them loyalty rewards (eg 10 per cent off their next membership subscription to your fitness club, 20 per cent off their next haircut or stationery order, a free gift).
- Make loyalty rewards incremental (eg 5 per cent off for customers who stay with you for a year, 10 per cent for customers buying from you regularly for two years or more).

Handling complaints

Customer care is not about handling complaints, it is about ensuring that you get things right in the first place, thus removing the causes of complaint. Inevitably, though, even in well-run businesses things do occasionally go wrong, and you need to be ready to respond properly and to correct errors.

Complaints fact file

- People are generally very reluctant to make formal complaints, but most will grumble to others about poor service.
- Of all dissatisfied customers, 96 per cent make no complaint!
- However, they do tell seven others how bad you are.
- 13 per cent will tell at least 20 others.

Responding to complaints well is really important. Here's why. Let's say you have 100 dissatisfied customers in any year: 96 of them will not complain at all; about 12 of those will tell 20 others how dreadful your company is; and 84 will tell 7 others. In other words, your 96 dissatisfied customers – of whose existence you are blissfully unaware – will deliver 828 powerful negative advertisements for your company. Is that what you want? No. Then start by developing channels that enable your customers to tell you that they are unhappy. For example:

- an official complaints procedure set out in a friendly leaflet;
- easy-to-complete complaints cards and boxes to post them in;
- customer satisfaction surveys;
- a customer care officer;
- comments cards;
- suggestions boxes.

A well-publicised, friendly and courteous, fair, easy-to-use and prompt complaints procedure is a must for encouraging complaints. Develop a system that works for your own business. Once you start getting complaints, you have a golden opportunity to transform dissatisfied customers into satisfied ones. Research in many companies shows that a dissatisfied customer who is dealt with well and sent away happy is more likely to be loyal to you than one who has never had cause to complain. Of course, the only way you can make unhappy customers happy again is to encourage them to complain.

True story

British Airways carried out a survey among its customers, and discovered that of all those who experience problems but make no complaint, half do not intend to use the airline again. This contrasts with the customers who are dissatisfied and do complain – just 13 per cent of this group will defect, the same rate of defection as among the satisfied group! The lesson? Encourage complaints and use them to help you improve what you do.

Give your staff guidelines on how to deal with customer complaints, both oral and written. They might be something like this:

Complaints over the telephone

- However angry or unreasonable you think the caller is, always remain polite and helpful.
- If there has been a delay in answering the call, or you need to put a caller on hold, apologise for keeping them waiting.
- If a caller is complaining about something outside your remit, explain this to them and helpfully point them in the right direction.

- Never leave a caller feeling that they have been abandoned or dealt with in an unsatisfactory way. Ensure that they get to speak to someone, or that you arrange for someone to call them within a specified time.
- If it is your fault, always say sorry and offer (without waiting to be asked) to do what you can to put things right.

Complaints in writing

Dealing with written complaints gives you time to think, so it can be easier than a complaint made face to face. Be careful not to get into a position where letters are toing and froing for months on end because with each letter you are raising more issues than you address. If the complaint seems to grow with each letter, why not suggest meeting to discuss the problem face to face? Always offer to visit the complainant; never expect them to have to come to you, though make that an option. Make yourself available at a time that is most suitable to them, even if it's an evening or weekend. Point out that they can bring someone else to the meeting to support or help represent them. Follow up any meeting with a letter thanking the complainant for their time and summing up the position.

Take action

Marketing-led companies should encourage complaints, not regard them as threats. Complaints are a bit like free research; they can provide you with data on where you are failing and an opportunity to put it right. To do this you need a system for ensuring that there is an opportunity for a complaint to result in a policy or service change or improvement. If your office is inaccessible for people with pushchairs, and no toys are available in your reception area for the many parents who need to bring their children with them, a visit will be an ordeal, even if the service you offer is, in other respects, first class. Perhaps you have failed to notice

True story

Edinburgh's legal profession is noted for its stuffiness. One firm of lawyers, in the city's exclusive Charlotte Square, offers customers help in lifting their pushchairs into the office, gives children toys to play with, will warm up bottles and babyfood, allows women to breastfeed their babies, and has a supply of potties and nappies for emergencies. Not only is this good customer care, it is very good for business. Word has got around that there is a legal firm with a difference – it's warm and human. Their good customer care has given them a competitive edge. A small investment in customer care has led to a big increase in their profile and their bottom line.

this shortcoming. A complaint can identify it for you and give you a chance to put it right, thus further improving your service. But this will only come about if the person dealing with complaints feeds them through to someone with responsibility for taking corrective action.

I once made a legitimate complaint to a hospital. Months later I discovered that they were continuing the practice I had complained about; no action had been taken as a result of my complaint. The image I held of the hospital was damaged by this discovery, and I was left feeling that they had no genuine interest in patients' views. Your customers will feel like this if you do not act upon their complaints.

True story

I completed a comments card at a restaurant and asked if they would contact me with a response to a suggestion I made. I never heard from them again. They never saw me again; their discourtesy lost them a customer.

Always aim to turn complainants into ambassadors. It can be done, as the following true story shows:

True story

I ordered some adhesive address labels as a birthday present for a friend, but the company sent the labels to my friend rather than me, thus baffling her (she had no idea where they had come from) and spoiling my gift idea. When I complained by telephone, the company apologised, gave me the labels free, and offered to send me a complimentary set for my own use. They followed this up with a very apologetic letter. I was impressed and will feel confident about using the company again and recommending them to others.

The dos and don'ts of customer complaints

DO:

- show empathy;
- listen;
- let them make their case;
- sympathise (regardless of where the blame lies);
- apologise – if it was your fault;
- propose corrective action;
- do more than the minimum;
- offer compensation if appropriate.

DON'T:

- say 'It's not my fault' – remember corporate responsibility;
- interrupt – it will infuriate the complainant;
- jump to conclusions – they are probably wrong;
- argue – you will gain nothing and will only antagonise;
- lose your temper – it won't help;
- accept responsibility until you are sure it's your fault – that doesn't stop you from sympathising though;
- be patronising – you might get a punch on the nose!
- blame others – remember corporate responsibility again.

True story

I had been having problems with my mail for weeks. I complained to the Royal Mail, who said they would investigate. Weeks passed and I heard nothing. I chased them several times and was told that my complaint was still being investigated. More weeks passed. I phoned again only to discover that all the correspondence relating to my complaint had been lost. They eventually admitted that they were in the wrong and had compounded the problem by handling the complaint badly, and having poor systems that led to the papers being lost. They offered me £5 compensation. I pointed out that this derisory sum hardly covered my phone bill to them, let alone the time I had spent pursuing the complaint, or the enormous inconvenience I had been put to. Their response? 'We don't have to give you anything at all. This is a goodwill payment.' It didn't create any goodwill!

Now over to you

A customer has made a complaint about your receptionist and you send the following reply (see Figure 19.2(a)). What is wrong with it?

Figure 19.2(a)   Letter in reply to a customer complaint (version one)

Mrs Valerie Johnson
37 Glendoon Road
Trumpington

29 August

Dear Mrs Johnson,

Thank you for your letter of 22 July. We note your complaint and apologise for any distress or inconvenience caused.

Please let us know if you have any other suggestions or complaints about our service in the future.

Yours sincerely,

Eleanor Davies

Eleanor Davies
PA to the MD

Discussion

There are a number of mistakes with the letter:

- It reads like a standard letter sent out to all complainants. This makes the complainant feel that:
  - (a) in your eyes they do not deserve a personal reply;
  - (b) you receive lots of complaints and the only way you can cope with the volume is by sending standard letters.
- It took over a month before a reply was sent.
- The sender of the letter is a junior member of staff, which will make your complainant feel that you do not attach much importance to complaints.
- You do not say what you intend to do to remedy the situation/make sure it never happens again.

You should be sending letters that are more like this (see Figure 19.2(b)):

Figure 19.2(b)   Letter in reply to a customer complaint

Mrs Valerie Johnson
37 Glendoon Road
Trumpington

25 July

Dear Mrs Johnson,

Thank you for your letter of 22 July. I was very concerned when I read it and an immediate investigation was carried out.

Our receptionist was asked why she was rude to you. She said she was under considerable stress that day, having received news of the death of a close relative. That is of course no excuse for rudeness, though we hope it goes some way to explaining her out-of-character behaviour.

As a result of your complaint we will be taking a close look at the training of our reception staff, to ensure that something like this never happens again. Once we have carried out a full review and come up with recommendations for improving our reception service we shall contact you again to let you know what action we intend to take. In the meantime, I hope the enclosed box of chocolates will go some way towards restoring your faith in us.

The receptionist concerned has written a personal letter of apology to you (enclosed).

Please call me if you feel that this complaint has not been dealt with satisfactorily or if you have any other concerns you would like to discuss. My direct line is 967 6784. I would also be interested in hearing from you if you have any thoughts or ideas of your own on how our customer care could be improved.

Once more, we are genuinely sorry for what has happened to you.

Yours sincerely,

Sally Jacobs

Sally Jacobs
Managing Director

Discussion

This is better because:

- It was sent promptly, within a matter of days of the complaint being made.
- It clearly demonstrates that complaints are taken seriously and dealt with by senior staff.
- It shows that immediate action was taken and follow-up action is planned (it's not enough to take action, you need to tell the complainant what you are doing).
- It gives the complainant an opportunity to discuss it further (an offer which is unlikely to be taken up, though it's still worth making) and to come up with ideas and be involved in making customer care better.
- The box of chocolates, although just a token, shows they care.

Never issue bland and uninformative letters in response to complaints, unless you want to antagonise the complainant. If you need to carry out lengthy enquiries before responding fully, always send a holding reply within 48 hours, to show that the complaint isn't being ignored. Say when the complainant can expect to hear from you again. But above all, try to set up your business in such a way that complaints are minimised or avoided.

20 Communicate for business success: how to have excellent internal and external communication

Communicating clearly and regularly is a vital part of business success. Communicate well with your customers, suppliers and staff (if you have any) and you will be sparing yourself plenty of grief. Reduce customer complaints, make your orders to suppliers clearer, and avoid the situation where poor communication leads to your staff letting you down and damaging your business.

Many a marriage has failed because of poor communication. No relationship can survive without it, and as marketing is about relationships, communication should lie at its heart.

Brushing up on effective communication can pay dividends for even the smallest business. Here are some common examples of poor communication that illustrate what I mean:

- You go into a shop and ask the assistant if she has a particular dress in a different colour. She takes the dress and, without saying a word, walks away. You guess that she's going to the stockroom to check, and will be back shortly. How much nicer if she had smiled and told you this!
- You are at the Post Office standing in a really long queue. Two of the counters are open but a third is closed even though a member of staff is

sitting at that counter behind the closed sign. She might be doing some important work, you don't know. What you do know is that everyone else in the queue is wondering the same thing as you, 'Why don't they open that till and help clear this queue?'

- You are passing a shop and see something in the window you would like to buy. On pushing the door you discover it is locked – at 11 am on a Saturday morning! You look in vain for a note to say why it is closed or when it will reopen.
- You place an order for a new washing machine and are told that delivery will be in two to three weeks. After four weeks you have heard nothing and the machine still hasn't arrived. You call the store from work, only to discover that they tried to deliver the machine to your home that morning while you were out.
- You telephone a company to leave an order. It's 5.05 pm on Friday. No one answers the phone and there is no answering machine to allow you to leave a message or to tell you the company's hours of business.

What each of these stories has in common is poor communication. These businesses have either failed to consider the information needs of customers, or have worked on the basis that we must all be mind-readers.

You will probably communicate with your customers:

- face to face;
- in writing (by letter, fax, e-mail);
- on the telephone.

How good are you at it? Do you always get in touch with customers to keep them up to date? Do you acknowledge customers when they enter your premises? Do you follow up on orders to ensure that everything is OK? Here are some occasions when communication is called for:

- to inform of delays;
- to inform of difficulties or problems;
- to inform of alterations to arrangements.

Your customers must feel that you are thinking about them and that you are aware of them and their needs.

True story

One Saturday I was queuing in Sainsbury's to pay for my groceries. Each till had enormous queues, bar one (which was closed). Everyone was grumbling about the closed till and complaining to each other that it should be opened. Finally I asked a member of staff, who told me that the till was broken. Had the store placed a sign to this effect, it would have avoided considerable customer dissatisfaction.

When it comes to effective communication, be friendly, clear and succinct. Be aware that the message sent is not always the same as the message received. To avoid crossed wires, always:

- give the necessary background and introduction;
- give all the necessary facts and details;
- leave out the irrelevant.

Catering for special needs

About one in six people have some kind of hearing loss, so it's likely that you will have customers who are in this category. The Department of Health produces useful literature on the issues surrounding people who have a hearing loss. The Department's contact details are: Department of Health, PO Box 777, London SE1 6XH, tel: 0800 333 777, fax: 01623 724 524, Web site: www.doh.gov.uk.

The Royal National Institute for the Blind produces *See It Right*, a really good guide to producing information for Britain's 1.7 million blind and visually impaired people. It is available from RNIB, 105 Judd Street, London WC1H 9NE, tel: 020 7388 1266. You can get some basic information on producing material for visually impaired people by referring to pages 131–32 of this book.

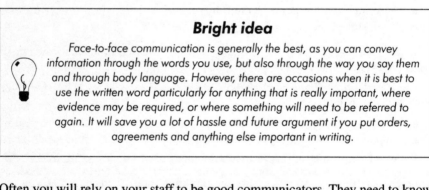

Bright idea

Face-to-face communication is generally the best, as you can convey information through the words you use, but also through the way you say them and through body language. However, there are occasions when it is best to use the written word particularly for anything that is really important, where evidence may be required, or where something will need to be referred to again. It will save you a lot of hassle and future argument if you put orders, agreements and anything else important in writing.

Often you will rely on your staff to be good communicators. They need to know what you expect of them, so issue guidelines if necessary. For example, staff may be required to:

- acknowledge a customer within 20 seconds of entering your shop;
- welcome diners and give them a menu within one minute of being seated;
- telephone customers if an order will take more than 48 hours to process;
- write to customers if an item is out of stock, asking if they would like to wait for new stock to arrive (give time scale), cancel or alter their order.

You cannot expect your staff to be skilful and committed communicators if you never communicate with them yourself. First you must get your own house in order.

Getting it right on the inside

Internal or employee communications is an area much neglected, even by many companies with a good external profile. Enjoy the benefits of good internal marketing – fewer industrial relations' problems, increased productivity, decreased absenteeism and better timekeeping – even for very small businesses. Now there is a lucrative internal communications industry with specialist consultants who collect fat fees for their expertise. There is no need for you to employ one of these consultants, even if you can afford to do so. Good internal communication uses many of the same techniques as good external communication, and the same principles lie at its heart.

Staff and your image

Knowledgeable, informed staff who feel valued provide a better service for customers, are more committed, more motivated, less likely to be off sick and to want to change jobs. They are more willing to be flexible in their approach and to put themselves out for you, so it makes sense to consider their needs. Enlightened companies who see their staff as people and not as machines recognise that staff have a right to be treated well and to know what is going on where they work.

Even if you have just two or three employees, your staff are probably your most valuable asset. Improving communication with them is crucial to your public image, for they are your ambassadors. You are judged on their performance, so the impression they give will shape the image you have. Thus the impression they give will be shaped by how you treat them.

The British car industry during the 1970s was notorious for its constant strikes and industrial relations problems. By contrast, the Japanese car manufacturers who set up here did very much better in this respect, and much of their success was put down to the fact that they kept staff informed, involved them in decision-making, and made them feel part of the company. Other foreign companies based in Britain, such as Ford, now pay great attention to staff and their information needs, employing a large communications team to keep everyone abreast of events and developments. You will not have at your disposal the resources of a large company, but that's no excuse for being a poor communicator.

The main area of communication breakdown in any organisation is between managers (or the owner) and staff. Many managers and proprietors assume that because they know something, others will know it too, which is often not the case, even in quite small companies. In bigger companies the organisational hierarchy means that many staff are denied quite basic and necessary information, whether intentionally or not. They have to rely on the grapevine, which, while it can be extremely effective, is also often a way of spreading false rumours and unhelpful speculation. Many a strike that should never have happened took place because people relied on the grapevine for their information, being starved of it by their seniors.

There are numerous companies which have a caring image as far as the public is concerned, yet are, unintentionally, bad employers, due in part to their poor communication systems, or even complete lack of them. Setting up a system should be easy if you are a small business, but for bigger organisations, formal procedures need to be put in place to inform staff of news and developments. You can choose from:

- *Noticeboards*　The humble noticeboard is so often overlooked as a communications tool. Start using yours now!
- *Team briefings*　Suitable only for the larger companies, you write a brief and managers go through it with their staff. The advantage is that all staff receive the same message at the same time, so it is particularly useful for companies with more than one office.
- *Staff meetings*　It's an old idea but a good one. Some companies ask staff to suggest topics to go on the agenda for the next meeting, giving staff a chance to air issues that are important to them. Even very small companies should have a regular staff meeting, even if it happens only every month or two.
- *Newsletters/news-sheets*　These can be glossies or cheapo in-house efforts, they can appear at a frequency of your choosing, and can be chatty or formal. All it takes is a word processor and a photocopier! (See Chapters 11 and 12.)
- *Staff training sessions*　In-house sessions are a great way of bringing the team together and examining an issue or problem. You don't have to be a huge corporation to organize some training.
- *Question time*　If you have a large staff, an occasional 'question time' can be beneficial and fun. This is a chance for staff to find out what they want to know. Make up a panel of managers or directors to field the questions.
- *Roadshows*　If you have lots of offices, staff not based at head office might feel neglected or isolated. Get off your butt and go and see them.
- *Listening circles*　This is where managers listen to staff and all of their concerns. It's a chance for staff to have a good moan in a non-threatening environment.
- *E-mail and 'intranets'*　Bigger companies may have a computer network that allows the use of electronic mail between staff, and access to information online (such as staff handbooks, internal phone directories, and so on).

These are all useful ways of ensuring that staff know what is happening and understand why. Remember that communication should be a two-way street; it's all very well to talk to staff, but you need to listen too.

Internal communications surveys

If you employ a lot of staff, or you have more than one office, it can be difficult to get communications right, or even to know where you are going wrong. The best way of uncovering communication blockages is to draw up a staff communications questionnaire. An example of some of the questions you may want to consider can be found on the sample communications questionnaire that follows in Figure 20.1.

Figure 20.1 Communications questionnaire

At Widgets & Digits we are committed to good communication, and as a first step in improving communications across the board, we are focusing on internal communications. Who better to ask for views than you, our staff? Tell us where we are going wrong and pass on your ideas for doing it better. You can do this by filling in and returning this questionnaire. We will publish the results in August and you will be sent a personal copy of the findings.

Many thanks for your help.

Sasha Sutcliffe

Sasha Sutcliffe

1. In which part of Widgets & Digits do you work?

Head Office   Devon office   Aberdeen office   Warehouse

2. Your job grade?

Grade 1–6   Grade 7–12

3. In addition to your immediate work team, with which part of Widgets & Digits do you identify most strongly?

Your department   Your office/region   The company as a whole

Other (please specify) ....

4. Please indicate whether you agree or disagree with the following statements. Tick only one box per statement.

	AGREE			DISAGREE	
	++	+	+/-	-	-/-
I feel isolated from other parts of Widgets & Digits	☐	☐	☐	☐	☐
My manager gives me all the information I need	☐	☐	☐	☐	☐
Communication within my work team is good	☐	☐	☐	☐	☐
I have to rely on the grapevine for the information I need	☐	☐	☐	☐	☐
I think my manager is interested in my views	☐	☐	☐	☐	☐
Management only tell us what they want us to know	☐	☐	☐	☐	☐
Communication works well between HQ and other offices	☐	☐	☐	☐	☐

5. How useful do you find each of the following as sources of information?

	VERY USEFUL	QUITE USEFUL	NOT USEFUL	DON'T KNOW
Team briefing	☐	☐	☐	☐
Staff newsletter	☐	☐	☐	☐
My manager	☐	☐	☐	☐
Noticeboards	☐	☐	☐	☐
Annual report	☐	☐	☐	☐
Memos	☐	☐	☐	☐
Noticeboards	☐	☐	☐	☐
Press cuttings	☐	☐	☐	☐

Other (please specify). . . . .

6. In general, how satisfied are you with internal communications at Widgets & Digits?

SATISFIED				NOT SATISFIED
++	+	+/-	-	-/-
☐	☐	☐	☐	☐

7. If in general you are not satisfied with internal communications at Widgets & Digits, please indicate the main causes of this. You may tick more than one box.

Not enough information   ☐

Too much information   ☐

Information received too late   ☐

Inaccurate information   ☐

Not enough contact with my manager   ☐

Not enough contact with other offices   ☐

Information which is not relevant to me   ☐

8. Do you have any suggestions for improving internal communications at Widgets & Digits? (Please specify.)

9. Which of the following Widgets & Digits publications do you receive? (Please tick.)

Annual report ☐   Staff newsletter ☐   Leaflets ☐

Thank you for completing this questionnaire. Please return your completed questionnaire in the envelope provided by **Friday, 17 July**.

Having found out what is happening in your company, and where communication is breaking down, publish the findings for staff and – most important of all – take steps to correct and improve your communications. Having highlighted the problem areas, it should be relatively easy to put procedures in place to address these. It is best to involve staff in devising ways of tackling communications problems, perhaps by setting up a communications review group which comprises representatives from all of your offices as well as different grades of staff.

Feedback to staff is crucial if you want their support in improving the way you operate internally. In feeding back the information to staff, try to set out the main findings in a meaningful way. The sample feedback sheet in Figure 20.2 shows how you could tackle it.

Figure 20.2   Communications questionnaire feedback

WIDGETS & DIGITS STAFF COMMUNICATIONS
QUESTIONNAIRE

SUMMARY OF FEEDBACK

Thank you for taking the time to fill in the recently circulated communications questionnaire. The response was fantastic, with 95 per cent of forms being returned by the deadline. Here is the promised feedback of the main findings.

We asked who, in addition to your work team, you most strongly identify with. Clearly we are failing to build a strong corporate feel, for only 5 per cent of staff said that they most strongly identify with Widgets & Digits. Most of you identify most strongly with the office where you are based.

Those working at Head Office do not feel at all isolated from Widgets & Digits, but staff in the regional offices do, to a large extent. The most isolated staff of all are those working in the warehouse.

Most of you feel that your manager gives you the information you need, though staff at Head Office are less happy in this respect. Managerial staff are generally better informed by their managers than are clerical staff.

While most of you feel that communication in your own work team is good, over 70 per cent of staff are still having to rely on the grapevine.

Most of you (80 per cent) believe that your manager is interested in your views, yet the same percentage think that managers only tell you what they want you to know.

Staff at Head Office think that communication between Head Office and the other offices is good, though 77 per cent of staff in the regions strongly disagree.

The staff newsletter is the most useful source of information, followed closely by team briefing. The annual report is generally considered a poor information source.

Most of you are reasonably satisfied with internal communication at Widgets & Digits. Of the 10 per cent who are not, managers cite the main cause of dissatisfaction as being information overload, while clerical grades say it is due to lack of information. Ideas suggested for improving communication range from management roadshows to the regional office to the use of electronic mail. All ideas put forward will be evaluated and there will be a round-up published in the next issue of the staff newsletter.

Anyone wanting a copy of the full findings should contact Sasha Sutcliffe at Head Office.

Don't let them down

Staff can sometimes let a company down, damaging its reputation, but companies often let staff down. Any damage to reputation caused this way can only be described as self-inflicted. Many businesses behave well with their existing personnel, only to treat prospective staff very shabbily. An Industrial Society survey found that many companies failed to write to applicants who were not shortlisted, treated interviewees discourteously, and were unnecessarily slow in telling applicants the outcome of their interviews. The author of the report wrote, 'Organisations will spend thousands of pounds on public relations, and yet many of them fail to understand that people who seek jobs with them will tell their family and friends if they have been poorly treated.'

True story

Some years ago I applied for a job with a public relations consultancy. I went to a lot of trouble preparing my application but received nothing in return, not even an acknowledgement. I phoned to check that they had received it; I thought it might have been lost in the post. They said they would check and ring me back, but they didn't bother. Later that year I needed to engage a PR agency for a project I was working on; guess who was not on my list of possibles? If you treat potential employees this way, they won't support your business in the future. Nor will anyone they tell about it.

Don't use poor administrative support or lack of budget as excuses for failing to acknowledge job applications. It costs nothing to state in the job advert that an SAE should be enclosed, nor to be properly organised for interviews, and to be welcoming and professional. You should aim to leave those not offered a job with a feeling of disappointment at not having the chance to work in your company – and eager to apply to work for you in the future – not one of relief at a narrow escape.

The success of your company lies in the commitment of your staff. Without everyone's support, you will be straining to create and maintain a good service and an image to match. Treat them well, keep them informed and involved and you will get the very best out of your staff. If you don't, you will damage their faith and they will damage your reputation.

Part 3

The professionals

Introduction

There will be times when you simply cannot do a marketing job in-house. Perhaps you do not:

- have the time;
- have the skills;
- have the equipment;
- want the responsibility.

That's when you need to bring in the experts. This section looks in detail at working with professionals in a range of marketing disciplines.

True story

A Dublin-based copywriter was interviewing someone for a junior copywriter's job. His portfolio looked impressive, until the interviewer noticed some of his own work, carried out while he was at a London agency! The moral: if in doubt, take up references to be sure that your experts are as good as they claim to be.

There are some basic guidelines that apply when working with any outsider, whether a designer, printer, marketing research consultant or advertising agency. These are:

- know what you want to achieve from using an external expert;
- have a clear, written brief;
- choose your consultant or supplier carefully;
- having gone to them for their expertise, for goodness' sake listen to them and allow them to guide you – after all, that's what you are paying them for.

True story

I was engaged by a client to write their annual report. They gave me an oral brief, which is what I worked to. Having written copy that perfectly matched the brief, I presented my work to the client. 'We've changed our minds,' they said. 'You caught us at a time when we were feeling a bit negative, so we gave you an unnecessarily gloomy brief.' I went away and rewrote it to the new brief, all the time ensuring that my style was the right one for their intended audience. The client then hacked about with my work, adding unnecessary detail in a different style. The end product was a hotchpotch that failed to address the needs of the audience and cost them a lot of money in copywriter's fees. A heartfelt plea – if you engage an expert, listen to their advice!

21

In the picture: putting photographers into focus

It is said that a picture is worth a thousand words. That may be true, but many business photos fail to live up to this. This chapter will show you how to find and commission a professional photographer. Find out how to write a comprehensive brief, how to compare prices, even how to use a photo library.

If you want really effective photos, start with a good photographer. Poor pictures will spoil your publicity material. You want your products, premises and personnel to look good. They will look their best through the lens of a professional, so go and find one. If you get stuck, contact the picture editor of your local newspaper and ask them to recommend an affordable, efficient, reliable and imaginative freelance photographer. Alternatively try the British Institute of Professional Photography (Tel: 01920 464011), who have members nationwide.

See a number of photographers and look at their portfolios to assess their work. Good product photographers are not necessarily good people photographers, so you might need to use different photographers for different assignments. Product shots may require studio work, so you will have to satisfy yourself that your chosen photographer has the premises to handle the job.

Bright idea

Try to choose a specialist PR photographer rather than one who specialises in weddings or portraits. But beware of those who tack 'PR/press' on to a long list of other specialisations – no one can be expert in everything.

Comparing prices

Don't select a photographer just on price; good photographers are rarely cheap. Price, though, should be a factor. As pricing policy varies from photographer to photographer, do ask exactly what they charge for. Here are some of the items that you may be billed for:

- *Rates*   Some charge hourly and others charge a session rate, which is a day or half-day.
- *Materials*   Find out what they will bill you for (eg film) and whether you will be charged at cost price or with a hefty mark-up.
- *Prints and slides*   What do they charge for these? This can really add to the bill.
- *Contact sheets*   These are like very small prints, but they are all printed on one large sheet of photographic paper, enabling you to view the prints in miniature, before selecting those you want made up full size. Some photographers will charge you extra for a contact sheet.
- *Expenses*   Find out what you will get billed for (including the mileage rate, and whether you will be charged travelling time).
- *Speed*   Many photographers charge extra for rush jobs.

Bright idea

Some photographers charge a small attendance fee, and make their money from selling you prints. Others charge a higher fee, but their prints are very reasonably priced. Find out the likely full cost of the job, and pick the photographer who will be most cost-effective for your requirements.

The brief

Having found your photographer, provide a schedule and/or brief (see Figures 21.1, 21.2 and 21.3), which will include:

- A description of the photographic assignment including dates, how long it will take and whether shooting will take place indoors, outdoors or both.
- Full details of names, addresses, etc to be visited by the photographer, along with a schedule.
- An indication of what you plan to do with the photographs/how you intend to use them.
- Whether you want prints or slides. Slides are much more versatile, though they do cost more. If you give lots of presentations, opt for slides. Prints

can be made into slides, but it's not cheap. Slides are easier to store, but prints are easier to view – you don't have the hassle of setting up a light box or projector. The drawback with prints is that they are not as hardy, and are more prone to damage.

Figure 21.1   Briefing/confirmation letter

DESIGNS ON YOU
181 Howard Street, Elliesville
Tel. 67113

Spike Wilson Photography
78 Donovan Way
Elliesville

1 May 1998

Dear Spike,

A note to confirm our booking and to give you further details of the brief we discussed on the telephone today.

We manufacture stick-on 'stained glass'. Our product looks very similar to real stained glass, but costs a great deal less. (A small sample is enclosed.) We require colour transparencies for our new sales brochure (a copy of our last brochure is enclosed for information). Our aim is to show our product in traditional settings, thus giving it an authentic and up-market image. The last thing we want is for people to regard our product as sticky-back plastic! That is why we have gathered a range of props for you to use to add an air of sophistication to the photographs. You will be supplied with pieces of antique pottery, pretty statuettes and small pieces of sculpture, for display on the sills of the windows you will be photographing. When you visit people's homes, remove anything inappropriate that they have on their window-sill and replace it with one of the props. (We have forewarned people that you will be doing this!)

The shoot should take less than a day, starting at 9 am and finishing no later than 3.30 pm (see enclosed schedule). Aleisha Davies, my assistant, will accompany you, provide transport and introduce you to the customers who are letting us use their homes in the brochure. You should call at our office on 31 May at 9 am and ask for Aleisha.

As agreed, your fee will be £500 inclusive, to cover your time, materials and expenses. Payment will be made on receipt of transparencies, which are required no later than 1 July. We will require you to assign the copyright to us and have enclosed a form relating to this for you to sign and return.

Please contact me if you have any queries. Otherwise, Aleisha will see you here on the 31st.

Yours sincerely

Janine Dolan

Janine Dolan
Managing Director
Encl.

Figure 21.2   Photographic schedule

ASSIGNMENT	Colour transparencies for sales brochure
DATE OF SHOOT	31 May
SCHEDULE	

9 am   Meet Aleisha Davies at Designs on You, **181 Howard Street**

9.30 am   **Mrs Templeton, 13 Mayville Gardens**
                Mrs Templeton lives in a 1930s' semi, where she has used one of our art deco designs in her cloakroom. We would like your photo to have a 1930s' feel to it. Use the flapper girl statuette in this photo and the Clarice Cliff vase.

11.00 am   **Mr Cunningham, The Lodge, Lullingworth Village**
                Our product was used extensively during the refurbishment of The Lodge, a beautiful Victorian house. Mr Cunningham's home is full of fantastic antiques, so perhaps you could make use of these for an opulent period feel. We require at least three different windows, each showing a view of the room but keeping the window as the focus.

1.00 pm   **Susan Joyce, 10 Bellfield Street**
                Ms Joyce's house is a modern Wimpey home. She has used designs from our contemporary range to add character to her home. We wish this photograph to show how our product can provide modern houses with a touch of class and individuality. If possible, we would like one of the shots to show Ms Joyce's cat, Timmy, relaxing on the window-sill.

2.00 pm	Sandwiches in car *en route* to our factory in the **Canning Industrial Estate**. One of our staff, Joe Tailor, has agreed to be photographed. He is in his late 50s and has a very characterful face. Although our product is made on large machines, we want a picture that suggests (without directly saying so) that it is made in the age-old way – a bit like real stained glass. Joe looks like an old-fashioned craftsman, which is why we have chosen him. He will have various tools available as props.
3.00 pm	The session will end at around 3 pm/3.30 pm. You will be returned to Howard Street to collect your car.

Figure 21.3   Photographic brief

Introduction
Designs on You wishes to add to its stock of photographs for use in its promotional, exhibition and display material. We require a wide range of photographs showing our product in manufacture and in use. We also require shots of our staff at work.

Our product
We manufacture stick-on 'stained glass' in a wide range of traditional and contemporary designs. Our product looks similar to real stained glass, but costs a great deal less.

Approach
We wish to give our photographer a relatively free hand in deciding how best to undertake this commission.

Our needs
Our aim is to have a stock of photos which show our product in use. We want to show beautiful windows in attractive homes. It is important than each photo focuses upon the window, while also including a little of the surrounding room. Anything visible in the surrounding room should be appropriate. The image we are seeking is up-market, sophisticated and quality. Antiques, traditional furnishings and expensive ornaments should be put in view if available.

We also require shots of the product during manufacture. Although it is machine-made, we would like to emphasise the hand-finishing elements and the quality control aspect.

As for staff shots, we want our staff to look friendly yet professional. We require photos of a selection of staff in our factory, at our mail order depot and at head office.

We have asked 20 of our customers in different parts of the country for their assistance with this project (by allowing their homes to be photographed). The photographer would need to liaise with these people to make the necessary arrangements. (A complete contact list will be supplied.)

Requirements

We require the photographs to be supplied as colour transparencies, two copies of each. The total number of photographs taken should be in the range of 400 to 500. The photographs should be ready by 1 July 2002.

The photographs should be numbered and accompanied by a brief note of the names and locations of people pictured.

Copyright

We will own all photographs and will expect the photographer to assign copyright to us in writing.

Reference material

For reference and background information we have enclosed copies of our promotional material and product samples.

Confirm the booking in writing, including as much information as possible so that your photographer knows what to expect, what equipment to bring and what film to use. Advise your photographer of any dress code; if it's a black-tie event, will the photographer be expected to wear dinner-dress? Warn your photographer if wellies or specialist clothing is required. If it's an invitation-only event, will the photographer need an invitation to get past the door?

Bright idea

Have a good tidy up before your photographer arrives. Ensure your office, shop or factory looks a credit to you. Rearrange plants, pictures and other decorative items so that the areas being photographed look their best. Make sure staff look good too. If it's a colour shoot, wear bright and attractive clothing and use cheerful backdrops. Prepare for the shoot and have any props to hand.

Creative images

You will see that the sample brief and schedule were very detailed. They explained why the photos were needed, how they would be used and what props would be required. The person commissioning the photos knew exactly what they were looking for and what image they hoped the photos would convey. It is best to prepare detailed instructions for your photographer. If you just leave them to get on with it, what you get might be unsuitable or disappointing. Photographers are not mind-readers, so tell them what's in your head.

The ideal photographer will combine technical competence with a great eye for a picture. In my experience the bulk of photographers are OK at the former but weak at the latter. Many are unimaginative, so don't rely on yours to find an interesting idea. Discuss your ideas and have a few suggestions ready. Try to avoid pictures of:

- directors sitting around a table;
- hand-shaking shots;
- straight product shots;
- group shots;
- photos of meetings or large gatherings.

Bright idea

If you see photographs you like in magazines and brochures, cut them out and keep them. You can then show them to your photographer as examples of the sort of thing you are looking for; this can be much easier than trying to describe it.

The most effective product shot I have seen was for Velux windows. Rather than showing windows, it showed a stylish penthouse-style loft conversion featuring Velux windows. A shot of the dark, cobwebby loft before conversion sat alongside. The change was dramatic and attention-grabbing. A straight product shot of a Velux window would not have had this effect. Imagination, anticipation and planning were required to get the shots, but the hard work paid off. Think how you can liven up product pictures. Showing them 'in use' is a good ploy.

Bright idea

While you have a photographer working on an assignment for you, get him or her to take some head and shoulders shots of your key staff. These are useful for popping into press packs, and will not add much to your bill if the photographer is working for you in any case.

Try to anticipate your photographic needs, in order to maximize the value of your photographic budget. If you commission a photographer to take some pictures for your new brochure, and you know that two months later you will be producing your customer newsletter, get the photos for that taken at the same time.

Catalogue your photos so that you know what they show, when they were taken and by whom. And don't forget to ask your photographer for the negatives, so that you can get prints made up by a photographic lab if necessary, which could work out cheaper or easier for you.

Picture libraries

There may be times when you need a professional picture, but can't commission a professional photographer. This is where a picture library comes in. Picture libraries give you access to an enormous range of images, to the world's very best photographers, to photographs taken in faraway locations, to pictures using special effects, and so on. So if you need a top quality picture of a happy family enjoying a beach holiday in the Caribbean, for example, and commissioning your own would be impossible, contact a picture library. For a one-off top quality image, it may be much cheaper to use a library than commission your own photographer, particularly by the time you have added in the costs of models, travel to an exotic location, props, etc.

Using a library is easy. Ring up and describe the kind of picture you are looking for, and they will either locate something suitable (generally they will come up with more than one picture), or suggest that you come in and have a look yourself. If you ask the library to find your image, they may charge you a search fee (of around £20–£35), though this is usually waived if you then decide to buy the picture.

The cost of a picture varies, depending on which library you use, how you intend to use the picture (eg a slide presentation or in a brochure), what the circulation will be, whether it will appear on the front cover or an inside page, how large it will be, and so on. Generally the fee is for a one-off use; you do not buy the rights to the photo.

When briefing a picture library, be as specific as possible about the kind of picture you have in mind. Don't just ask for a photo of 'someone shopping', as this raises too many questions: Male or female? What age? What ethnic origin? In a supermarket? A corner shop? A market? A clothes shop? What era? 1950s? 1990s? USA or UK?

Most libraries produce free catalogues, often on CD, though they are not comprehensive; a catalogue can only show a fraction of a library's stock of tens of thousands (often millions) of images.

There are general libraries with a wide range of images, and specialist ones, for example those specialising in scientific or nature photos.

Across the country there are over 300 photo libraries (though the highest concentration is in the London area). To find out where they are, contact the British Association of Picture Libraries and Agencies (BAPLA) (Tel: 020 7713 1780).

Copyright

Question: When you commission a photographer to take photos of you, your staff and your products, who owns the copyright?
Answer: The photographer.

You might have done the commissioning, provided the subject matter and paid for the work, but under the provisions of the Copyright, Designs and Patents Act 1988 the copyright belongs to the photographer. When a copyright owner (your photographer) authorises another person (you) to publish their work (eg in your sales brochure), they are in effect granting a licence. This can be done orally, for example, over the telephone, though it's always sensible to get something in writing, too. Usually you need not worry too much about licences, as a licence is usually implied by your commissioning a photograph for a particular purpose. If, however, you go on to use the same photos in another publication, strictly speaking you should get another licence. It's unlikely that your photographer would actually require you to do this, though you should be aware of the possibility. If you want to be sure of avoiding any such problems, get the copyright assigned to you (in writing) when you commission the photos.

DIY photography

This chapter is about using the professionals, but inevitably you will occasionally need to take your own shots. Few DIY-ers are as good as they think they are, but here are some professionals' tips to help you sharpen your focus:

- When you look through the viewfinder, watch out for extraneous matter. Don't let stray people, litter or anything else invade your photo.
- Try to take close-ups whenever possible. Most amateur close-ups (or 'tight' shots) are better than wider shots.
- Avoid crowding too many people or too much activity into a shot. Keep it simple.

Bright idea

You can get photographic help and advice on the Internet. There is an on-line version of the magazine Practical Photography (called Image Connect). You can contact professional photographers for tips and answers to your questions. You will also find tips on getting better shots, tutorials on techniques, and where to go to find the cheapest second-hand equipment.

Using your photographic material to good effect

It is amazing to discover how many businesses spend money on getting quality photographs taken, and then never make full use of them. If you invest in good photographs, make sure they work for you. Some ideas for using your photographs include:

- *Exhibitions* Use your photographs to make up exhibition boards of your work or your products, for display in your reception and at formal exhibitions and conferences.
- *Sales presentations* Use slides to brighten up talks and sales presentations.
- *Thank yous* If you take pictures at events, it's nice to send copies to principal guests.
- *Publicity material* Use your photos in leaflets, brochures, Web sites, newsletters and annual reports.
- *Newspapers* Send appropriate photos to accompany news releases. (Make sure they are captioned, as they may get separated from your release. Newspapers prefer 8" × 6" pictures. Always send them in card-backed envelopes, as creased pictures are useless.)
- *Decoration* Mount your best photos and get them framed, for display in your reception area, meeting rooms, shops and other outlets.
- *Induction* Use slides for showing at staff training and induction sessions.

22 *You've been framed: how to make a promotional video*

A good video can be a powerful promotional and sales tool. Read on to find out what's involved in getting one made, what it will cost you, and what to watch out for.

We have all seen video nasties, those horrible home-made efforts with an out-of-focus camcorder. They are living proof that making a video involves more than picking up a video camera and pointing it. Videos take months of work and cost thousands of pounds. Some small businesses find that the time and money are worth it if they end up with a first-class sales tool, an effective promotional vehicle or a useful information film.

The advantages of video are:

- it's an excellent way of showing your product in use;
- testimonials on video are more powerful than written ones; a real person whom you can see and hear is more believable than a printed testimonial;
- you can show things in a way that would be impossible using static pictures or words, really bringing your products to life;
- it requires less effort for the audience than some forms of publicity; watching a video is easier than working through a written sales pack;
- a well-produced video can use music, voice-overs, graphics and moving pictures to create a powerful and motivating picture;
- you can use video in your reception/foyer, to promote your company to a captive audience of people waiting to be seen;

- you can use video at exhibitions and conferences as an added extra;
- you can use video to support and enliven sales presentations;
- video is still a relatively novel sales tool, so people mailed a video are more likely to watch it than if they were to receive a brochure.

The disadvantages of video are:

- the cost (production costs, duplication, packaging, etc);
- the time involved;
- the disruption to the company during filming;
- the damage to reputation that can be caused if you do a bad/unprofessional job.

Video is probably the most expensive promotional medium you are likely to use, so consider whether there is a cheaper, easier or more effective way to achieve a sale. If there is, use it.

DIY videos

If you have set your heart on a video, please don't make your own. Friends might tell you that your video of cousin Sharon's wedding was brilliant, but that does not make you a Steven Spielberg! Making a video yourself is very time-consuming, stressful, and the end product will look home-made and unprofessional. You have perhaps seen video diaries on TV and thought that you could produce your own company video. The clips used on TV are inserted into professionally produced programmes and therefore look far more slick than if you produced one that was entirely filmed on a camcorder with no professional editing. People expect company videos to be produced to the same high standards as they get daily on TV. If your efforts are amateurish, what will people think of your company?

Bright idea

A halfway house between DIY and full-blown professional is the local college. Some offer companies a chance to have a video made by students, though you are still likely to have to pay a fee to the college, albeit a smaller one than you would pay a professional.

The brief

You will need to find a production company to make your video. Prepare a brief before you set off to talk to companies. Work through the following questions; your answers will form the basis of a brief:

- Why do you want to make a video?
- How will you use the video? Where will you show it? (eg mailshot it to homes or businesses/show it at reception.)
- Who will it be aimed at? What audience?
- Is it a general promotional video, a sales video or an information one?
- What will its focus/key message be? What information will be included? (List everything that *must* be covered and anything that is desirable.)
- Where will it be filmed? How many locations?
- When do you want it ready? (It will take around four months from start of project to finish – assuming everything goes according to plan.)
- How long will it last?
- Do you need a celebrity? If so, why? Who?
- Will you require graphics? What sort? (Tables? Charts? Animation?)

Gather your responses and set them out in the form of a brief. See Figure 22.1 for an example of a sample brief.

Figure 22.1   Video brief

Cumberledge Quality Components
'Bold as Brass' promotional video

Background to Cumberledge Quality Components

Established in 1963, we are an innovative manufacturing company making top quality machine components. We have a first-class reputation in France and Germany, where we are market leaders, yet in Britain we are little known. Although we make a standard range of products similar to those produced by our competitors, we have a unique selling point. We are the only company to manufacture exclusively in brass. Although our products cost a little more (around 10 per cent), their life expectancy is 90 per cent greater. We are, therefore, much cheaper in the long run.

Reason for the video

Our sales team make cold calls to various companies. They are frequently met with little interest. When we are able to get the benefits of our product across, buyers are all too ready to place an order. The problem is that they do not respond to our mailshots or sales calls. We hope that a video will pave the way for sales visits and convey product information in an accessible way.

Audience

Buyers at factories making small machinery such as lawnmowers, sewing machines and small electrical domestic appliances.

Where will it be shown?

It will be sent to factories for viewing on-site using domestic video equipment. Product samples will be enclosed in the mailing.

Messages:

- Our components cost 10 per cent more, but last almost nine times as long.
- Although a UK company, we are market leaders in France and Germany.
- We are fully accredited and all our manufacturing exceeds the stringent UK and European standards.
- Our sales team comprises skilled people with industry experience who can offer product advice to companies.

Communication of the message

We wish to show our manufacturing plant, with its hi-tech equipment, in order to show the quality origin of the product. We also need to show the product range. In addition, we wish to convey the quality of the sales team by showing them in a training session. There will also be two interviews with satisfied UK customers.

Locations:

- our manufacturing plant in Exeter
- a satisfied customer in Bristol
- a satisfied customer in Walthamstow, London
- our sales team training centre in Camden, London

Graphics:

- visuals to illustrate the benefits of our product compared with others
- a map to show where our products are in use

Required audience response/action:

- interest in the product and excitement about the savings that could be made
- eagerness to see a sales rep and to find out more

Length

It must not exceed 10 minutes.

Required by

Our next major sales drive begins in September next year, so the videos would be required no later than mid-August. Ideally we would like delivery in early August.

Technical talk

Videos are made in different formats. VHS (which stands for video home system) is the standard domestic format. Your home video recorder will be VHS. Domestic camcorders and their smaller sisters, the palmcorders, take VHS and 8 mm tape, respectively. If you make a video on VHS or 8 mm it will lose so much quality during copying and editing that it will be unsuitable for showing; the image will be fuzzy and grainy.

The next notch up is S-VHS (or super VHS). If your budget is really restricted, choose a small, local production company and ask them to make your video on S-VHS format. Unlike VHS, S-VHS will give you acceptable quality.

One up from S-VHS is Betacam or its equivalent, the format used by broadcasters. If you can afford it, go for the better quality offered by Betacam. (£8,000–£10,000 is the going rate for a ten-minute promotional video on Betacam.)

Whatever format is used to make your video, the final film will be copied ('dumped down') on to VHS tape for use in a domestic video recorder. So just because a tape is played on VHS, it does not mean it was made on VHS equipment. The Hollywood blockbuster you hire from the local video shop will be played on your VHS recorder, but it was made on top quality film.

Choosing a production company

Always talk to several production companies. As to which companies, go by recommendation if you can. If not, try the *Yellow Pages*. A few local authorities produce a 'screen industry directory', which will list other production companies and associated services (such as companies specialising in duplication – making copies of your video). There's also an organisation – IVCA, the video industry's trade association – which produces some useful background information on producing a video. (Telephone them on 020 7512 0571.)

Look for a company that is affordable, professional and enthusiastic. Always arrange a meeting, never just book a company over the phone. Ask to see a 'show reel' (a compilation of their work) so you can see what they are capable of. Don't rely on the show reel alone, as this will contain only the best bits. Watch a few complete videos, too.

Discuss your brief, ask for their comments, thoughts and ideas.

Bright idea

Some production companies are fluent in techno-speak. If you don't understand what they are saying, don't be afraid to say so. If they can't explain it in simple terms, find a company that can.

The three stages of video-making

The three stages of making a video are:

1. *Pre-production* This involves research, preparing a story outline (or synopsis), storyboarding (a running order and detailed plan of what shots are to be filmed, where and how) and scripting.
2. *Production* This is the actual filming.
3. *Post-production* This term covers everything that happens after filming, such as off-line editing (rough editing using cheaper equipment) and the next stage, on-line editing (the final editing, carried out on top quality equipment); adding graphics, sound and voice-overs, credits and titles, etc.

The cost

Ask for a costing based on your brief. Be sure you understand what is included in the quote. You may need to find extra money, over and above your budget for the filming and editing, to pay for:

- *Music* If you intend to have music of some sort, you will need to commission an original score (which is expensive), or pay the necessary copyright and seek the necessary permission to use someone else's music (this, too, is costly). Alternatively, you can use a copyright-free recording. Copyright-free music can be a bit tacky and muzaky, but it is a low-budget option. Your production company can advise you on copyright, commissioning, etc. (Never use music without the necessary permission: if you are caught, you will be heavily fined and your video will be grounded.)
- *Packaging* The cover design on the video case will probably not be included as part of the fee, so you will need to budget separately for its design, printing and finishing. Also, don't forget the labels that stick to the face and the spine of the video. These, too, will need to be designed and printed.
- *A celebrity* The price you are quoted should include the cost of a voice-over (but always check). If you want to use a celebrity, that will be extra. See below for advice on this.
- *Subtitles and signing* You might decide to make your video as accessible as possible by adding subtitles and/or a signer (for deaf viewers). If your video is one to promote hearing aids, perhaps subtitles are essential. This adds significantly to costs and it will lengthen your production time scale.
- *Duplication* You will want more than one copy of your video, and each extra will cost you anything between £1 and £10. Your production company can arrange this for you, though you may find it cheaper to arrange your own duplication by ringing around.

- *Support material*   It is likely that you will want to produce something to accompany your video; it could just be a covering letter and order form, or perhaps a more expensive catalogue or brochure. Build this into your costs.
- *Contingency*   What happens if one of your key interviewees falls ill on the day of the shoot, or your essential outdoor shot is rained off? You'll need to build in a contingency of 10 per cent just in case.
- *The mailing*   If your video is being direct-mailed (see Chapter 16) remember to budget for post and packaging, plus the other direct mail costs.

It is as well that you are aware of these extras from the start so that you don't run out of money for unexpected additional items.

Bright idea

It's a good idea to get consent, preferably in writing, from anyone who is going to appear in your video. It has been known for people to come back at a later date arguing that they didn't know what you were planning to do with the film, or that you misled them. The consent form should outline what the footage is being used for, so that you are fully covered.

The contract

Your chosen production company will issue you with a contract; read it very carefully before signing. If it contains clauses you are unhappy about discuss them and renegotiate if necessary. Agree in writing what their quote includes and what it doesn't. When you accept a quote, your acceptance letter should stipulate that any additional costs must be agreed in writing before go-ahead. Payment terms also need to be spelt out (for example, half the fees payable on completion of filming and the balance on delivery of the video).

Bright idea

Ensure you are the copyright holder of your video; get it in writing when you agree a contract. If you don't, copyright will remain with the production company. They will also retain copyright to all footage (known as 'rushes') shot for, though not necessarily used in, your film. Get this copyright too, or you might find your material popping up in someone else's video.

Build into the contract a penalty for delays. This is particularly important if you need the video for a particular date – perhaps in time for a product launch. Find out about arrangements your production company has in place to avoid delays caused by staff being sick or essential equipment being stolen or breaking down.

Bright idea

Check that you are not responsible if your production company's equipment is stolen or damaged on location.

Stars on screen

You can (if your pocket is big enough) use a famous face to front your film. The right celebrity can inject a bit of oomph, give you added credibility, and serve as a subtle endorsement. Select a suitable celebrity. A video for your mail order gourmet food company would gain from being presented by a top chef, famous foodie or well-known restaurateur. Your interior design franchise would benefit from having someone like Lawrence Llewelyn-Bowen to front it. Ensure that your chosen star is skilled at this game; sounding natural when reading from an autocue is not a talent everyone has.

Your production company may be able to advise you on celebrities and locate one for you. Alternatively, contact celebrities through their agents or through one of the many companies specialising in famous people. Debrett's *People of Today* CD ROM will help you pinpoint the right celebrity. For example, if you want a TV personality who likes golf, no problem. The five-minute search will throw up various names. Always get a contract so that your celebrity can't suddenly pull out if a better offer comes along.

Length

Most companies start off with a 30-minute video in mind, perhaps because this is the length of many TV programmes. Yet most promotional videos are between 5 and 15 minutes. Deciding how you are going to use the video will help you settle on the length. A video for your reception should be very brief, as people will pass through fairly quickly. Something to be mailshotted to people's homes can be a little longer.

> ### *Bright idea*
> *Assign someone from your company to accompany your production crew on filming days. You or your staff will have a better idea of what you are looking for, and will be on hand to provide guidance, check that everything is going smoothly and to sort out any problems.*

Promoting your video

Given the cost of making a video, you must justify the expense by making full use of it. Get it working for you if you want to see a return on that investment. Show it at every opportunity. Send out copies to key customers. Publicise it through a news release to your trade press. Have a write-up in your customer newsletter. Know up-front how you will make full use of it and be ready to put your plans into action as soon as you receive delivery of your completed videos.

23 *Absolutely fabulous: how to choose and use a PR consultant*

If you are interested in bringing in consultants to help you with your PR, this chapter is a must. It could help prevent you making costly mistakes or getting ripped off, and will show you how to develop a successful relationship with a consultancy.

Before you speak to any PR consultants, be clear about why you need them. What do you hope to achieve? Would it be better to appoint someone in-house, perhaps even in a temporary or part-time post? If you are certain that you would benefit from using a consultant, write a brief which sets out your objectives, and circulate it to three or four PR consultants. If you can, approach consultancies recommended to you by people or companies you trust. Alternatively, use the Institute of Public Relations' PR Matchmaker Service (the IPR is the professional body representing PR consultants – Tel. 020 7253 5151 or www.ipr.org.uk). It will provide you with details of those in your area who specialise in your field. The IPR's register of members is organised according to specialisation and location. There is a small charge for the service, but it is free to IPR members.

True story

I was looking for a PR agency to award a contract to. I rang a few to ask for their brochure and client list and most were happy to oblige. One, however, quizzed me on why I wanted a brochure, demanded to know who I was, and was generally unhelpful and unfriendly. How could I ask a company to do my PR when they were clearly incapable of doing their own? Although they never knew it, that telephone conversation lost them the chance of £20,000 worth of business.

Try to select a consultancy that already works for a small business, or has done so in the past. Big companies usually have bigger budgets; if your consultancy is used to working for the 'big boys' they may have trouble adjusting their thinking to your scale of work.

Bright idea

Using a freelance PR consultant may be much cheaper than an agency. They will have much lower overheads and are more likely to be able to be flexible. The drawback, however, is that they will not have the backing of an organisation and colleagues to fall back on if they are sick or on holiday. Some freelance consultants work with associates; this can give you the best of both worlds.

What does a PR brief look like? The brief in Figure 23.1 covers the sorts of thing you should include in yours.

Once you have selected your prospective consultants (your shortlist is known as a 'pitch list') and issued them with the brief, set a deadline and then ask them in to do a presentation to you on how they would approach your assignment and what ideas they have. Get them to bring to the presentation a document setting out their approach and detailing their costs. Alternatively, go to their premises for the presentation; it's more time-consuming, but you get a better idea of who you will be doing business with. You do not have to pay a consultancy to do a pitch presentation; they will not expect you to. There is debate within the PR industry about whether consultancies should charge, but this has been going on for years and looks unlikely to be resolved. (Consultancies in Ireland, however, will charge you. The Public Relations Consultants Association Ireland members – representing 90 per cent of the consultancy business – now charge for 'creative proposals', unless they get the business, although they do not charge for credentials presentations.)

You can decide after the presentations whom you want to use, or whittle down your list and receive a further presentation from the best of the bunch. This will give you a chance to digest what you were told last time, and to ask any questions that have since occurred to you. Alternatively, if you are unhappy with all those you have seen, draw up a new pitch list and start again.

When assessing the performance of prospective consultants, ask yourself:

- Did they fulfil the requirements of the brief in their tender documents?
- Was their presentation confident?
- Did they come up with good ideas?
- Did they seem to understand what we are about?
- Did they handle questions well?
- Do I feel, from what I have seen, that I have confidence in them?

In addition to telling your prospective consultants about yourself, you need to know about them. Ask them:

- What experience they have of working for companies similar to your own. Ask for names of clients and details of projects. Don't hesitate to take up references.
- What knowledge and understanding they have of your business sector. If none of your consultants knows much about your field, ask them how they would go about building up their expertise.
- Who will be working on your account. Ask for their CVs, so you can be sure of their experience. (The people who present to you are generally not those who will be carrying out the work day to day.)
- How many staff they have.
- How long they have been established.
- What other clients they work for.
- Are the consultants who would work on your account members of the Institute of Public Relations (IPR)? How long have they been members?
- How they would evaluate the success of the work they carry out for you.
- Has the consultancy won any awards, such as the IPR's Sword of Excellence?

Don't be impressed if a consultancy says that it is a member of the Public Relations Consultancies' Association; this is a trade body set up to represent the interests of its members.

When deciding whom to use, you should obviously pick a competent consultancy, one you have faith in. But cost will be an important factor too. When you are quoted costs for PR consultancy, ask:

- Does this include VAT?
- What do you charge for photocopying, paper, faxes, etc? Are these charged at cost price? (Some consultancies charge exorbitant sums for stationery and administration, so be careful that you are not ripped off in this way.)
- Do you operate a mark-up system when you buy in services such as print or design? If so, what do you mark up by? (Most PR consultancies, if they use a designer, printer or photographer to do work for you, will add anything upwards of 17 per cent to the bill. If your consultancy marks up,

organise your own printers, etc if you want to save money and stretch your budget further.)
- What are your hourly rates? (Some consultancies operate an hourly or daily rate, but others charge a retainer. This is a flat monthly fee which you must pay whether or not you make use of your consultant. Retainers are normally charged for ongoing support, but a set rate, agreed in advance, will be charged for a project.)
- Do you charge time for travel?
- How do you account for expenditure? Do you issue itemised bills and timesheets?

Most consultancies will ask you what your PR budget is, and you will certainly need to have decided this internally. Whether you choose to share this information with a prospective consultant is up to you, although you will need to give them approximate guidelines to enable them to tailor their proposals to your likely budget.

Figure 23.1   PR brief

VIKING INSULATION: BRIEF FOR PUBLIC RELATIONS SUPPORT

About us
Viking was formed in 1989; turnover is £10 million. We manufacture insulation products such as pipe lagging, roof insulation and wall insulation. All our sales are direct to the trade; we do not deal with the consumer market. There are some very big, successful competitors in our field; indeed we are the smallest player. However, this gives us an edge in that we can be more flexible than our bigger competitors. We can, for example, tailor deliveries of our insulation products to the needs of the contractor, unlike our competitors. People who use us say that we are much friendlier and much more helpful than our rivals. The problem is that the majority of contractors do not know about us, or do not want to risk trying a new supplier.

Our PR objectives
We are seeking to appoint a PR consultant, initially for nine months, who can work with us to:

1. Raise our profile in the building/construction trade. We have carried out awareness research, which shows that just 10 per cent of our sector is aware of the company and its range of products. We aim to increase awareness to 70 per cent by the end of the year. We would expect our consultant to suggest ways of achieving this.
2. Publicise our customer-friendly approach, and the range of unique benefits we offer customers, such as multiple drops, split deliveries and telephone ordering.

3. Publicise our product range. The few contractors who know about us are not aware of the wide range of our products. We need to get this information across to our target audience. We would expect this to be done in a variety of ways, including through editorial in the trade press. We would expect to have had positive mentions in all our key trade papers by the end of the initial contract.

Following an assessment and evaluation after nine months, we may decide, budget permitting, to extend the contract. Ideally we are looking for a long-term relationship with a consultant.

Our budget
We envisage spending between £500 and £1,000 per month on fees, and have an additional £4,000 for design, print, photography and other publicity costs.

Working with consultants

Once you have selected a consultancy, make sure that you get the best out of it. For the relationship to work, your consultancy will need to have clear guidelines from you on what they can and can't do, and you will need to agree a work plan with them, with time scales and budgets.

Regular meetings are a must. Keep them informed and ensure they brief you on the work they have carried out to date. Most will provide you with a 'contact report' after each meeting. Rather like minutes, this will set out in note form what was agreed and who is to do it.

True story

A very large retail company looking for PR support was invited to the offices of one of the PR consultancies pitching for this lucrative account. The receptionist ignored the company directors for several minutes while she finished a telephone call to a friend. They were then kept waiting for a further 30 minutes by the PR consultants. Finally, when they were on the verge of leaving in disgust, the consultants asked them through to the meeting room. 'We decided to treat you the way you treat your customers, just so you know how they feel,' said one of the PR people. 'Use us and we'll help you tackle your poor customer care and your bad image.' They won the account! Good PR professionals will help you see things through clients' eyes.

If you enter into a long-term contract with a consultant, meet after six months specifically to review the work and check that you are happy with them and that everything is on target. Many consultants organise such review meetings as a matter of course, and may even ask you to complete a client satisfaction questionnaire at this stage. If yours does not, why not suggest that they do?

Never sign a contract with a consultancy that will commit you to them for more than a year, and always ensure that anything you do sign has a get-out clause, enabling you to terminate the contract, with due notice. Remember that PR is a buyer's market and there will always be consultants out there eager to help you, so do not remain with an agency if you are unhappy with them. Discuss the problems, and if they cannot be resolved, go elsewhere.

Having found a consultancy you are happy with, it generally makes sense to stick with them. The longer you use them, the more they will come to know and understand your work. There is, though, always the danger that they will become complacent, and for this reason, you might decide to ask them to take part in a competitive re-pitch for your account every three years. Many companies and public bodies employ this practice with their consultants to keep them on their toes and to ensure that they are getting the best deal.

Although your consultant is a supplier and not an employee, remember that they need to know what you are up to, just as a member of staff would. Tell them when your office is shutting down for a holiday, tell them if a new director or senior member of staff is to be appointed, tell them if you are planning something major or you have won an important new customer, and get them on your regular mailing list. If you want to ensure that you get the best out of your consultants, keep them informed. They can't come up with ideas for you if you don't tell them your plans. Make sure, too, that they keep you in the picture, particularly where your budget is concerned. If you have a set PR budget, ask your consultants to let you know when half of it is spent, and to give you a countdown as it runs out. If they don't, you may suddenly find that the budget is gone and you're only halfway through the year.

24 *Designs on you: getting the most from a designer*

Most small businesses will use a graphic designer at some stage, even if it is just for their letterhead. However often you use them, make sure you get the very best from them. This involves understanding how they work and what they need from you.

The first thing many worry about when considering a designer is cost. Thankfully, using a designer need not mean using an expensive design studio. There are many talented freelance designers who can do an excellent job on a very limited budget. The problem is finding them! I have come across some real cowboys masquerading as designers.

Finding your ideal designer

Not all designers are the same, even if they have received identical training from the same college. Some have limited creativity and a very set style of work, others are capable of great variation and have tackled wide-ranging assignments. A good way to find a designer is by recommendation, so if you have never used one before, ask your contacts if they can give you some names. Look through other (non-competing) nearby companies' promotional material, and if any look really good, get in touch and ask them who did the design work. (Some designers will put their name on their work, usually in very small print on the back of a leaflet or brochure, so try looking there first.) If all this fails, the *Yellow Pages* always provides a last resort, although you are only likely to find design consultancies advertising there; most freelance designers will not be listed.

Visit several designers (or get them to visit you) and ask to see samples of their work. Look for variety; if everything they show you looks too similar in style, you are probably in the company of a designer with little imagination. Ask about costs for the samples shown (of both design and print). See how good they can make low budget publicity look. Ask to see their two-colour work; that's the real test of their ability.

Also check for reliability; your chosen designer might be very talented, but if they are unreliable, you could be in for problems. Get references if you are unsure – talk to their clients and ask whether they are good at meeting deadlines. A designer I was using disappeared to New York for two weeks in the middle of a job! Needless to say, my client was less than pleased.

Once you select a designer, explain what your business does, what sort of promotional material you have produced in the past and what you thought of it (give copies to your designer), and what you are expecting from this assignment.

Briefing designers

Even a great designer will not produce a good job for you if they are given a lousy brief. Spending time talking to your designer will pay off in the end. For any design job you will need to supply some of the following information. How much you specify depends on how many decisions you are happy to allow your designer to make. If you are unsure, defer to the designer.

- *Colours* How many colours do you want to use? (The more colours, the higher the cost for design and print.) What colours? What about tints (see Appendix 1 for a definition)?
- *Copy* How much copy (text) will there be? (How many words?) Which bits of copy need to be placed where? If you have already written the copy, let the designer see it.
- *Size* How many pages do you want your finished document to be? (An A4 document is produced by folding A3 sheets, so remember that pages go up in multiples of four, ie if you planned on a 12-page document, but you now need to lengthen it, you must opt for 16 pages.) What size of page?
- *Folding* Will your leaflet be folded? If so, what type of fold? (There are many different ways of folding paper and some, such as 'staggered concertinas', to use a technical term, are more expensive to carry out and more complicated to design to than traditional folds such as gatefolds.

Your designer will show you different types of folds and explain the pros and cons.)

- *Visuals* How many visuals do you plan to use? Where do you want them placed? What type of visuals – photos, illustrations, charts, tables, cartoons? Who will provide them – you or the designer? (Using a picture library will cost you money, so if you have good photographs, use them.) The more charts and illustrations you ask your designer to originate, the bigger the bill you will receive for the work – illustration is much more time-consuming than straightforward page layout. Also you will need to check that your graphic designer has the ability to produce an illustration.
- *Guidelines* How much freedom does the designer have? Even if it's a lot, also give a few guidelines or some sort of briefing. Be clear on where the designer can make decisions, and where you want to have a say.
- *'Look'* What is the style or 'look' of your publicity material? Do you want something expensive-looking, with quality paper and classy illustrations, or a cheap and cheerful affair?
- *Function* What is the function of your publicity material? A poster that needs to be seen at a distance? A sales brochure that will be skimmed? A business report that will be read cover to cover?
- *Audience* Who will read your material? Children? Professionals? Young people? Pensioners? The intended audience will influence the design.
- *Paper* Decide the type of paper you want. Do you want a textured paper, a recycled one, something that is transparent or has a special coating? A decision will also need to be taken on the paper's weight. (Paper is described according to its weight in grams per square metre, or 'gsm'. Letterheads are normally around 100 gsm and magazine covers are generally 220 gsm to 250 gsm.) The colour of paper must be selected from a large variety. Your designer should be able to advise you on all of these, show you samples, and give you a rough idea of price.
- *Type* What typeface would you like? (Ask to see samples.) And what point size (size of type)? Do you want the type to be right-hand justified or unjustified? (In other words, do you want the text to have a ragged edge on the right-hand side, or to have a straight right-hand margin, as with your left-hand margin?) Do you want columns of text, as in newspapers? If so, how many? What 'weight' of type? Bold or normal, for example.
- *Special effects* A wide range of special effects is available to 'lift' your design. For example, gold embossing, blind embossing, varnishing, laminating and die cutting. Ask your designer what these are and how much they will add to the bill if you decide to use any of them.

Your designer should offer you guidance on the above points, and indeed you are paying for their best advice on technical matters such as paper and typefaces, so they should be recommending materials and styles that will be appropriate for the job. If they are not good at advising, and you are unclear about your own ideas, find another. In any case, it's always worth talking to two or three designers to get different perspectives and different quotes for the work. However, having found a good and affordable designer, you might wish to stick with them, particularly if they begin to build up an understanding of your work, a knowledge of your likes and dislikes, and a keen idea of the image you are looking for.

Bright idea

If you opt for a heavier paper for your publicity, it may affect the postage you have to pay when you mail it, thus pushing up your overall costs in a way you have not budgeted for.

Agree a fee and time scale before you proceed and get it in writing. It will be your only comeback if things begin to slip.

Fonts

There are thousands of different typefaces or 'fonts'. Thanks to clever computer technology, typefaces can now be manipulated to create new fonts. Here are just a few, to show the wide variety:

Times New Roman and TIMES NEW ROMAN
Courier and COURIER
Caslon Open Face and CASLON OPEN FACE
Gill Sans Serif and GILL SANS SERIF
Rockwell and ROCKWELL

Many designers like to play around with fonts. Allow them to use an original typeface by all means (as long as it is easy on the eye) but don't allow their creativity to stand in the way of clear and readable publicity. Ideally you want something that is both eye-catching and readable. A good designer should be able to provide this.

In addition to a great range of fonts, there are also many different point sizes (or sizes of typeface). The main text in this book is point size 10½ (including this sentence).

This is point size 20.

This is 30.

The good design checklist

Design is a matter of taste but you can apply some objective criteria as a check that the design work you have commissioned is appropriate:

- It should appeal to the target audience.
- The text should be easy to read and to follow, guiding your reader and highlighting the key points.
- The illustrations (cartoons, photos and drawings) should be appropriate for the audience.
- It should enhance your image.
- Your logo should appear on it.
- It should not appear too cramped or crowded.
- Neither should it be too blank or sparse.
- It should be well executed and neat/tidy.
- It should be appropriate for the use to which it will be put.
- It should make imaginative use of the colours available (this is particularly important if you have just one or two colours).

If you have chosen a competent designer and provided a good brief, your artwork should fit the bill. Sadly, though, not all artwork lives up to expectations, and it is helpful to be able to identify why the design doesn't work.

Spotting design faults

You would think that spotting bad design would be easy, for it would look terrible. The trouble is that much bad design actually looks really good; what makes it poor is that it is either inappropriate for the audience or for the use to which it is to be put.

Never go for a design just because *you* like it; always choose a style that will appeal to the audience the publicity material is aimed at. So a psychedelic leaflet with a 3D cover may not be appropriate for a special afternoon tea promotion aimed at the over-60s. Equally, traditional design may not be the best choice for the trendiest nightclub in town. So design that looks good is only part of the picture, it must be appropriate too.

Six common design faults

1. Text that is difficult to follow because of the way it has been laid out – it lacks a visual eye path to direct the reader.
2. Material that is hard to read owing to small print or clashing colours which make the text 'dance' before your eyes.

3. Material that is not very user-friendly because text has been superimposed over an illustration.
4. Material that fails to use typographical tricks to catch the readers' attention such as call-outs, boxes and bullet points.
5. A document that looks wrong for the purpose, such as a serious annual report that looks like a cheap newsletter, or a free brochure that looks so glossy that people are afraid to take one.
6. Design work that uses graphic devices to highlight words or phrases that are not the most important or interesting bits – your design should ensure that the best bits leap out from the page, so that if these alone are read, the reader will have picked up the key information.

Using illustrators

Graphic designers work mainly at computers, designing their work on an Apple Mac screen. They are good at planning page layouts, typesetting and working with text and typography. Some can also draw. However, for complicated illustration, it is best to use a professional illustrator. They might work with a computer, too, or use paints, brushes, pastels, collage and other techniques to achieve the right look. You might use an illustrator to:

● help with package design (labels, boxes, bags and packets);
● illustrate a report cover (perhaps for a really important report such as your annual report);
● design your company Christmas cards.

Some designers are good at illustration, but check first and ask to see their portfolio. You may need to use an illustrator and a graphic designer; often designers will recommend illustrators to you.

Working well together

When you take your copy to a designer, make sure that you deliver final copy. Be absolutely confident that what you hand across to the designer is, word for word, what you want to see in print. Too many people give their designer some text, see the designed version, then decide to rewrite it! It happens all too often, creating:

● *Frustration* It is very annoying for a designer to have to spend time keying in your text amendments, which may affect the design and create extra work.

- *Mistakes*   Once you start altering text that has already gone to a designer, you are relying on someone else to key in that amended text accurately. It is very easy for errors to creep in when you do this.
- *Increased costs*   The extra time spent keying in text and possibly fiddling about with the knock-on design complications will result in a bigger bill for you. Designers will charge for what are termed 'editors' corrections'.
- *Delays*   Obviously all of the above takes time, time which will not have been planned for. This will result in a delay.

In practice there is no problem in changing the odd word or two during design, but try as far as possible to deliver final text. If you start rewriting at this stage, you are asking for trouble.

Take your final text to your designer on disk (having first checked that your computer and theirs are compatible). Most businesses use PCs, and most designers use Apple Macs. While the two are not compatible, most designers will have conversion software to enable them to read your disk. Be sure to give them a hard copy as well, so they can check what's on their screen against what you have given them, for it has been known for chunks of text to disappear during conversion. The hard copy will allow them to scan it, should there be difficulties during the conversion. The benefit of supplying text on disk is that you do away with the need for retyping, and can thus avoid typing errors appearing. Make a second hard copy, but annotate this with instructions. Mark out which headings are main headings and which are just subheadings. Indicate which photos go where. Give as much guidance as possible on this annotated version.

Checking page proofs

Once the design is ready, you will be given a 'dummy' or some page proofs. If they are in colour, they will have been printed on a computer printer, not a printing press. This means that colours shown are for guidance only. They are not a true match. Sometimes colours appear far more vivid than the real thing will be. Ask to see the pantone match if you want an accurate indication of colours. Photos shown on page proofs will be produced using a low resolution scan and may look grainy and unclear. However, they will be properly reproduced for the printer. You will just have to take your designer's word for this.

As well as checking colours, check text and other details very carefully. Some designers do not pay enough attention to detail, failing to check their work before preparing a proof for the client. Even if you supply word perfect copy, it is easy for mistakes to appear in your artwork. In particular:

- Check your original text against the designed version. I have come across cases where a designer has somehow lost a whole section. Don't skim-read, read every word, every punctuation mark.

- Check that each bit of text is given the right emphasis – make sure that main headings appear as main headings, subheadings as subheadings, and so on. Your designer may not know what is meant to be a main or subheading, so it is easy for this to be wrong.
- Check maps and diagrams to ensure they are correct.
- Double-check figures, telephone numbers, page numbers, and so on.
- Ensure consistency of fonts, point sizes, etc.
- Look out for awkward line breaks, page breaks or word breaks. For example, if a word needs to be split between two lines, make sure the break is well placed – 'under[break]spend' is better than 'unde[break]rspend'.
- Pay particular attention to captions; unlike your body copy, captions are usually keyed in by designers, so it is possible for there to be spelling or punctuation errors here.
- Check that the right photo appears with the right caption – it is so easy for these to get mixed up.

The importance of checking artwork cannot be overemphasized. Any uncorrected errors at this stage will appear in the printed version. The fact that you handed over perfect copy will not guarantee that what you get back is error free. Once you sign off the artwork, the designer is no longer responsible for the errors. You are deemed to have checked and approved their work. When you have signed off the artwork, your designer may produce a 'cromalin' proof (depending on their facilities). This is a proof produced on photographic paper, which shows everything in accurate colours. You can make changes at this stage, but they will be costly. The cromalin proofs will then go off to the printer and plates will be made.

Have a go yourself

Put your proofreading skills to the test (see Figure 24.1). Circle all of the errors in the following piece of copy. Then go back and correct them.

Figure 24.1   Proofreading test

Proofreading made easy

Its not difficult to proof read, though it does take time, patience and an eagle eye. All to often misstakes are made. Some-times a word missed out. Or maybe a necesary peice of text is omited. You're job as proof-reader is is too spot mistakes and insure they are correctted. you must also look out for words that are mispelled. Frequently words like   accomodation, publically, vaccuum and goverment are spelt wrongly. Every libary has a supply of good dictionary, so theres no excuse. Every company should aim for excelence in it's publicity. Instal appropriat systems to gaurd against the likelyhood of of errors.

See how well you did by looking at the answers at the end of the chapter. There were 32 errors. If you missed anything, or got it wrong, you will need to brush up your proofreading skills. Remember that mistakes in your materials could cost you money or your reputation.

Copyright

When you commission a designer or illustrator, you might imagine that the work they produce belongs to you. It does not. So if you are entering into a contract with a designer, ensure you get them to assign the copyright to you. Simply write to them stating that in accepting the commission they are assigning copyright to you. If a designer objects to such a clause, don't use them. After all, why shouldn't you own what you have paid for? One good reason for ensuring you have the copyright is that you are covered in the event of a falling-out. Suppose you commission a designer to do a regular customer newsletter for you. A year later you have a major disagreement and find that you can no longer work together. You decide to use a new designer for your regular newsletter, but you don't want a new look. You like the newsletter's styling and want to retain it. If you do not have copyright on the design, your former designer could – in theory – prevent you from using it. Spare yourself possible hassle by getting copyright up front.

True story

I know of an organisation that failed to secure the copyright of its logo. Now it has to ask a design company for permission every time it wants to use the logo in some new way. Don't ever make this mistake.

Proofreading test – answers

The text from the test on page 323 is reproduced below. Mistakes are in bold, with the correction alongside in square brackets. How did you do? Not such a good proofreader as you thought?

Figure 24.2   Proofreading test (answers)

Proofreading made easy

Its [It's] not difficult to **proof read** [proofread], though it does take time, patience and an eagle eye. All **to** [too] often **misstakes** [mistakes] are made. **Some-times** [Sometimes] a word **[is]** missed out. Or maybe a **necesary** [necessary] **peice** [piece] of text is **omited** [omitted]. **You're** [Your] job as **proof-reader** [proofreader] is **is** [delete] **too** [to] spot mistakes and **insure** [ensure] they are **correctted** [corrected]. **you** [You] must also look out for words that are **mispelled** [misspelled]. Frequently words **like** [too many spaces after this word] **accomodation** [accommodation], **publically** [publicly], **vaccuum** [vacuum] and **goverment** [government] are spelt wrongly. Every **libary** [library] has a supply of good **dictionary** [dictionaries], so **theres** [there's] no excuse. Every company should aim for **excelence** [excellence] in **it's** [its] publicity. **Instal** [Install] **appropriat** [appropriate] systems to **gaurd** [guard] against the **like-lyhood** [likelihood] of **of** [delete] errors.

25

Getting into print: finding the best deal from a printer

This chapter will show you step by step how to choose a printer, put together a specification, secure competitive quotes, and ensure a quality finished product is delivered to you on time at an affordable price.

Every small business will need to use a printer at some stage. The first contact with printers is usually for start-up letterheads and business cards, with many businesses sticking with the same printing firm thereafter. Does this sound like you? Then you are probably not making the best use of your printing budget. The only way to make it stretch further is to shop around, using your basic knowledge of print production and print jargon. You can then make the best print and design decisions, ask the right questions of prospective printers, and secure the best price deal.

Bright idea

Gain an understanding of print production by visiting a printshop. Look at the machinery, and ask lots of questions. Most printers will be more than happy to give a prospective customer a guided tour. If you phone and are told it is not possible, perhaps that's a good indication that your chosen printer is not a terribly flexible, friendly and accommodating person. Do you really want to do business with someone like that?

A beginner's guide to print

When you want something printed, you take your artwork to a printer. If your artwork has been produced by a designer, it will be in 'camera-ready' form, or even 'film'. If it is camera-ready, it means that it is ready to be photographed by the printer and turned into film. Printing plates are made from this film.

If it is already on film, it has been taken a stage further by your designer, thus saving your printer a job. (When seeking quotes from printers, ensure they know in what form the artwork is arriving, as this will affect the cost.)

If you produce the artwork yourself in-house using DTP, you will probably have text and photos, though the printer will need to screen photos and prepare your artwork.

If you have raw text that has not been laid out (because you have not used a designer, and cannot do layout in-house), your printer will need to typeset your text and do some basic layout for you. Some printers have an in-house designer, and often this can work out a lot cheaper for clients than using a conventional design studio. If you are using a printer's own designer, read Chapter 24 and ensure that you are happy with what they can offer. Many printers do not have their own designer, but they will still offer you some basic layout assistance. The quality of this is variable, so do ask to see some examples first. Remember that designing and printing are two very different professions, so a good printer is unlikely to be a good designer too.

Once the printing plates are made and the machines set up, your job is ready to be printed. Some machines will print both sides of your paper at the same time; some will print several pages at once on one large sheet, cutting and collating them afterwards; some machines will print two or more colours at one time. Many printing machines require the paper to be run through again in order to print the reverse side or to add other colours. Find out what sort of machines your printer has, and what the pros and cons of this are for your particular print job.

Once the printing is over, your work will be cut and trimmed. If required, it will be folded, stitched or stapled. All of this is known as 'finishing'. It will then be boxed and delivered to you. Unless you ask for the plates to be retained (because you may need a future reprint) they will be scrapped.

How to choose a printer

Go for the right balance between price, quality and service. Never just open *Yellow Pages*, select a local printer, and book them for your job – unless you have money to waste. Choose a printer that can do a good job for you at a competitive price.

Bright idea

If you use a printer often, you should be able to negotiate a special rate or discount. Even if you are just an occasional user, consider joining forces with other small businesses in your area to see if together you can get a bulk deal. And remember that high price does not always mean high quality.

Some printers are cheaper for some items than others. One might be competitive for two-colour work but expensive for full colour. One might be great at letterheads but unable to meet the quality required for glossy brochures. Some can do small runs cheaply, while others will be more competitive for large runs. It all depends on the machinery they have and its suitability for your print job. That is why shopping around for every print job is a good idea. Your cheap letterhead printer may not be cheap for other print jobs.

Ask each printer what sort of work they specialise in. Get them to supply samples of material they have printed recently. (What they send you will be the best they have – not all their work will be that good.) Quality does vary enormously, especially when it comes to colour printing. Look at samples supplied:

- What is the overall quality like?
- What about the quality of colour reproduction? Are colours clear and true? For example, does the grass look the right shade of green?
- What about finishing? Is the work folded and stapled neatly? Are the pages cut square?

If the samples you are sent look scrappy, don't use the printer.

Many larger printers have a sales rep who will visit you, show you samples and explain what services are available. If you decide to go ahead with a job, your rep will be your contact point. They should keep you in touch with the job and how it is going. A good rep will get in touch afterwards to check that everything is OK and that you are satisfied with the work.

Bright idea

Always involve several people in proofreading your copy before it goes to the printer. At least one of them should never have seen the copy before, thus making them more likely to spot errors.

Getting quotes

Printers' prices vary enormously, so always shop around and get at least three quotations. Let your printers know that you are seeking other quotes, so that they come back to you with a more competitive price than they might otherwise offer. Small, local printers are generally cheaper than the high street quick-print shops. However, the high street places are often more user-friendly which is a bonus if you are new to the game.

Bright idea

If you are asking your printer to get your work typeset for you, see if you can supply text on disk in order to save the cost of retyping. Check first that your disk/software is compatible with your typesetter's.

Give a written specification to each printer, so that you can compare like with like. Check that your quotations include extras such as folding, finishing and delivery.

When getting quotes from printers you will need to tell them:

- *Print run* How many copies you need. A run-on (extra copies done at the same time) is much cheaper than a reprint (extra copies done at a later date), so if you are in doubt about how many you need, opt for a few extra, as this could save you considerable money in the long run. It is not economical to get small amounts (generally under 400) printed; high quality photocopying might be a better option.
- *Colours* For the inks (if you are unsure, ask to see the Pantone book – see Appendix 1 under 'Design and print jargon' for an explanation) and the paper (ask your printer to show you samples).
- *Paper* The type, weight, size (see below) and colour.
- *Size* Of paper and document (dimensions of page and number of pages – also known as 'extent').
- *Special* Any special finishes such as varnishing, embossing or laminating (if you don't know what these are, ask your printer to show you examples).
- *Other* Other requirements, such as finishing (folding and stitching, for example), delivery, VAT.
- *Delivery* A delivery date and delivery address will be required.

Cost and the factors affecting it

Some cost factors are obvious. Full colour printing, for example, is much more costly than just one or two colours. Having your documents folded or stitched will add to the cost too. There is, though, a less obvious factor that can seriously affect price. Let's say you are having a 16-page sales catalogue printed. It might be that 16 pages exactly fit a particular printing press, thus making best use of the machine's capabilities and minimising your costs. If you decide to up the number of pages to 20 (ie a 25 per cent increase), it could end up costing you double. The extra four pages would need to go on to a new plate and be run through the machine separately. Sometimes, asking for a page size just a few millimetres larger can add hugely to your print costs. Discuss any potential cost implications with your printer.

Bright idea

If you plan to have material printed in three colours, check it out with the printer first. Most printing presses are two-colour or four-colour. It might cost you very little extra to up the job to full colour.

Paper

Paper comes in different *sizes*. A0 is the largest standard size sheet, measuring 841 mm × 1,189 mm. A5 is the smallest, measuring 148 mm × 210 mm. Each 'A' size is derived by halving the size immediately above it. A5, therefore, is half the size of A4 (most letterheads are A4). A four-page A5 leaflet can be created by folding one sheet of A4. A four-page A4 newsletter can be created by folding an A3 sheet.

Paper also comes in different *weights*. The weight of a paper is denoted by 'gsm' or 'g/m²'. This stands for grams per square metre. Paper weighing 60 gsm will be very flimsy. Your letterhead is probably printed on 90 or 100 gsm. Your printer will want to know what weight you want your paper, and you should ask to see samples of the various weights. Obviously the heavier the paper, the greater the cost.

As well as size and weight, you also need to consider *type*. Papers come in a range of different types, from basic and cheap newsprint (used for printing newspapers) to expensive luxury handmade paper. Most if not all of your printing will be on a 'coated' paper known as art paper (which has a glossy finish) or matt art (which does not). Printers have a ready supply of white art papers, but if you want to use an unusual paper (eg a particular colour, or a paper that is textured) your printer will need to order it in. You will need to allow them time to place an order and get delivery of anything not in stock.

True story

A director was given sight of the final artwork for the company's annual report, to approve it before printing. Not knowing what 'final artwork' meant, he believed it was his final chance to influence the design, so he scribbled over it with comments. These were duly reproduced by the printer, and delivered a week later – all 5,000 annotated copies!

Briefing a printer

If you are using a designer to get your material produced, they may offer to deal with the printer for you, which can be useful. Your designer will produce a detailed print specification for your printer. Ask if they will add a mark-up to their bill for doing this. Some designers include a quote for print as part of their estimate for the whole job. They then pay the printing costs and invoice you for design and print, and while this all sounds very straightforward, it can work out more expensive. It is standard practice for designers (and PR consultants) to add an extra 17 per cent or more to printing costs, so be clear on this before you go ahead, and if necessary do your own print buying. It can save you a fortune if you know what you are doing.

If you have given the printer a good specification at the outset (on which he based his quote for the work), there is little more you need to do. Just confirm quantity, paper and so on (see above). If your specification has changed since the quotation, make sure you point this out very explicitly to the printer. Agree a timetable for the job and confirm this in writing. (Printers are not always too great at meeting deadlines; if yours is set out in writing, at least you have some comeback should delays cause you problems.)

Now sit back and await the finished product.

26 *Using a market research consultancy*

You can do marketing research in-house, but there are occasions when it is preferable, for a variety of reasons, to engage an outsider to undertake research for you. This chapter will show you how to select a market research consultancy, how to brief them, and how to make full use of their findings.

Once the preserve of the large corporation, now even small companies use marketing research consultancies to undertake research on their behalf – and many small and affordable consultancies have sprung up to cater for this demand. But if you think that commissioning a company to undertake your research will relieve you totally of the burden, you are wrong. Undoubtedly it is easier (albeit more expensive) to get someone else to do research for you, though there are still a number of tasks that have to be undertaken by you, namely:

- drawing up a research brief;
- drawing up a shortlist of companies to approach and selecting one to work with;
- interpreting the findings (although you can pay your research company to do this for you);
- deciding what action to take as a result of the research (you can ask your researchers to make recommendations as part of their brief).

You need to draw up a research brief so that you are clear about why you need the research, what you wish to discover, and how you will use the findings. It is also important to have a brief so that your researchers understand what exactly they are doing and to what end. A simple sample brief can be seen in Figure 26.1.

Figure 26.1 Research brief

MARIO'S LEISURE AND FITNESS CENTRE
RESEARCH BRIEF

Mario's is based in purpose-built premises half a mile east of the city centre. It offers a range of sports, leisure and beauty pursuits (see enclosed publicity brochure) mainly for adults, although a smaller selection of activities is available for children. We open Monday to Saturday from 10 am to 9 pm and Sunday until 8 pm. We were established five years ago and are open to members (£450 per year – all activities free) and non-members (£1–£5 per session, depending on activity and time of day/week).

Need for the research
One year after opening, Mario's had over 500 members and a further 1,000 regular users who were not members. Membership has now fallen to 200, and we have just 500 regular users. We want to know why people are not renewing their membership. We also wish to know from people using the Centre what they like most about it as well as what they dislike.

What we want to know
We would like to find out the following:

- Why people who were members have not renewed their membership.
- Would a loyalty discount of, say, 20 per cent have tempted people to rejoin?
- Why recent members joined (ie why they wanted to join a fitness centre and why they chose Mario's).
- What it would take to turn regular users who are not members into fully paid-up members.
- Children's activities: if we increased the range of these, would the Centre be used more often and if so, by whom (existing members, regular non-members, new people who have previously not used Mario's)?

What action we are considering/how we will use the research
We are considering increasing the range of activities on offer, particularly those for children. We are also looking at the benefits of membership and whether we need to incentivise members to rejoin. The research will provide us with the information we need to take these decisions. If activities are identified by users as being unpopular, we will consider changing, scrapping or replacing them.

Sample
We are unsure about this and would require our researchers to indicate the type and size of sample and how they would select it.

Methodology
We would like our researchers to recommend an appropriate and cost-effective methodology for this assignment.

Report
We would like a detailed report setting out all the findings. In addition we require a summary report that will set out clearly the main points in an easy-to-digest way. We require visual presentation on the main findings (bar charts, pie charts, etc) plus accompanying explanatory narrative. Any qualitative observations picked up during the survey may be included, in addition to the quantitative findings. We also require our researchers to make recommendations to us on future action.

Time scale
We require tenders for this assignment to be with us by midday, 30 April. We intend to have selected a market research agency by 31 May and to have the research underway by the end of June. The results of the research must be with us by 31 July.

If it is a headache, take an aspirin

Always discuss your brief with more than one consultancy. Each will have its own style and a distinctive approach to carrying out your brief, so aim to speak initially with three or four to give you a range of perspectives. Go by recommendation if you can. Alternatively, talk to the market researchers' trade body, the Association of Market Survey Organisations (AMSO). They can be contacted on 020 8444 3692 and will provide you with information on the types of research on offer and companies with expertise in specific sectors. There is also an organisation for those who commission marketing research, the Association of Users of Research Agencies, which can be contacted on 020 7831 5839. And if all of this sounds like a headache, why not take ASPIRIN. This is an acronym that summarises the stages involved in choosing a consultancy:

A   Ask around – see if you can get any recommendations.
S   Source the market – see what else is available.
P   Prepare a brief – see above.
I   Invite market research consultancies to present to you (at your premises or at theirs) – see below for what to ask them.
R   Review their approach, proposals and presentations. Decide who to use.
I   Invite the successful consultancy to start.
N   Negotiate and agree the project plan and contract.

When asking around, speak to other businesses they have carried out research for. Try to find out what work was undertaken, whether they were any good at it, whether the work was carried out on time, whether the consultants were helpful and whether they underperformed in any of the tasks.

When you come to interview consultants, find out the following from them:

- Do they understand what you are looking for and why?
- How would they tackle it – are their suggestions practical and cost-effective?
- How many consultants would be involved? You need to find out who these would be (they may not be the people presenting to you) and what their relevant experience is for the job.
- Whether trained interviewers will be used and what training they will have received.
- What the market research consultancy's experience is of undertaking work for your sector.
- What the fee would be.
- Whether this would be inclusive, and if not, what the extras would be.
- Do they anticipate any problems or difficulties and if so, how do they propose to solve them?
- Are they flexible – in other words, are they able to cope with a brief that may change, or a time scale that might differ to the original?
- About the consultancy – how long has it been established, who else have they worked for, what other projects or commitments they will be undertaking at the same time as your project?
- Can they provide references?

You may also like to consider:

- Did they come across as professional?
- Did they seem to be able to think on their feet?
- Did they impress with their understanding of you as an organisation and the need for this research?
- Did they appear keen to do the work?
- Did they have any interesting and helpful observations to make on the brief?

Your meeting with consultants should be two-way; you need to find out what they can do, and they need to find out more about you. If you aim for a meeting format that is informal but structured, you will make it easier to achieve this.

Bright idea

Many colleges and universities offer a cut-price research service using their students. This might be worth looking into if budget is a problem. Contact your local colleges to see if they can help

Once you have made a decision, call the successful company and commission them. Ask them to sign a contract with you which sets out your terms, expectations, deadlines, performance measures, payment details, etc. Write to the unsuccessful firms to notify them. Hold a preliminary meeting with the successful firm and get the research underway.

Now act upon your research!

Research reports all too often sit on a shelf gathering dust. Once you have gone to the trouble of commissioning research, do act upon the findings. What do they say? How does this affect your work? What do you need to do/change? Is further research required? Sit down with your researchers and talk it through, take their inputs on board and draw up an action list based on the findings of the research.

If you want to know more about marketing research, read Chapter 18.

27 Choosing an advertising agency

If advertising forms one of the central planks of your promotional strategy, if slick and professional adverts are essential for your business, or if you want to use TV and radio advertising, you will need the services of an advertising agency. This chapter will explain the different types of agency, it will show you how to choose the right one for your business, and how to prepare a written brief.

Advertising is at the glamorous end of marketing and some advertising agencies' fees would put a small company out of business. But now that small businesses are using advertising more, there are many small agencies supplying this market at reasonable rates.

An advertising agency can:

- come up with ideas for adverts that achieve your objectives;
- advise on where, when and how to advertise;
- prepare artwork for you and oversee production of TV and radio adverts;
- buy advertising space and air time for you.

There are three main types of agency:

1. creative agencies;
2. media independents;
3. full service agencies.

Creatives

These deal with the creative side of advertising, coming up with clever ideas and doing all of the artwork for you. They are 'fee-based'; you agree a fee in advance and they will carry out the work on your brief for that agreed fee. They can do more than straight advertising and will take on the design of corporate identities, exhibitions and other publicity material. (Do not confuse them with graphic designers. Graphic designers are experts at design and layout, but most know little about devising an advertising campaign and placing adverts.)

Bright idea

Select adverts that are designed to be effective, not those which have been produced to win creative awards.

Media independents

These specialise in buying space in the media and do no creative work at all. Because they buy in large volume they can save you money. Media buyers may take as little as 2 or 3 per cent commission for buying space for you, which compares favourably with full service agencies. They can also help you with media planning.

Full service agencies

These agencies combine creative teams with in-house media buyers, giving you everything you need in a one-stop shop. You may pay more for this inclusive service, but it is less hassle and is perhaps the best starting place if you are new to advertising. Full service agencies get an automatic 10 to 15 per cent discount from the media when they buy space. Traditionally this money is used to fund the creative work on big advertising campaigns. However, for small campaigns you will probably have to pay a fee for creative work, planning and the management of your account. Generally full service agencies concentrate on 'above-the-line' advertising (in the media), although they also offer 'below-the-line' services such as brochures and other promotional material.

Which one?

You will find plenty of advertising agencies eager for your business. Go by recommendation if you can. If you don't know anyone who has used an agency, look at the advertising of small, non-competing businesses in the press and contact the companies whose advertising you like. Ask them which agency they use. With the growth in the number of small agencies and freelance advertising consultants, finding affordable advertising help is easier than it used to be.

Contact at least three agencies with your written brief (see Figure 27.1). Ask the agencies to let you know whether or not they are interested in your business. Some may turn you down because your budget is too small or because there is a conflict of interest with another client. If they already handle the advertising account for a widgets factory, you may get turned away if you too make widgets. (You might decide that you can't do business with them anyway in that case.) Some agencies operate a 'Chinese walls' system, which enables them to work for competing clients. Set a deadline and ask the selected agencies to get back to you by then with ideas on how they would tackle your campaign.

Figure 27.1   Advertising brief

The Toy Hospital
Advertising Campaign Brief

About us

Our business, which officially begins trading in four months' time, will specialise in repairing/restoring valuable antique toys – everything from collectors' teddy bears and other soft toys to automata, dolls' houses, games, tinware, bikes, rocking-horses and pedal cars. We will offer a national service from our premises in Worthing, arranging collection of clients' toys by Securicor, and returning repaired toys in the same way.

As we have not yet launched, no one has heard of us; we have no pedigree and no profile. We want to launch ourselves using a combination of press advertising and editorial obtained via PR. (We have already engaged a PR consultant and would expect our advertising and PR people to work closely to create a complementary and coordinated publicity campaign.) We hope to generate considerable interest in the lead-up to our opening, and to sustain interest once we are up and running. We are currently negotiating to get one of the *Antiques Roadshow* presenters to be at a photocall for the grand opening (which will feature a one-armed teddy bear in an ambulance!), and possibly also to endorse us in our press advertising.

We have produced 'The Antique Toy Restoration Information Pack', which will be available free to any enquirer. This will be promoted by coupon response adverts.

Our messages

Our advertising must explain what we do, the sorts of toy we can repair and how quality restoration can add value to antique toys. We need to convey that we are skilled, professional restorers. We have a good selection of dramatic 'before' and 'after' photos of toys. No toy is beyond saving.

Our audiences

Mainly we will do business with serious collectors of antique toys and specialist dealers. However, we also hope to generate income from museums and from people with just one beloved but shabby teddy bear or similar.

Our advertising objectives

1. **To inform antique toy collectors and dealers about our service**.
2. **To get them to send for an information pack**. We expect to receive 200 requests for packs within the first month of our first adverts appearing. Respondents' details will be put on our database and they will be direct mailed at a later date.
3. **To attract custom**. As a direct result of the press adverts we expect to get 100 customers in the first three months. Long-term we wish to negotiate contracts with 50 per cent of Britain's toy museums.

Initially we are looking for a set of one-off advertisements in the antique trade press to launch the business and meet the above objectives. We will then look to build upon the initial push by developing a rolling advertising programme to maintain awareness, interest and custom.

Our budget

Our advertising budget of £25,000 must cover all media space and all creative work, project management, etc. We are aware that this is relatively small, given what we are hoping to achieve, but remember that advertising will be backed up by carefully targeted PR.

Bright idea

Ask agencies you are talking to for the names of the last six clients they have lost, for whatever reason. Telephone those companies and get the inside story. It's only worth going to this trouble if you have a really big advertising budget with a lot resting on it.

Look through the submissions and invite agencies which have impressed you with what they have submitted to do a presentation (known as a 'pitch'). Ask them to do a 'credentials presentation' – a general presentation on themselves, what their strength/expertise is, which advertising campaigns they have worked on, etc. Also ask them to explain to you how they would approach your assignment and what ideas they have. Get them to bring to the presentation a document setting out their approach and detailing their costs. Alternatively, go to their premises for the presentation; it is more time-consuming, but you get a better idea of who you will be doing business with.

Bright idea

Advertising agencies will show you examples of their work. Ask when the work was done, who it was done by, whether that team still works for the agency and whether they will work on your account. There's no point in engaging an agency because you liked the samples, only to discover that the people responsible for them left three years ago.

Some agencies will ask you for a fee just for pitching. This is to cover the time and materials involved in preparing ideas for you. Decide whether or not you are willing to see agencies who expect payment at this early stage.

Select an agency from those you have seen or, if you are still not sure, draw up a new pitch list and start again.

When assessing the performance of prospective agencies, ask yourself:

- Did they fulfil the requirements of the brief in their tender documents?
- Was their presentation confident?
- Did they come up with good ideas?
- Did they seem genuinely enthusiastic about our account?
- Did they seem to understand what we are about?
- Did they handle questions well?
- Do I feel, from what I have seen, that I have confidence in them?

Tell your prospective consultants about yourself, and find out about them. Ask:

- What experience they have of working for companies similar to your own. Ask for names of clients and examples of their work. Take up references.
- What knowledge and understanding they have of your work. If none of your consultants knows much about your field, ask them how they would go about building up their expertise.
- Who will be working on your account. Ask for their CVs, so you can be sure of their experience, and samples of their work, so you can be sure of

their skill. (The people who present to you may not be those who will carry out the work.)

- How many staff they have.
- How long they have been established.
- What other clients they work for. Is there an actual or potential conflict of interest?
- How they intend to evaluate the success of the work they carry out for you.
- If the agency has won any industry awards.

Select an agency that has relevant experience. If you are doing radio or TV advertising, it is important that your agency has worked in these fields before. Some agencies specialise in press work, and are very good at this, but have limited experience of broadcast advertising.

Bright idea

If you are concerned that your agency may become complacent, let them know that they will be required to take part in a competitive repitch for your account every three years. This is common practice and keeps agencies on their toes and ensures that you are getting the best deal.

You might find the table shown in Figure 27.2 useful for comparing one advertising agency with another. Give each agency marks out of ten for each category. (Replace the given categories with others relevant to your assignment.) One is the lowest score and ten the highest. You may decide not to go for the highest overall score, but to opt for an agency that scores well all round. It is up to you.

Figure 27.2 Table for evaluating advertising agencies

Criteria	Agency 1	Agency 2	Agency 3
Understanding of our needs			
Experience in this field			
Creativity and ideas			
Approach to the advertising campaign			
Team involved			
Confidence and competence			
Total cost			
Total score			

Once you have chosen your agency, make it a profitable partnership; share your thinking, listen to their ideas, and generally try to establish and maintain a good working relationship. The harder you work at keeping them informed, the harder your adverts will work for you. Better adverts equal bigger profits, so it is in your interest to keep the relationship going. That means, for example, making sure your agency knows about any new product or service developments. This will keep them up to speed and allow them to come back to you with further ideas and suggestions. When briefing your agency on new products, they might find it useful to be given a completed pro forma along the lines of the one set out in Figure 27.3. If you use a PR consultancy, copy it to them too. Remember that the more your agency knows about you and your products, the more in tune it will be. You will gain from this.

Figure 27.3 New products' pro forma

Product	Features	Benefits	Market	Price
Phoenix paint	Fire retardant	Can upgrade standard doors to fire-safe ones	Trade – builders, developers, architects, etc	£10 for 1-litre tin
	Available in a wide range of colours	Can be mixed to match existing decor		Discounts for bulk purchases
	Water-based	Brushes wash out in water and no toxic or unpleasant smells. Environmentally friendly		
	Available in gloss, matt and satin finishes			

Appendix 1:
A plain English guide to marketing and PR jargon

Like any jargon, marketing and PR-speak can be impenetrable to the outsider. Let this glossary help to demystify it for you. If you are reading other marketing books you can refer to this user-friendly definition of terms to help you. Many of the terms and concepts outlined below are dealt with in more detail in the relevant chapters of this book.

General marketing jargon

Cause-related marketing (CRM)
CRM is sometimes known as 'strategic philanthropy' or 'socially responsible marketing'. A company with an image, product or service to sell, builds a relationship or partnership with a 'cause' or a number of 'causes' for mutual benefit. Cadbury's 'Strollerthon' – an annual sponsored mass participation walk through London – is an example of this. Save the Children benefits from the cash raised from the event, while Cadbury's gets publicity, goodwill, a database of participants and a chance to give out product samples at the event. In 1994, for example, Save the Children got £250,000 from the Strollerthon, and subsequent research revealed that 52 per cent of walkers perceived Cadbury's as a caring company. CRM is much bigger in the USA than here. Indeed, 64 per cent of US consumers are likely to switch to a brand linked with a cause, price and quality being equal, and 84 per cent says it gives them a more positive image of the company. Research carried out in the UK at the end of

1996 showed that 86 per cent of consumers choose a product associated with a good cause, price and quality being equal. Sixty-one per cent of consumers would change retail outlet to support a good cause. While some big name companies in the UK are using CRM, few small companies do so (even though it is a marketing tool that is as appropriate to small business as to large).

Cross-selling
This is where you use information about a customer's purchases to sell them other products. For example, you might try to sell software, or a modem, to someone who has a computer.

Diversification
This involves complete change. You are developing new products and offering them to new markets, a risky strategy.

Four new Ps
In 1981 a further three Ps were suggested for service industries: people (the attitude of staff, behaviour, training, commitment, etc); physical evidence (the surroundings in which a service takes place, its furnishings and decor, noise levels, layout, etc); and process (policies, procedures, etc). Norman Hart, Britain's first professor of PR, suggests that P for 'perception' should be added to the classic four Ps.

Market development
Here you take your existing products, but you promote them to new target markets.

Market penetration
This is where you take your existing products to your existing markets. Your aim is to capture a bigger share of this market, or to reach previously unreached potential customers.

Market segmentation
To be effective you need to 'know your market'. That makes it sound as if you have just one market, made up of one type of person. It is important to recognise that not all markets are uniform. Most are made up of subgroups or segments. You need to spot the segments in your market and identify what makes one different and distinct from another, and to tailor your approach to these distinct markets. Spotting the subgroups in your market is called market segmentation. Your market might be segmented **geographically** (eg if you have clear regional differences); **demographically** (sex, age, lifecycle or family size); socio-economically (income, occupation, social class, etc); **psychographically** (in other words, according to the type of person who buys, their personality or lifestyle); and/or **behaviouristically** (how often they buy from you, what they look for from you, etc).

Marketing mix
The term 'marketing mix' refers to the four Ps – product, price, place and promotion – and it is important to know which of the Ps are the key influencing factors for your market.

Niche markets
A niche market is one that is small and specialist, for example skate-boarding computer whizz-kids. It can be very profitable catering for niche markets, as they are generally not targeted by anyone else and therefore are crying out for products or services to meet their needs. Often they are prepared to pay handsomely, and with no competition the way is open for companies to make good profits. Equally, you are more vulnerable. If something happens to your niche, or another player (competitor) appears, you could find that you have no other market to provide services to, or that your expertise is so specialised that you cannot diversify.

Niche products
A niche product is simply a product or service developed to meet the needs of a particular niche market (see above).

Place
'Place' is the bridge that connects buyers and sellers. It ensures that the product and customer are brought together, thus creating an opportunity for the customer to buy. It may mean distribution – getting the products to the places where they can be available to consumers. If you make baked beans, you need a distribution system that enables you to get your tins out of the factory and into the shops where they will be sold. Clearly in manufacturing the 'place' P is a really important one; tins of baked beans stacked in a factory are of no use to anyone – they need to be placed where they can be bought. But place also has a use, as a concept, to service-providers. Just as those making a product need to know how to get it to the customer, you too need to consider how to get the consumer to your service. For example, are there parking meters near your restaurant?

Price
This is obvious. Less obvious is how to use price to your advantage. See Chapter 6 for details.

Product
We tend to think of products as things – such as a tin of baked beans or a packet of washing powder. 'Product' can also cover services.

Product development
This is where you develop brand new products, but offer them to your existing target markets.

Promotion
This is the aspect of marketing that we most readily associate the word with. Indeed, this is often what we mean when we talk about marketing. Promotion involves promoting your service or product, but the question is, 'Promote it to

whom?' Are you promoting it to the people who use it or those who pay for it? Those who use are not always those who pay. Children's pasta products, for example, are paid for by adults, but advertising for Postman Pat spaghetti is not aimed at them; it is targeted at children, as they are the major influencing factor on how and what food is bought in a household. Supermarket chain Asda did some research into consumer buying habits and discovered that children exert a strong influence over what their parents buy in supermarkets, to the tune of almost £2 billion a year. A survey backed by The Co-operative Bank found the same thing, that children use 'pester power' to influence their parents into buying something. The promotional tools used and the messages promoted will differ, but the need for promotion to both audiences remains. Promotion involves advertising, leaflets, posters and other methods to reach target audiences.

Prospects
A prospective customer.

SWOT analysis
SWOT is an acronym. It stands for:

Strengths: what you are good at, what you do well, what factors are in your favour.

Weaknesses: what you are poor at, what factors are against you.

Opportunities: what external opportunities there are for you to develop new services or to attract new customers, etc.

Threats: what external threats could affect you, for example, new legislation or competition.

A SWOT analysis is simply an examination of your company's strengths and weaknesses, and the opportunities and threats which it faces. Once you have carried out a SWOT analysis, you can start to build on your strengths and, where appropriate, do something to address your weaknesses. Remember that a threat to one company can be an opportunity to another.

Take one
Quite simply, 'take ones' are publicity leaflets left where people can take one, often in leaflet dispensers or display stands.

Telemarketing
This is marketing by telephone. In-bound is where a customer calls you, and out-bound is where you call the customer or prospect. Telesales is where you sell by telephone. Telemarketing is more about developing relationships, handling enquiries or managing customer accounts.

USP
This is an acronym for unique selling point (sometimes also called 'unique selling proposition') – it is the thing that differentiates you from all the others. For example, there might be scores of architectural practices, but your USP is that you are the only one set up exclusively for owners of small historic properties. No one else is offering that service. It is what makes you stand out from the rest.

Marketing research jargon

Customer profile
A customer profile paints a picture of the sort of person who buys from you – for example, middle-aged *Telegraph* readers with two incomes, grown-up children, living in the south of England and interested in outdoor activities.

Demographics
This relates to population characteristics such as age, sex and family size.

Methodology
This is jargon for how you intend to get the information you need when doing research. For example, you may decide to use a postal questionnaire plus depth interviews with a sample of customers.

Primary data
Primary data are not ready-made. You have to gather them yourself, or commission someone else to do it for you. They are thus more expensive and potentially much more time-consuming than secondary data (see below).

Samples
With the exception of the government's ten-yearly census, no survey can cover the whole of the population. Researchers use instead a 'sample', which is a smaller group that is representative of the 'population' they wish to survey. By surveying a representative sample, rather than the entire relevant population, your survey is made more manageable and affordable.

Secondary data
Secondary data are material that already exists (as opposed to primary data, which you gather yourself). It includes, for example, government publications and statistics (eg the *Census of Population*, the *Family Expenditure Survey*, reports from the Registrar General, *Monthly Digest of Statistics and Social Trends*). Large reference libraries are an obvious starting point when tracking down secondary data.

Advertising jargon

Above-the-line
This is an advertising term which refers to paid-for advertising using press, radio, TV, cinema and billboards.

Advertising rate card
Newspaper and magazine advertising departments produce a rate card which sets out what an advertisement costs according to where it is in the publication, its size, whether it is colour or black and white, etc. It also contains production

information such as deadlines and the form in which you need to submit your advert.

Advertorial
An advert that is designed to look like editorial.

Below-the-line
This refers to advertising and promotion via media other than 'above-the-line' media such as direct mail, exhibitions, promotional brochures and give-aways (such as promotional pens, balloons and key-rings).

BRAD (British Rate And Data)
This monthly publication (which can be consulted at large reference libraries) sets out the advertising rates of a wide range of publications, from daily newspapers to women's and special interest magazines. It also contains circulation information (see below).

Circulation
Circulation figures tell you how many people *buy* a particular publication. 'Readership' figures tell you how many people *read* a publication. Usually readership figures are higher than circulation ones; a newspaper or magazine will frequently be read by more than just the person who bought it.

Classified adverts or 'smalls'
These are small adverts which comprise lines of text. There is no design element. They are usually charged by the line, so advertisers often abbreviate their copy to fit as many words in per line.

Display adverts
These are creative adverts which have been professionally designed and laid out. Often they will incorporate photos or illustrations.

Facing matter
This is when your advert is placed alongside editorial, rather than being buried in an advertising section surrounded by other adverts.

Island position
Advert surrounded by editorial.

Knocking copy
Copy that criticises a competitor. For example, Scotrail Sleeper Service produced an advert criticising the British Airways shuttle service from Scotland to London. It said, 'You've BA chance of reaching central London by 8 am if you fly.' Easyjet, an airline flying from Scotland to Luton, retaliated by placing an advert saying, 'Snailtrack [with a picture of a snail with the British Rail logo on it] Fast Track [with a picture of an aeroplane]'.

Recall tests
Recall tests are used in advertising research to see how many of a sample of respondents remember having seen an advert.

Run-of-paper (ROP)
You do not get to choose where in the publication your advert appears; it is placed at the publisher's discretion.

Single column centimetre (scc)
This is the unit of vertical measurement that is used to measure the size of an advert and therefore its cost.

Solus position
There will be no other advertisements adjacent to your own. This means it will not have to compete for attention with other adverts.

Special position adverts
You can specify if you want your advert to appear in a special position, such as the front page or near the leader column. If you are running a business selling educational toys and games, you may opt for your advert to be placed on the education page. The price of your advert will depend on where in the paper it is placed. There can be a waiting list for the best positions, as these are often booked up in advance.

Direct mail jargon

ACORN
This acronym stands for 'A Classification Of Residential Neighbourhoods'. It classifies people and households according to the type of neighbourhood they live in. People in a particular neighbourhood will probably share similar lifestyles, social characteristics and behaviour. There are 38 different neighbourhood types and 11 different 'family group classifications'. Using the information it is possible to produce mailing lists that will enable you to target very precisely so that you can reach only 'high-status, non-family' areas, or 'unmodernised terraced houses with old people'. There is a similar system called MOSAIC.

Active customer
Generally an active customer is one who has purchased from you (or sent for information from you) within the last 12 months.

Coop mailings
This is when two or more non-competitive businesses come together and have their information or promotional material inserted into the one mailing. Sharing the costs is a cost-effective exercise.

Cost per conversion
You add together all the costs of a direct mail campaign and divide by the number of orders received. This gives you your cost per conversion and it is a good way of working out whether your campaign has been a success in terms of the response it generated.

De-dupe
Short for de-duplicate, this is when you remove duplicate names from a mailing list.

Door drops
Door drops are mailings (leaflets, packs, etc) that are unaddressed, delivered to households by hand, not in the mail. Strictly speaking this is not direct mail, it is direct advertising.

Fulfilment
This is when you process an order or a request for information. Fulfilment houses are specialist companies geared up to dealing with mass enquiries/orders. If you expect the response to your mailshot to be huge, you might need to consider using a fulfilment house.

Gone-aways
This is a term used to refer to mail returned by the Royal Mail to the sender because the intended recipient has gone away or the address is wrong or non-existent. Such mail is also known as 'returns'. Gone-aways are a waste of money; when you get one you must update/amend your mailing list accordingly.

List broker
A specialist who can help you find the perfect mailing list. You can get a list of approved list brokers from the Direct Marketing Association (see Appendix 2).

List cleaning
Mailing lists need to be kept up to date if they are to be of any use. List cleaning involves correcting names and addresses, removing those who have moved away or those who have not responded to your mail within a designated period (eg after four mailings or within one month).

List exchange
Sometimes you can exchange your mailing list with another non-competing business likely to have a similar customer profile. This can be a good (and free) way of getting a quality list.

Mailing house
You can arrange to have your direct mail addressed, collated and despatched by a mailing house.

Member get member (MGM)
This is when an existing customer sends in the name of a friend or relative who may be interested in receiving information from you. This technique is used a lot by big companies, who offer incentives to people to get them to send in details of friends. It can sometimes be an effective way of building up a mailing list of interested people.

MOSAIC
See ACORN above.

Piggybacks
A piggyback is when you enclose your literature in another company's existing mailing, for example by inserting a flyer into another (non-competing and complementary) business's customer newsletter. This is a cheaper way of doing a mailing. Businesses can make money this way too, by offering a piggyback service in their own mailings.

Media relations jargon

Broadcast monitoring companies
A number of companies specialise in monitoring radio and TV output, and can ring you up to alert you that you have had a mention. They can also provide transcripts of programmes and video and audio tapes. They are expensive, but can be useful for the bigger companies or big campaigns.

Broadsheet
Broadsheets are longer, more rectangular in size, such as *The Times*. They are sometimes called 'the qualities' because of their more serious treatment of news.

Chief reporter
As the name suggests, the chief reporter is more senior than other reporters and generally gets the best and most interesting assignments. They are usually more experienced than other reporters on the paper.

Editor
This is the top job on a newspaper. On larger papers it is generally a management job rather than a hands-on writing position, although the editor often writes a leader or comment column. On small papers and free papers, the editor can also be a reporter of sorts. The editor is responsible for the content, tone and style of a newspaper.

Embargo
A request to the media to withhold publication or broadcast of information until a specified date/time. Embargoes are not always respected, so don't rely on them.

Journalist/reporter
There are specialist reporters or correspondents (such as business, health and consumer correspondents) and general reporters who have to write about a very wide range of issues but who may specialise in none.

Media invitations
If you want to let the media know about an event, news conference or photocall, issue them with a media invitation setting out briefly what is happening, where, when and why.

News editor
The news editor selects the news, decides where in the paper it will appear, and assigns reporters to follow up particular stories.

News releases
Sometimes referred to as 'press releases', they are stories written in newspaper style by PR people. Releases are issued by companies to the media in the hope of securing press or broadcast coverage for a story.

Photocalls
If you are organising an event and are seeking publicity for it, consider whether it has 'photo opportunity' potential. If so, set up a photocall, where you invite newspaper photographers (and possibly TV, too) to attend at a certain time to take pictures. Invite them by issuing a media invitation (see above) – sometimes also known as a photocall notice.

Press cuttings bureaux
These companies will send you cuttings on your company or your market sector from a massive range of publications. They are expensive, as they charge a reading fee and an amount per cutting, so are suitable only for fairly large companies doing a lot of media work, or for one-off, high profile campaigns.

Press officers
Press officers are in-house specialists who deal with media relations and are a contact point for journalists seeking information.

Press or media statement
If you are asked by the media to comment on something, or to answer questions on a particular issue, you might find that you are unable or unwilling to do an interview. By issuing a press statement – a written response – you can avoid an interview while at the same time getting your point across.

Press or news conference
This is an event held specially for the media to brief them on an important issue, a new product or service, or something that is generally very news-worthy. If you can achieve the same effect simply by issuing a news release, do not go to the trouble of holding a news conference.

Sub-editor
Cutting stories to fit the space and headline-writing are two of the main responsibilities of the sub.

Tabloid
The terms 'tabloid' and 'broadsheet' (see below) simply refer to the size of a newspaper, with tabloids being smaller and squarer, like the *Sun* or the *Mirror*. People often refer to tabloids as 'the popular press', and regard their coverage as trivial, over-sensational and based too much on celebrities and TV shows.

Video news releases
A 'video news release' (VNR) is a news story produced on video to broadcast quality. They are expensive (£5,000 to £15,000), so generally they're the preserve of big companies. Like conventional paper news releases, they are sent out to TV newsrooms to be used as the producer sees fit. Those that make it on to the screens are presented as if the programme did the filming, carried out the interviews and so on. Viewers cannot tell the difference between a VNR and a report complied by the TV station's own news team. Broadcasters say

that they don't like them, yet with increased pressure on news teams, VNRs do get used, as they are a cheap and easy way for broadcasters to get news. With the growth in satellite stations, there is a ready market for video news releases.

Design and print jargon

Call-out
A short extract from the main text, which is repeated as a subhead within the text, in order to draw attention to it.

Colour-separated camera ready artwork
This is artwork that arrives in a form ready for printers to process. The original colours have been separated using special filters.

Contact sheets
These are miniature prints which are reproduced in strips (rather like negatives) on a large sheet of photographic paper. They allow you to view and select your prints without the expense of getting them made up to full size.

DTP
This acronym stands for desktop publishing. Special computer software can enable you to do attractive layout, which you then print out on your laser, inkjet or bubblejet printer.

Dummy
A designer will produce a mock-up for you of your leaflet, newsletter, brochure, etc so that you can approve it or comment on it before completion of the final design. This is known as a dummy.

Finishing
This is the final stage of the print production process, where the document is made ready for use by, for example, being cut, stitched, glued or guillotined.

Full colour printing
This is produced using the four-colour process. Your designs are split into their four original colours, yellow, magenta (red), cyan (blue) and black, using special filters. This is known as colour separation.

Gatefold
A leaflet folded so that its two edges meet in the centre.

gsm
Paper is referred to by designers and printers according to its weight. Typical notepaper is around 100 gsm, or grams per square metre. Magazine covers are much heavier, weighing in at around 220 gsm.

Halftones
This is a photograph which has been 'scanned' or 'screened' by a printer to turn it into a series of different sized dots which give the appearance of a continuous tone.

Initial caps
This is where a word is in lower case letters, but the first letter uses a capital, such as England or Denise.

Justified text
Justified text produces lines of text of equal length. Unjustified text has a distinctive ragged or uneven right-hand margin.

Landscape
This is a format where a document is longer than it is tall, rather like most landscape paintings. In other words, it is like a horizontal rectangle, with the longer edge at the top and bottom.

Pantone colour
There are many different shades of the same colour, so in order to ensure consistency, designers and printers use something known as the Pantone Matching System (PMS). Every shade has a Pantone number to identify it.

Picture library
This is a commercial library containing thousands of photographs which cover every conceivable subject. You can borrow photos and use them, as long as you pay a fee and acknowledge the photographer or picture library in your credits. If you need a special picture, your designer should be able to track it down for you through a library. (See Chapter 21 for further information.)

Point size
Typefaces are measured in points. Most books, magazines and letters are typed in 10 or 12 points. The higher the number, the larger the type size.

Portrait
This is an upright rectangle, where the shorter edge is at the top and bottom – rather like most portrait paintings.

Reversed out
This term describes the process by which the image or words themselves are not printed, but the surrounding area is. The text or image thereby appears to take on the colour of the paper.

Serif and sans serif
These are typeface classifications. Serif (or Roman) typefaces have 'tails' on many of the letters. Sans serif typefaces (such as Univers) do not have tails (or serifs). Sans serif faces look easy to read, but experts recommend a serif typeface such as Courier for maximum readability. With sans serif faces it can sometimes be difficult to distinguish between a lower case 'l', an upper case 'I' and the number '1'.

Tints
These are made up of tiny dots that give the effect of a shade. If you are printing in dark blue, your tints would be in shades of lighter blue. For black ink, tints are grey, for red ink they are pink. Effective use of tints can give the illusion of another colour.

Typo
Short for typographical error, a typo is a misprint or misspelling. They are sometimes known as 'literals'.

Upper case
Capital letters.

Appendix 2:
Useful addresses

This is far from a comprehensive list, though it covers the main companies and organisations you may need to contact, as well as the key magazines and handbooks.

Marketing

The Chartered Institute of Marketing
Moor Hall
Cookham
Maidenhead
Berks SL6 9QH
Tel: 01628 427500
Web site: www.cim.co.uk

The CIM was established in 1911 and has over 50,000 members. It is a membership organisation offering a range of services including training, professional qualifications, a library and information service, and consultancy. It produces various publications, including a journal, newsletters and marketing reports.

Marketing
Haymarket Publications
174 Hammersmith Road
London W6 7JP
Tel: 020 8606 7500

A weekly marketing newspaper.

Marketing Week
Centaur Communications Ltd
12–26 Lexington Street
London W1R 4HQ
Tel: 020 7439 4222

A weekly marketing magazine.

Marketing Pocket Book
NTC Publications
World Advertising Research Centre
Farm Road
Henley-on-Thames
Oxfordshire RG9 1E7
Tel: 01491 411000

This pocket book is published annually for the Advertising Association by NTC Publications and costs £16.95. It contains a vast array of marketing information covering a wide range of subjects.

Marketing World
Web site: www.marketing-world.com

A marketing magazine on the Internet.

Advertising

Advertising Association
Abford House
15 Wilton Road
London SW1V 1NJ
Tel: 020 7828 2771

This trade association runs courses and publishes industry statistics.

The Advertising Standards Authority
2 Torrington Place
London WC1E 7HW
Tel: 020 7580 5555
Web site: www.asa.org.uk

Established in 1962, the ASA provides independent scrutiny of the advertising industry. It investigates complaints and ensures that the system operates in the public interest. It is independent both of government and the industry. The ASA produces a monthly report detailing companies which have been investigated for breaching the advertising codes, and you can subscribe to this free of charge.

The Committee of Advertising Practice
2 Torrington Place
London WC1E 7HW
Tel: 020 7580 5555

The CAP is the self-regulatory body that devises and enforces the British Codes of Advertising and Sales Promotion. These are reproduced in a free guide, available from the above address. CAP also offers free copy advice on your advertising and promotions, to help you ensure they meet the codes. Tel: 020 7580 4100. They will also advise 'Webvertisers' – companies who advertise on the Internet. And they produce a free leaflet on advertising on the Internet. Tel: 020 7580 5555 for a copy of this.

The Incorporated Society of British Advertisers Limited
44 Hertford Street
London W1J 7AE
Tel: 020 7499 7502

The ISBA represents the interests of the majority of British advertisers. It can offer organisations help with selecting advertising, promotional and direct marketing agencies, and offers training and a range of useful publications and briefing papers.

Advertising Agency Register
26 Market Place
London W1W 8AN
Tel: 020 7612 1200

This independent organisation will give you the names of advertising agencies suitable for your brief.

Campaign Magazine
Haymarket Publications
174 Hammersmith Road
London W6 7JP
Tel: 020 8606 7500

A weekly publication focusing on the advertising industry.

Bus advertising

Viacom Outdoor
28 Jamestown Road
Camden Wharf
London NW1 7BY
Tel: 020 7482 3000 or
0800 22 66 33

This is one of the largest bus advertising companies in the country. It can arrange for you to advertise on buses in your area or nationally.

Bus ticket advertising

Image Promotions
Ticket Media
Units 2 & 3 Maple Works
Old Shoreham Road
Hove
East Sussex BN3 7ED
Tel: 01273 726325

Image Promotions has organised over 95 per cent of all bus ticket promotions in the UK. It has links with over 100 bus companies in all major towns and cities. The company can help you with planning and advice, bus company bookings and liaison, artwork and design, printing, delivery and campaign monitoring.

Market research

The Market Research Society
15 Northburgh Street
London EC1V 0JR
Tel: 020 7490 4911

Founded in 1946, the Market Research Society is the professional association for those involved in compiling or using research. It has around 7,500 members and offers them a monthly magazine and quarterly journal. The Society produces an annual training programme which includes such courses as questionnaire design, marketing skills and training the interviewer trainer. Courses are open to non-members, although a higher fee is charged. They also produce a free directory of organisations providing market research services.

Raymead Ltd
Geneva House
3 Park Road
Peterborough PE1 2UX
Tel: 01733 890790

Raymead sells software to help you set up databases that will enable you to have a clearer picture of your customers.

General research

Press Association Library
P A News Centre
292 Vauxhall Bridge Road
London SW1
Tel: 020 7963 7011

This library holds over 14 million news cuttings on every subject from 1926 onwards.

British Library Newspaper Library
Colindale Avenue
London NW9 5HE
Tel: 020 7412 7353

English, Scottish, Welsh and Irish newspapers from 1700 are housed here.

Office for National Statistics
Family Records Centre
1 Myddelton Street
London EC1R 1UW
Tel: 020 8392 5300
E-mail: enquiries@pro.gov.uk
Web site: www.pro.gov.uk

Direct mail

The Direct Mail Information Service
5 Carlisle Street
London W1D 3JX
Tel: 020 7494 0483

For industry statistics, research and general information on direct mail usage, trends, etc, contact the DMIS.

The Direct Marketing Association
DMA House
70 Margaret Street
London W1W 8WS
Tel: 020 7291 3300

This body represents the direct marketing industry. It produces a very useful code of practice covering direct mail, the use of gifts, incentives and prizes, prize draws and competitions. It also produces a list of accredited list brokers, agencies, consultants and mailing houses.

The Institute of Direct Marketing
1 Park Road
Teddington
Middlesex TW11 0AR
Tel: 020 8977 5705

The IDM organises educational initiatives, including the Direct Marketing Diploma, to improve the knowledge of direct marketing.

Direct Mail Accreditation and Recognition Centre
248 Tottenham Court Road
London W1P 9AD
Tel: 020 7631 0904

Established in 1995, DMARC is an independent accreditation scheme to ensure that direct mail suppliers adhere to the best practices and self-regulatory guidelines of the industry. They produce a free handbook, available from the above address, and a list of recognised agencies, mailing houses and other specialists.

Royal Mail Mailsort
This is a Royal Mail service which offers discounts (ranging from 13 per cent to 32 per cent) for large mailings sorted by you. If you are sending at least 4,000 letters in one go, and you can sort them geographically, you could get a good discount. Talk to your local sales centre on 08457 950 950 for details. The Royal Mail offer a range of services to support direct mail campaigns, including Freepost, Business Reply and Door-to-Door. Ask them for details. They also produce a useful *Direct Mail Guide*.

Precision Marketing
Centaur Communications
St Giles House
50 Poland Street
London W1F 7AX
Tel: 020 7439 4222

A weekly direct marketing magazine.

Marketing Direct
Haymarket Publications
174 Hammersmith Road
London W6 7JP
Tel: 020 8606 7500

A monthly magazine on direct marketing.

Mailing lists

There are many different mailing list companies, and this list is by no means comprehensive.

MarketScan
8 Duke's Court
Chichester
West Sussex PO19 2FX
Tel: 01243 786711

MarketScan will also assemble and post mailings for you. And they can arrange 'shared' mailings, where you share your mailing with one or more non-competing organisations. This can more than halve your costs.

Financial Times Business Lists
5th Floor
Number One Southwark Bridge
London SE1 9HL
Tel: 020 7873 3000

Royal Mail Address Management Centre
4 St George's Business Centre
St George's Square
Portsmouth PO1 3AX
Tel: 02392 838515

The Royal Mail have an address management database on CD-ROM. It is called PAF, the Postcode Address File. It contains 25 million addresses and allows you to cross-reference with census information, local authority ward codes, etc or to check that addresses are correct before adding them to mailing lists.

DMA Directory of List Owners, Brokers, Managers and Builders
DMA House
70 Margaret Street
London W1W 8SS
Tel: 020 7291 3310

This body represents the direct marketing industry. It offers a list brokering advisory service.

Mailing Preference Service
DMA House
70 Margaret Street
London W1W 8SS
Tel: 020 7291 3310

Members of the public can register their details with the MPS to help cut down on the amount of 'junk mail' they receive. The MPS produces a list of everyone who has contacted them to say that they do not want to receive unsolicited mail, and this list is made available to list owners, who then remove these people from their lists. Hopefully this makes everyone happy: Consumers do not get unwanted mail and companies do not waste money writing to people who are not interested. You can buy a copy of this list for £100 plus VAT. (Consumers wishing to add or remove their names from mailing lists should write to the MPS at Freepost 22, London W1E 7EZ.)

Telephone Preference Service
This is a similar service to the one outlined above, only it covers direct marketing via the telephone. It is supported by, among others, the Direct Marketing Association. Ring British Telecom on 0800 398 893 for details.

The Office of the Data Protection Registrar
Wycliffe House
Water Lane
Wilmslow
Cheshire SK9 5AF
Tel: 01625 545745

The ODPR offer free advice, guidance notes and information on the Data Protection Act. A free video is also available.

Promotional merchandise

The British Promotional Merchandise Association
Bank Chambers
15 High Road
Byfleet
Surrey KT14 7QH
Tel: 01932 355660
Web site: www.bpma.co.uk

Promotions News
Published six times a year, this is the newspaper of the BPMA (see above). It is full of adverts from companies publicising the promotional items they produce. These range from cheap biros, balloons and carrier bags right through to tasteful branded gifts.

Rocket Badge Company
38 St Pancras Way
London NW1 0QT
Tel: 020 7533 6767

This company produces a wide range of badges.

Mainline Promotions
Collins Court
High Street
Cranleigh
Surrey GU6 8AS
Tel: 01483 271171

This company produces promotional textiles, clothing and bags.

Craft Emblems
Aspen House
14 Station Road
Kettering
Northants NN15 7HE
Tel: 01536 513501

Craft Emblems will source a variety of promotional items.

London Cardguide Limited
68 Brewer Street
London W1R 3PJ
Tel: 020 7494 2229

This company pioneered the idea of promotional postcards. They produce post-cards and distribute them to selected cafés and restaurants across Britain.

Public relations

The Institute of Public Relations
The Old Trading House
15 Northburgh Street
London EC1V 0PR
Tel: 020 7235 5151
Web site: www.ipr.org.uk

This is the professional body which represents around 5,000 PR professionals. They have a database of PR consultants and can give you details of consultants working in your locality or specialising in your business sector.

The Public Relations Consultants Association
Willow House
Willow Place
Victoria
London SW1P 1JH
Tel: 020 7233 6026

The PRCA can help you find a PR consultancy. They run a free referral service, though they will only recommend their own members, who tend to be the more expensive consultancies.

IPR Journal

This quarterly publication is published by the IPR.

PR Week
174 Hammersmith Road
London W6 7JP
Tel: 020 8606 7500

The weekly magazine for people working in PR.

Press cuttings bureaux

Romeike Media Intelligence
Hale House
290–296 Green Lanes
London N13 5TP
Tel: 020 8882 0155
www.romeike.com

Durrants Press Cuttings
28–42 Banner Street
London EC17 8QE
Tel: 020 7674 0200

The Broadcast Monitoring Company
89½ Worship Street
London EC2A 2BE
Tel: 020 7377 1742

EDS Presscuttings
25–27 Easton Street
London WC1X 0DS
Tel: 020 7278 8441

McCallum Media Monitor
10 Possil Road
Glasgow G4 9SY
Tel: 0141 333 1822

Paperclip Partnership
Unit 9
The Ashway Centre
Elm Crescent
Kingston-upon-Thames
Surrey KT2 6HH
Tel: 020 8549 4857

All of the above offer a national service and some have local offices.

We Find It (Press Clippings)
103 South Parade
Belfast BT7 2GN
Tel: 02890 646008

Specialises in Northern Ireland newspapers and magazines.

Broadcast monitoring

The Broadcast Monitoring Company
89½ Worship Street
London EC2A 2BE
Tel: 020 7247 1166

Tellex Monitors
Communications House
210 Old Street
London EC1V 9UN
Tel: 020 7566 3100

The above offer a national service, and also have offices in the North of England and Scotland.

Video news releases

Medialink
7 Fitzroy Square
London W1T 5HL
Tel: 020 7554 2700

TV News London Limited
Northway House
High Road
London N20 9LP
Tel: 020 8445 3500

Lion's Den Communications
75 Valetta Road
London W3 7TG
Tel: 020 8576 6500
Web site: www.lionsden.co.uk

Complaints about the media

The Press Complaints Commission
1 Salisbury Square
London EC4Y 8AE
Tel: 020 7353 1248

The Broadcasting Complaints Commission
7 The Sanctuary
London SW1P 3JS
Tel: 020 7808 1000
Web site: www.bsc.org.uk

Index